LEGAL PLURALISM
IN CONFLICT

LEGAL PLURALISM
IN CONFLICT
COPING WITH CULTURAL
DIVERSITY IN LAW

Prakash Shah

With a foreword by
Professor Roger Cotterrell

London • Sydney • Portland, Oregon

First published in Great Britain 2005 by
Glass House Press, The Glass House,
Wharton Street, London WC1X 9PX, United Kingdom
Telephone: + 44 (0)20 7278 8000   Facsimile: + 44 (0)20 7278 8080
Email: info@cavendishpublishing.com
Website: www.cavendishpublishing.com

Published in the United States by Cavendish Publishing
c/o International Specialized Book Services,
5824 NE Hassalo Street, Portland,
Oregon 97213-3644, USA

Published in Australia by Cavendish Publishing (Australia) Pty Ltd
45 Beach Street, Coogee, NSW 2034, Australia
Telephone: + 61 (2)9664 0909   Facsimile: + 61 (2)9664 5420
Email: info@cavendishpublishing.com.au
Website: www.cavendishpublishing.com.au

British Library Cataloguing in Publication Data

Shah, Prakash
Legal pluralism in conflict: coping with cultural diversity in law
1 Minorities – Legal status, laws, etc – Great Britain
2 Legal polycentricity – Great Britain
I Title
342.4'10873

Library of Congress Cataloguing in Publication Data
Data available

ISBN-10: 1-90438-558-3
ISBN-13: 978-1-904-38558-5

1 3 5 7 9 10 8 6 4 2
Printed and bound in Great Britain

Contents

Acknowledgments   *vii*

Foreword   *ix*

1   Introduction: Legal Pluralism as a Tool for Ethnic Minority
    Studies   1

2   Ethnic Minority Legal Studies: Towards a Jurisprudence of
    Difference   27

3   The other Incoming Tide: The Diasporic Challenge to the
    British Constitutional Order   43

4   Criminal (in)Justice in a Plural Society: South Asians and
    the English Law on Homicide   67

5   Attitudes to Polygamy in English Law   89

6   Bangladeshi Legal Pluralism and English Law   123

7   Expert opinions on South Asian laws in immigration
    cases   141

8   Who do we think we are? British nationality in the
    European context   149

Conclusion   173

Bibliography   179

Acknowledgments |

This book emerges out of the contributions and effort of many persons besides the present writer. Due respect must be paid to my mentors, Professsor Werner Menski at the School of Oriental and African Studies (SOAS), University of London and Dr Roger Ballard, Director of the Centre of Applied South Asian Studies at the University of Manchester, without whom there would be no book and no writer. Thanks should also go to my many colleagues for creating the healthy research environments in which I have been fortunate enough to work, in particular, at SOAS, the University of Kent at Canterbury and, more recently, at Queen Mary. I have had many valuable discussions and received critical feedback in staff seminars and, sometimes more crucially, in departmental corridors! They are too many to all be named and I hope they will not take offence at being referred to in the collective. Particular thanks should, however, go to Professor Roger Cotterrell at Queen Mary.

Parts of this book have been aired at various seminars and conferences and/or been previously published elsewhere. Thanks are due to organisers of all of those academic meetings as well as the editors and publishers of the journals where material has been previously published. All material has been revised and updated for the present book. What is now Chapter 2 was presented at the Association of Law Teachers' Annual Conference, 24–26 March 2002, University of Greenwich, London and at the Socio-Legal Studies Association Conference, 3–5 April 2002, University of Wales, Aberystwyth. It was later published in (2003) Vol 37, No 1 *The Law Teacher*, pp 18–35. Versions of what is Chapter 3 were previously presented at the conference on 'Global Migrations/Domestic Reactions: A Comparative Constitutional Perspective', 24 May 2002, Oxford Brookes University, Oxford; at the Department of Law, University of East London, 20 February 2003; and at the Association of Legal and Social Policy Conference: 'Disagreement, Dissent and Disobedience', University of Newcastle, 3–5 April 2003. Versions of Chapter 4 were presented at the Australian Law and Society Conference, University of Newcastle, New South Wales, 8–10 December 2003 and at the National Critical Lawyers' Group Conference, 'Justice in the 21st Century', 7–8 February 2004. Attendance at the Australian conference was kindly funded by the Department of Law at Queen Mary. Chapter 5 was previously published at (2003) Vol 52 *International and Comparative Law Quarterly*, pp 359–400. Material in Chapter 6 was presented at the conference on 'Bangladeshis in Britain: Changes and Choices, Configurations and Perspectives', 25 May 2002, London Guildhall University, London. A version of Chapter 7 was presented at the seminar of the Association of Sri Lankan Lawyers in the UK, 11 July 2003, London and subsequently published in (2003) Vol 17, No 3 *Immigration, Asylum and Nationality Law*, pp 192–96. Chapter 8 was previously published in (2002) Vol 16, No 2 *Immigration, Asylum and Nationality Law*, pp 82–96.

Foreword |

The most basic and, at the same time, the hardest problem for law is to balance equality and difference. The mantra of justice demands that we treat like cases alike and unlike cases differently. However, because each event, relationship or individual has distinct features, law has to deny the relevance of some of this distinctiveness if government through rules is to be possible. Choosing criteria of relevance, law applies these criteria and assigns cases to categories. For a long time, in Western societies, the idea of a stable legal balance of equality and difference – the basis of the rule of law – has been closely linked with liberal individualism. The abstract individual is at the centre of liberal legal thought: each individual, as far as possible, should be treated legally as equal with all others, so that people acquire different positions before law only as a result of their voluntary acts. Difference before the law is supposed to result only from rational choices pursued by individuals. The residual legal position is thus one of equality – a deliberate official blindness to differences of, for example, gender, race, ethnicity or religion that seem generally part of an individual's inherited or assumed identity, rather than a consequence of chosen projects.

This broad legal approach with its many merits has gradually been challenged in ever more fundamental ways. In part this is surely a consequence of the fact that liberalism *as a practical attitude* (rather than as a focus of sophisticated philosophical debate) has become deeply impoverished: socially ignorant and ethically barren. Putting the individual and individual choices at the centre of everything has too often become a justification for a lack of concern to understand the social world at large: its complex, fragile tissue of stable relations of trust and power. It has also become an excuse for selfishness, for insistence on one's own rights and interests, whatever the wider social consequences or contexts. The social theorist Emile Durkheim famously contrasted a morally acceptable individualism with egoism. For him, individualism, as a personal value, is a moral concern for *all* individuals in their human specificity; by contrast, egoism is a blind, essentially amoral concern for self alone. Egoism sees *only* the self, as in a mirror: it treats the collective goods of culture instrumentally; or, at least, as of secondary importance alongside selfish personal goals.

For many reasons, including those that Prakash Shah writes about in detail in this book, liberalism's subordination of difference to an abstract individualism has become increasingly problematic. Even in mainstream legal thought, feminism, critical race theory, gay/lesbian legal studies and other developments have heralded a new *jurisprudence of difference*. This asserts that law's social environment can no longer be thought of as made up merely of individuals addressed equally by law. Law addresses – not necessarily explicitly or directly – groups of many kinds. Law means different things to different people and has different consequences for them in the light of a plurality of religious beliefs and practices, ethnic identifications and historical patterns of collective experience. The growth of distinct populations that, during their settlement history, have brought different ways of life from foreign places of origin is hardly a new phenomenon in British history. But its recent scale is striking and the vital challenge now is to create a sound legal framework for Britain as a society of stimulating diversity, but also of solidarity and individualism in Durkheim's specific sense – involving a constant reaching out to others across cultural divides.

Dr Shah's book should be seen as part of this exciting project, a marker in the development of a field of legal studies that will surely become increasingly rich and diverse in coming years. As a colleague, I know of his successful efforts, through a range of popular courses, to develop teaching about ethnic minorities and law. With this volume he makes his ideas more widely accessible.

The book deals with such themes and issues as the recognition of polygamous marriages and of cultural defences, the interaction of South Asian legal traditions and the official legal system, and the role of experts in immigration cases and more generally in fostering understanding of cultural and legal pluralism. Dr Shah persuasively advocates a legal pluralist perspective in law teaching and legal scholarship and an outlook that links law to ideas of community, including transnational and 'translocal' networks of community having boundaries not coterminous with those of the nation-state. His arguments are often controversial. He writes with passion and is never afraid to state strong, thoughtful conclusions. His book will surely help to stimulate interest in the field of ethnic minority legal studies. And this field – broadly conceived – will be fundamental to the effort to shape British society and its law to balance equality and difference in a manner appropriate to the 21st century. In coming decades, the responsibility of managing – nationally and transnationally – the peaceful and respectful interaction of contrasting cultural allegiances can only grow in importance.

Roger Cotterrell

Professor of Legal Theory
Queen Mary, University of London
April 2005

Chapter 1
Introduction:
Legal Pluralism as a Tool for Ethnic Minority Studies

According to the British Census of 2001, people who belong to an ethnic minority are now said to have risen to some 8% of the UK's population, and to some 9% of England's population. The magnitude and growing importance of these people, who are themselves from diverse origins in Africa, Asia, the Caribbean and Latin America (and a considerable number of mixed-origin people), has given rise to an appreciable scholarship on their legal position(s) (in particular, Pearl 1986, Poulter 1986, 1990, 1998, Bradney 1993, Hamilton 1995, Pearl and Menski 1998, Jones and Welhengama 2000), and this book presents a series of critical essays as an addition to the growing field of ethnic minority legal studies in Britain. It is therefore crucially concerned with the problem of cultural diversity and law, and the question of the fate of law in plural societies, which is an issue that arguably reaches worldwide proportions (Welhengama 2000, Ghai 2000, UNDP 2004), although our focus here remains fixed on Britain.

In using the term 'cultural diversity', I follow Bhikhu Parekh (2000a: 3–4) in his concern to address what he refers to as 'communal diversity', as distinct from 'perspectival diversity' which is that deriving from groups that dissent from prevailing ideologies such as feminists, or 'subcultural diversity' which is that deriving from groups that broadly share the values of the dominant society but entertain or evolve their own beliefs, practices or lifestyles such as gays and lesbians. This communal diversity exists when there are 'several self-conscious and more or less well organised communities entertaining and living by their own different systems of beliefs and practices' (Parekh 2000a: 3). Other writers (for example, Cohen 1974, Ballard 1976) have tended to refer to such communities as 'ethnic' groups, although the concept of ethnicity signifies not only these common cultural elements, but also emphasizes boundaries between one group sharing these and its 'others', as well as often having politicised connotations.

Given the picture derived by recent Censuses, it continues to be ever more critical to rise up to the theoretical challenges that force us to re-evaluate the concept of law in a culturally diverse, plural society. This requires us to examine the direction in which this modern society can make the transition from a concept of law that is regarded as homogeneous despite prevailing diversities, to a postmodern conception that is reflective of its cultural diversity.

1.1   Legal pluralism

This book relies on the basic theoretical propositions of legal pluralism. While there is not one but several theories and theorists of legal pluralism (see Griffiths, J 1986, Merry 1988, Griffiths, A 2002 for overviews), I have tended to rely mainly on the work of Masaji Chiba (1986, 1989, 1998) and Werner Menski (2000a). This is because both scholars take a broad perspective of comparative law which includes consideration of non-Western, as well as Western jurisprudence. Their theoretical perspectives have therefore been more thoroughly tested for the demands of an intercultural world.[1]

Legal pluralists argue for a more or less holistic conception of 'law', while tending to be critical of the position in Western 'model jurisprudence' (Chiba 1986: 1) in which a monistic conception of law has dominated. This latter concept of law was once a political claim but it has penetrated legal theory to the degree that 'law' is generally regarded, presented and taught as that law which is made and recognised by the state (Santos 2002: 89–90). While Western in origin the idea has also dominated legal thinking in many parts of the world through the export of legal modernity by colonialism or by voluntary adoption in an effort by ruling elites to 'keep up' with Western trends. Thus, the West may be the home of legal modernism, but it is 'now a state of mind rather than a geographical region' (Kakar 1982: 5). In company with other legal pluralists I do not accept that law should or can be reductively presented in such a narrow way. Not only is it conceptually inadequate, it is also experientially unsustainable, as law throughout the world is found to contain multiple founding elements. Modern jurisprudence is also found to be repressive of other traditions, within and outside the West (Glenn 2000: 50–51), and their contributions to legal thinking.

---

1   At various points in the preparation of this book there has been criticism from reviewers that I have not used the work of Brian Tamanaha (notably 2001). However, I did not find his work to have been as well tested for different cultural contexts as the work of the above writers. I also did not share to the same degree his concern to assert that 'law' is necessarily a separately identifiable category, given that it is inevitably an interlinked phenomenon. Nor do I agree with Tamanaha that legal pluralism necessarily entails an anti-state ideology which views non-state law as 'good'.

So how can law be conceptualised in a more accurate and validating sense, one that accounts for its inherent plurality? Several writers have proposed a threefold structure of law, and it might be the case that we are looking at a kind of emerging constitutive triad among the basic law-founding elements. Chiba earlier (1986, 1989: 131–40) saw law as constituted of 'official law', 'unofficial law' and 'legal postulates'. Each of these concepts is used in preference to the triad identified by Chiba (1989: 134–38) as already existing within Western conceptions of law as indicated by the terms 'positive law', 'customary law' and 'natural law', because he finds them too linked to the Western tradition to be of value in a multicultural world.

Official law then corresponds to that law which is made by the state as well as that which does not originate in the state but is nevertheless sanctioned by it (Chiba 1989: 139). Unofficial law is that which 'is not officially sanctioned but which is in practice sanctioned by the general consensus of a certain circle of people whether functioning in correlation with official law, or complementing, opposing, modifying or even undermining it' (Chiba 1989: 136). Official and unofficial law were later classified by Chiba (1989: 177–80) as the first of the 'three dichotomies of law in pluralism'.

Legal postulates in turn are defined as 'the system of values and ideals specifically relevant to both official and unofficial law in founding, justifying and orienting the latter' (Chiba 1989: 139). Legal postulates therefore consist of established legal ideas (natural law, equity, justice, *dharma, sharia,* and so on); religious precepts; social and cultural postulates related to the fundamental social structure (such as the caste system, stratification, the system of lineal descent, clan unity, exogamy, individualism or the traditional philosophy of national character, that is national philosophy); and political ideologies, which are often closely connected with economic policies (Chiba 1989: 139–40). Later, Chiba (1989: 178) added 'legal rules' to his scheme. They are defined as 'formal verbal expressions of particular legal regulations to designate specified patterns of behaviour'. These rules are easier to isolate than legal postulates but they coexist together and interact, and possibly also conflict in some circumstances leading to the annihilation of one or the other. Legal postulates and legal rules therefore constitute the second of Chiba's 'three dichotomies'.

Chiba (1986: 7–8) also drew a distinction between indigenous and received law, which became the third of his 'three dichotomies'. Both were defined in relation to his work on Asian legal systems. Thus, he defines the former broadly as being that law which 'originated in the native culture of a people' and narrowly as that which was already in existence prior to contact with the West. In the latter definition the indigenous law would already be a mixture of multiple influences as in the presence of Islamic law and its combination with pre-existing laws in South Asia prior to British intervention. Received law was defined as that law which is accepted or imposed upon contact with the West. More recently, Chiba refers to 'transplanted law' in place of received law, the former being described as that 'which was received from foreign cultures or imposed by foreign countries' (1998: 241), but, even more interestingly, as 'law transplanted by a people from a foreign culture' (1989: 179). In our context it will be relevant to note that a process of legal transplantation has been occurring in Britain and throughout Europe with the onset of large-scale immigration. This process can be regarded as a sort of 'reverse colonisation' (Menski 1997a: 67) or 'globalisation from below' (Bryceson and Vuorela 2002: 7), or as another sort of 'incoming tide' (Lord Denning in *Bulmer v Bollinger* [1974] 2 All ER 1226),[2] having multiple legal influences, although largely suppressed by the ideology of legal monism prevalent in Western countries. Not only that: the parallel process of migrants and ethnic minorities being exposed to British or European legal culture can also be regarded as a process of transplantation leading to the further 'hybridisation' of their lived legal cultures. Such processes of 'transplantation' have further important implications that I will need to flesh out further below and throughout the rest of this book.

Meanwhile, Chiba talks about other processes that also have implications for our study. In particular, he speaks (1998: 233–34) of 'trans-state law' in place of his earlier references to 'international law' or 'world law'. The international law or world law concepts may be construed as being quite state-centred since it is states that are generally credited with making or unmaking international agreements. While Chiba admits of such law 'by official treaty', as manifested in the influence of EU law across European countries, he also regards 'unofficial agreements' as coming within his definition of trans-state law. Recognition of this legal influence is vital for us too as it can help to account for the creation and maintenance of 'transnational' (Bryceson and Vuorela 2002) or 'translocal' (Ballard 2001b) communities, with their own forms of trans-state law that also carry legal implications for the societies through which they navigate. Turkish and Kurdish communities, for example, are spread throughout Europe nowadays and they may marry, trade or chat online by 'unofficial agreements' as they actively seek to retain and renew connections with their 'home' areas, and to make new

---

2   The evocative passage in Lord Denning's speech in the case, which concerned the effect of the European Economic Community membership in UK law, reads: 'But when we come to matters with a European element, the treaty is like an incoming tide. It flows into the estuaries and up the rivers. It cannot be held back.'

ones. Indeed, Chiba (1989: 139) had earlier defined unofficial law in a broad, inclusive sense as that 'which is authorised by the general consensus of a certain circle of people, whether of a country or within *or beyond it'* (emphasis added). This arguably takes into account the trans-state nature of the unofficial level of law.

Chiba's initial triad is mirrored in Menski's (2000a) enunciation of three 'law founding elements' of 'state', 'society' and 'religion or ideology' in his detailed study of Asian and African legal systems within a global context. In fact, he argues that those elements can also be applied to the legal study of Western societies and thus constitute a model of potentially universal application. That state law should figure in any account of 'law' is hardly contentious, but Menski's study shows very importantly that states in the Asian and African traditions were not, at least in premodern times, conceptualised as being the Austinian sovereign or the Napoleonic law maker, as a subtle balance operated among the three law founding elements. Whenever the state may be in danger of being hijacked by over-ambitious rulers, the other two elements come to rein it in by asserting themselves. Therefore, it appears that Asian and African legal systems have in-built accountability mechanisms premised on non-positivist ideologies. Thus it was that Islamic scholars attempted to control their states by critical insistence on reference back to religious elements of law (Menski 2000a: 238–47); and the Chinese experiment with 'legalism', China's home-grown variant of positivism, supported by the Ch'in dynasty between 221 and 206 BC, collapsed through the reassertion of Confucian self-control mechanisms (Menski 2000a: 469–77). Were similar reasons responsible for convincing Indians to rid themselves of their British rulers?

Thus, for Asian and African legal systems, if not for other components of the world's legal cultures, there is a quite distinct approach to the place of state law. Additionally, there is a strong emphasis on self-regulating customary laws (the 'society' element), on the one hand, and religion as a preferred means of assisting self-control, on the other. For our immediate purposes it is critical to study the interaction between Afro-Asian diasporas, whose legal baggage has a markedly sceptical attitude to the capacity and legitimacy of significant intervention by the state, and the state-centred, or 'legal centralist' (Griffiths 1986: 3) assumptions of the British legal system. Positivist assumptions of law makers and enforcers will be read, if not necessarily articulated, as inappropriate interventions in societies premised on the principle of self-regulation. This mismatch leads, on the one hand, to the constant reassertion of ethnic minority laws, but can, on the other hand, often lead to the development of conflict situations on which this book has much to say. I am tempted to read Gandhi, who belonged to an earlier generation of the Indian diaspora, in this light, given his excoriating critique of the British state system as frustrating traditional modes of individual and societal self-regulation (see Parekh 1989: 110–41).

As with Menski (2000a), who sees law as far from being autonomous but intimately connected with other culture-specific elements within society, Chiba too is concerned to underline that law must be studied as an aspect of the total culture of a people. But if 'law' is characterised by the co-existence of diverse components, then how is it that a whole legal order, or what Chiba (1989: 162) calls a 'socio-legal entity', can hold itself together? He (1989: 140) accords some importance to the legal postulate of a country as it is that element that is:

> ... the foundation of its official and unofficial law which it also justifies and orients. It thus includes not only consonance or indifference but also, to a limited extent, nonconformity, opposition, conflict or struggle among laws, because each legal postulate underlies each system of official or unofficial law, which it may supplement, oppose, modify or even undermine. A minimum integration should be preserved within the whole structure of law of a country, in order to maintain the legitimacy of the official law, especially state law.

In a subtle way, therefore, Chiba indicates what Menski too finds about the balance among the different law founding elements. Primarily with reference to the transplantation of foreign, Western laws into the Japanese legal system in its effort to modernise, he attempts to identify how it was that the 'cultural crisis' (Chiba 1989: 155) that this process precipitated was managed by the Japanese legal order. The success or failure of reception of foreign legal elements, consistent with the maintenance of the Japanese cultural identity, Chiba argues, is dependent on the basic legal postulate which enables a people to maintain its cultural identity. He calls this the 'identity postulate of indigenous law' (Chiba 1989: 157). 'It is an attribute which is indispensable to every system of law which wants to remain culturally independent' (Chiba 1989: 157), and it is what guides people in choosing how to reformulate indigenous law and transplanted foreign law in order to maintain their cultural identity. However, the fact of this mixture in the history of legal systems explains his choice of the new term, the 'identity postulate of a legal culture' (Chiba 1989: 166–67). Crucially for us, he points out that competition between different postulates, whether in space or in theory, is unavoidable, and that these postulates must reach accommodation or integration under a more inclusive one. 'This means that each people must not only cherish their own identity postulate of indigenous law, but also they must constantly endeavour to reformulate its content, so that it can maintain itself in this competition as circumstances change' (Chiba 1989: 157). Pierre Legrand's (1997: 45n) recommendation to comparatists to elucidate what he calls 'para-*mentalités*' that could account for differences of legal culture within the *same* jurisdiction seems to be leading us in the same direction. Current discussions about the reformulation of 'Britishness' (Parekh 2000b, Phillips 2004) could also be read in this light.

I identified above two directions of legal transplantation in the context of my study of the interaction between ethnic minorities' unofficial laws and the official British legal system. What Chiba indicates here with reference to the Japanese experience of transplanted, foreign law could also apply to both the British legal system and Britain's ethnic minorities. The major qualification to be made here is that in the Japanese case, 'Westernisation' of the Japanese legal system or, rather, the 'Japanisation' of Western legal codes was a strategic move to modernise, initially in the face of pressure exerted by Western states for concessions to be granted to their nationals but which persisted in other senses into the aftermath of the Second World War. The circumstances were therefore somewhat different from those prevailing today in Britain. However, it can be argued that the basic lessons of legal transplantation, and what Chiba subtly indicates about the capacity to adjust to new circumstances, should be one of the key tests for the British legal system's adjustment to the presence of diasporic legal cultures, as well as for the transplantation of British legal ideas and models among members of these groups. Indeed, parallel issues are now arising in Japan, which also faces the presence of diasporic minorities.

But if much of the capacity for coping and adjusting is to depend on the identity postulates of law then it should be asked: What is the identity postulate of the British legal system which faces the inescapable fact of the transplantation of 'foreign' legal cultures on the soil over which it seeks to assert territorial jurisdiction? After all, as Chiba (1998: 241) notes, it is the identity postulate that is 'the integrating principle to re-organise individualised constituents into a truly workable legal pluralism'. I pursue this problem in section 1.3 below, after specification of two of Chiba's chief theoretical concerns, which can be read as the integrating features of the chapters that follow.

1.2   Legal pluralism in conflict and in subjectivity

As seen above, Chiba maintains that there is a varying interaction between the different elements of legal pluralism, but he has recently noted that scholars have neglected the study of legal pluralism in conflict. He argues (1998: 230):

> ...the expression 'law in conflict' is theoretically a conceptual contradiction, in so far as peace or stability is one of the essential features of law, and that

it is in practice no more than an irregular phenomenon to be corrected even when found. I will not outright reject such a view of the nature of law, but I cannot help admitting frequent cases of the conflicting coexistence of plural legal systems. The legal pluralism in conflict thus forms another issue of mine.

Further on, Chiba (1998: 237) elaborates on the above:

> My emphasis on conflict is never to encourage it, but rather to discourage it by devising a way to manage it wisely. According to the established sociological theory, social conflict functions negatively against social order, but it also works positively by revealing the defect of the existing order for improvement. The same applies to the case of conflict in law. We hope law will prevail without conflict, but in reality we cannot do without any conflict in law. What is expected of us living under law is never to try to simply disregard or hate conflicts, but to manage them wisely in response to their nature and our social ideals. Accurate observation of conflicts in law is indispensable to manage them wisely, without which legal pluralism would not survive in peace.

These observations about conflict in legal pluralism have a crucial bearing on our study, since the situation of ethnic minorities under English law is full of such conflictual situations, some of which are discussed in this book. On the one hand, there are obvious instances such as the periodic 'urban disturbances' involving large numbers of ethnic minority people in British cities. But conflict is often handled silently without anyone necessarily knowing about it, partly due to the elasticity of the laws of ethnic minorities themselves, particularly where their legal postulates stress conflict avoidance.[3] That does not mean that it goes away, and it will be no great revelation to realise that conflicts can psychologically accumulate to result eventually in negative effects for a wider portion of society.

In addition to highlighting the lack of studies on conflict, Chiba also draws attention to the need to focus on the motive, will and decision of the recipient under legal pluralism which he calls 'law in subjectivity' (1998: 238). Modern jurisprudence, he argues, excludes this personal factor because of its emphasis on 'law in objectivity'. He continues (1998: 239):

> ... the essential importance of the subjective perspective [is] that a person under legal pluralism is not only a passive recipient of legal regulation but

---

3 There is an implicit critique here of policies that are premised on conflictual, adversarial models of official legal protection such as access to courts. Much of the uproar after a group of 19 Chinese people died in Morecambe Bay in February 2004 was about providing legal protection in such form, but one wonders whether persons brought up in a society which lays stress on conflict avoidance would view things in the same way.

also an active agent for the law by his/her choice of an alternative legal rule among the plural. The choice is made to support one of the plural standards, ie, to reject the other ones. The supporting choice may need no special mention, for it signifies the "productive and creative" function of the law. The rejective choice, on the contrary, needs special attention, for it may cause minor or major conflicts in the whole legal order, whether passively by evasive behaviour ... or positively by "destructive" behaviour of personal criminality ... When these choices are accumulated, they may result in collective resistance to or even revolution of the legal order in force.

Further on, from his data on law among non-Western peoples, Chiba (*ibid*) notes:

First, a person under legal pluralism may stand in the position of legal ambivalence between conflicting legal rules. Thus he/she is aware of being legally entitled to choose one of them and reject the others. Further, he/she is encouraged to make that choice on the ground that it is culturally justified. Finally he/she may be proud of the choice as a cultural privilege for its traditional value... In sum, being accompanied by cognition of cultural pride, the recipient's choice may produce a considerable effect upon the working of legal pluralism, whether positive or negative and manifestly or latently.

Chiba therefore links the culturally dependent subjective choices that individuals, as agents of change, have available to them within legal pluralism, and the potential for conflict situations to develop. These passages also have a crucial bearing for our study as ethnic minorities in Britain today are dealing with dilemmas about how to reconcile the often conflicting legal choices before them, leading to forms of legal 'hybridity' (Menski 1993); 'cultural navigation' and 'code-switching' (Ballard 1994: 30–33); chameleon-like behaviour (Menski 2002a); and the constant deployment of 'proxy selves' in different situations (Ballard 2003). Exposure to the powerful influences of the homogenising institutions of the modern state (Parekh 2000a: 179–85) and its legal system introduce an unevenness in the freedom with which legal negotiations and choices take place, deepening the sense of conflict in legal pluralism.

This study takes inspiration from Chiba's argument that it is essential to observe conflicts within legal pluralism, the better thereby to highlight and to manage them 'wisely', and to address this from the subjective perspective of the recipient of legal pluralism. The studies presented in this book all deal in one way or another with conflict situations between the British official legal order on the one hand, and the unofficial laws of ethnic minorities on the other. Thus, we find that in each of the areas studied – teaching about ethnic minorities in law schools, the nature of the British constitutional order, polygamy, legal reconstruction amongst

Bangladeshis and the treatment of this phenomenon by English official law, homicide amongst South Asians, interventions by experts in the immigration law sphere, and the regulation of immigration and nationality laws in the context of European Union membership – there are marked conflicts that pull the members of the minorities concerned, as well as the official British legal system, in different directions. In particular, we observe deep conflicts between the state-centred assumptions of official law with its own baggage of legal postulates derived from Protestantism, modernism, positivism, individualism and white supremacy, and the postulates governing ethnic minority communities with their own kinship networks and religious spheres that are used to negotiate the manner of legal reconstruction in the diaspora. Returning to the discussion above about the capacity of the British legal order to manage conflicts, we now need to discuss the question of its 'identity postulate'.

1.3   Seeking the identity postulate of British/English legal order

There is a 'cultural crisis' already underway at the heart of the British identity, with the conflicting pulls of decolonisation; American hegemony; Europeanisation; regionalisation vis à vis the Celtic nations; and – probably considered the least important of all – the presence of ethnic minorities from more far flung parts of the globe, many of them previously under colonial domination (Cohen 2000). The legal order has adopted different policies to manage the above problems: creating the Commonwealth to replace the imperial system; supporting the American effort to alter the international legal order in light of its interests; belatedly adjusting the *grundnorm* of its constitutional system to accommodate membership of the European Community/Union; and devolving constitutional powers to Scotland and Wales, and accepting power sharing in Northern Ireland. Of chief interest to us is the mode of adjustment, if any, which is adopted vis à vis the ethnic minority population of non-European cultural origin. In this context both the 'ethno-cratic' and 'techno-cratic' visions in British law come to be relevant.[4]

---

4   The term 'ethno-cratic' is used by de Sousa Santos (2002: 247–51) to indicate how particular ethnic or national groups claim to represent the State, thereby universalising what are basically specific political-cultural principles. The term 'techno-cratic' is most immediately an adaptation of Legrand's (1996: 235) phrase 'technicians of the national law', describing those law teachers who derived their concept of law from the unexamined presuppositions of a particular legal system rather than through a deeper reflection on the ontology of law.

1.3.1 The balance of law founding elements in Britain

Some writers have observed that the spur to legal development in England may have been the contact between the Normans and Muslims in the Mediterranean area and further development a result of the Talmudic legal tradition, especially in the area of commercial laws (Makdisi 1990, Glenn 2000: 208–14). In earlier times, Catholic universalism had some influence on legal development and, since Henry VIII's reformation, Protestant individualism as state-centred orthodoxy in religion has had a considerable impact in the operation of the English social and legal order. As Jones (1998) shows, the Henrician revolution was a key turning point in British history, when isolationist perspectives of English nationhood and law, particularly the common law, were formulated and institutionalised with lasting implications.

It was the Normans, themselves immigrants to Britain, who initiated the process of moulding the chthonic British laws into a state-centred, official law (Milsom 1969). A key role in forging this centralising, *common* law was acquired by lawyers and judges. As Glenn (2000: 208) remarks: 'If "modernisation" is a European process, the common law was the first to do it, in its own way, but as part of a larger process.' Indeed, England's capacity for piecemeal absorption of various components into its national social and legal order through lawyers' and judicial activity, albeit with often violent resistance from the Celtic nations, has marked it out as having developed a tradition that is quite distinct in comparison to its continental European counterparts, who ultimately resorted to Roman-inspired codification as the preferred means of consolidating their state systems into some sort of unity. Scotland, on the other hand, remains in an intermediate position, having followed the Roman legal tradition after initial dalliance with the common law (van Caenegem 1987: 119), while retaining an official legal system quite distinct from the English and Welsh model. Such basic differences in history may be responsible for hindering the process of unification of laws in the European Union, if such a thing is possible at all.[5]

The common law tradition is therefore certainly distinct from law in the Napoleonic tradition.[6] The latter is arguably more committed to the

---

5   One would do well to read Pierre Legrand (1997) who highlights the threat posed to the 'plurijural' character of European legal systems by the prospect of a European civil code.

6   Remarkably, Rosen (2000: 38–68) places Islamic law and common law in the same larger category of 'common law' systems of law, as distinct from 'civil law' and 'reciprocity-based' legal systems. This last category would be called 'chthonic' legal systems by Glenn (2000) and Menski (2000a).

supremacy of the state and its capacity to intervene in social life, whereas in the British system it is difficult definitely to identify what the division between 'public' and 'private' is (Dyson 1980: 115, Poulter 1998: 26–29) or, as the Afghan writer Idries Shah (1999: 17) remarks, even what the 'state' is. These aspects seem to provide clues to the fundamental British legal psychology, which is a basic unwillingness to commit oneself either way. In recalling the frustration of a French writer who could not understand the 'English inability to devise a system', who could see the effect but could not find the mechanism, Idries Shah (1999: 146) responds:

> But the English proceed otherwise: they feed their minds with facts, keep opinions at a low level, and seek an answer as and when one is needed. That is the basis of case-law as opposed to codification, of custom rather than rule – and of the enormous inventiveness of the British.

Thus, there is a relative tendency to keep one's options open in order to react when it is necessary to do so, rather than forcing oneself into a corner. This cultural aspect has had a crucial legal bearing, and accounts for the huge area of discretion that is built into all sorts of legal provisions in Britain.

It may be this cultural attitude that has also led some commentators to remark upon the common law's genius as an institutionalised means of ensuring social responsiveness and adaptability (Rosen 2000: 48–50, Glenn 2000: 215–28) and therefore also its potential to respond to the demands of an ethnically plural social base (Joppke 1998: 233–34). However, the common law is itself sharply conditioned by some culturally specific elements, and also carries within it the capacity to act as a culturally *homogenising* institution. Roger Cotterrell (2004: 4) recently noted that the rootedness of law in culture has often been celebrated in Anglo-American legal traditions and treated as being of considerable political significance, but as he points out: 'These assumptions seemed, until recently, unproblematic because the *unity of culture* was an object of faith in classical common law thought' (emphasis added). The balance between the chthonic and the lawyers' laws gradually shifted over time so that the history of the common law came to be largely written as one of judicial decisions that are *nationally* applicable rather than as analyses of the laws of *various* British peoples. By the 20th century, local custom retained only a marginal status as a source for the common law, a fact that has significant implications for the encounter of the laws of ethnic minorities and the British legal system, as well as being partly responsible for the failure of legal science to discern the nature of legal reconstruction among ethnic minorities. The 'techno-cratic' and 'ethno-cratic' elements of the British legal order therefore appear to combine in suppressing the influence of other traditions.

Of course, legislation is far from being unknown to the British system, but with the rise of figures such as John Austin, political sovereignty as the supreme basis for determining legality won many advocates. Recourse to legislation as a preferred mode of law making in late modern times has had even more dramatic consequences for the uniformising aspects of the official, modern legal order. Again, as Roger Cotterrell (2004: 5) explains:

> The rise of legal positivism shifted attention from cultural bases of law to its political sources in legislation and obscured the issue of the consequences of cultural change. Only recently, with interpretation elevated to a central concern of legal theory, has the nature of legal interpretive communities attracted sustained attention. Consequently, the patterned differentiation of the social (by gender, class, race, ethnicity, sexual orientation, religion, etc) has also become a matter for inquiry bearing on the nature of law.

Elsewhere, Cotterrell (2003: 209–36) speaks of the development of a 'jurisprudence of difference' through which was mounted a multilevel critique of the assumptions of modern law.[7] This book too can be read as part of the process of elucidating a 'jurisprudence of difference' that sheds light on legal theory as a result of cultural change and which, therefore, has fundamentally to question the homogenising and uniformising presuppositions of the official legal order.

1.3.2 Managing legal pluralism in conflict?

What are the chief elements of the British strategy for coping with legal pluralism? There are at least three strands of response, each unsuccessful in resolving conflict in legal pluralism, and partly also responsible for exacerbating it. The three strands are immigration law, race relations law and, most recently, what I call ethnic minority legal studies. While the first two responses are really legal strategies adopted by the state, the third is an academically focused discussion about the right place of ethnic minorities within the overarching framework of the British legal order.

As discussed in various chapters in the book, immigration law came to be identified in the post-war period as responsible for managing cultural diversity in Britain and, although it ultimately does not appear to

---

7 Cotterrell includes in this 'critical race theory', which seems to be a largely United States-centred debate and has curiously never made much impact in Britain. Thus, legal studies that take critical positions on the social relations of class and gender tend to dominate the field. This is now changing of course with the emergence of race-focused literature (see eg, Bowling and Philips 2002), and the more widely focused field of ethnic minority legal studies mentioned at the outset of this chapter.

have succeeded, it still remains a major site of legal conflict. David Jackson, a legal academic and a judicial officer as the Vice President of the Immigration Appeal Tribunal (IAT), writes (1996: 3): *1999 ?*

> Immigration Rules are said by some to be both racist in purpose and racially applied; by others to be racially neutral but appearing to apply primarily to non-whites simply because predominantly they form the categories who, because of poor conditions at home, seek entry into this country. Regrettably the structure of immigration control in the UK has traditionally been and continues to be the result of reaction to events as they are seen to be, rather than planned development.

While in true judicial style assessing both sides of the case, as it were, Jackson comes up with a judgment that appears highly ambiguous and delivers a message that seems quite perpendicular to the issue of racism that is apparently being discussed. A key point in this passage, however, seems to be that immigration controls have not been planned and that this is to be regretted. Is Jackson's regret in fact about the development of a sizeable ethnic minority population? That planners failed to foresee that allowing Afro-Asian immigrants to enter Britain in the early post-war years would result in the immigration system not being able to control the tide of kinsfolk that would follow? It may well be that in years to come the history of immigration control, modelled on a 'strong state' ideology (Young 1998: 42) but with the reality of the 'leaking tap' of immigration (Menski 2002b: 46), will be read as a failure of attempts to prevent the establishment of ethnic minority communities in Britain. We already find leading commentators, albeit not yet in law, asking whether it is realistic for states to control immigration (Castles 2004).

So the horse had bolted, as it were, and attention shifted to asking how the legal order at large would cope with the presence of the new ethnic minorities. In the earlier periods of British history, judicial decisions had come to ratify racial discrimination in social life. With the large-scale immigration of people from parts of the British Empire and Commonwealth, judges were seen by some as supporting majoritarian 'white' racism that led reformers to argue that the legal system no longer served to protect 'coloured' minorities, and to make the case for the introduction of anti-discrimination legislation (Lester and Bindman 1972). Thus, legislation came to be introduced in a society in which neither great portions of the public nor its judges accepted that racial discrimination was in itself a questionable virtue. Far from allowing the vaunted capacity of the common law to evolve piecemeal and thereby to assimilate the new ethnic minorities, the preferred method was to enact legislation that might act as a signal that the state was ready to address the concerns of, and provide redress for the wrongs done to, those minorities.

In fact, the reception given to the Race Relations Acts makes a fascinating case study, illustrating several aspects of the functioning of the British legal order. It demonstrates the key gate-keeping function of British judges, since they can considerably influence how and whether a statute comes to be effective, even when the predominant custom of the British constitution remains that it is parliament that is sovereign! After all, it is judges who created that doctrine and they can probably change it should the need arise – as they have eventually done in order to reconcile to the supremacy of European Community law. In the case of the Race Relations Acts, however, several writers have argued to the effect that judges effectively subverted the reformist aims of the legislation (Griffith 1991, Gregory 1987, Jones and Welhengama 2000: 73–82). The judges had after all been, in Ashis Nandy's (2002: 5) terms, 'oversocialised to their own disciplinary histories' which presumed the notion of freedom of choice and contract, and therefore freedom to discriminate.

The presence of the legislation has, far from tackling widespread xenophobia in Britain, tended to act as a *limit* to the recognition of cultural differences within its changing social order. It represented a stratagem to accommodate the ethnic minority presence by individualising ethnic conflict and ended up selectively privileging some ethnic groups (Jones and Welhengama 2000: 27–50), while preventing the conception of ethnic and cultural pluralism in more comprehensive terms. It allows ethnic minorities to claim to be treated the *same* as their white counterparts but does not readily allow them to rely on their *differences*, thus sustaining the homogenising impulse of the British legal order. If, therefore, a small minority of people were seeking to initiate legislation as a means of provoking the development of a 'jurisprudence of difference', it does not seem that the legislation or its practical application were enough to secure a right to be different in British law.

The Race Relations (Amendment) Act 2000 now places a duty on public authorities to have 'due regard' (another non-committal phrase) to the need to eliminate unlawful racial discrimination and to promote equality of opportunity and good relations between persons of different racial groups. There are various specific duties on public authorities too, in particular on educational institutions. Quite how one unpacks the implications of this legislation will depend on the perspective that one takes about the capacity of official law to challenge and to change societal and institutionalised practices and attitudes. In this respect, the late Antony Allott (1980: 224–36) wrote critically about the earlier versions of the Race Relations Acts which have subsequently been echoed by those who were initially more optimistic about the capacity of official law to effect social change (for example, Bindman 1992). Official stipulations will remain mere paper guarantees until we develop challenging perspectives on what living in a plural, multicultural society entails, and what the place of legal thinking in this tricky equation can be.

Since the 1980s we have seen a strand of legal scholarship emerging that attempts to get closer to addressing the question of how the British/English legal order could and should respond to the Afro-Asian presence. The most prolific writer here must be Poulter (1986, 1987, 1990, 1998), who addressed the question of how far English law should recognise ethnic minority 'customs' by reference to what he called 'core English values', although his solution was oddly to refer to *international* treaties as the main reference point for judging whether ethnic minority customs should be allowed to be continued in Britain. The identity postulate of English/British law for which we are searching was therefore still not clearly defined. This is perhaps unsurprising in light of the foregoing discussion, since a core English value seems to be that there is a basic desire to avoid principle and a preference, instead, for case-by-case analysis. As with our general discussion of the common law, this should not be taken to mean that this tradition is devoid of culture specificity. Poulter himself argues that it is *English values* that should determine acceptability of ethnic minority customs and traditions, only that the question of *what* those English values are is sidestepped by him.

This approach is highly unsatisfactory for a number of reasons which I have discussed elsewhere (Shah 2000a). Among my criticisms is that Poulter overlooks the highly competitive environment in which putatively universalising human rights treaties exist. After all, such treaties are only one, official component of legal pluralism, and therefore their assigned function as the exclusive benchmark for legitimate legal choices amongst ethnic minorities cannot be justified. What role have Britain's ethnic minorities had in the conclusion of any such treaties? Secondly, Poulter (1998: 111) argued that 'it is quite erroneous to focus upon "traditional" value systems in the search for universal human rights'. This underlines the exclusivity that Poulter wished to accord to one strand of thinking within the Western legal tradition and can, at the same time, be read as suppressive of the world's chthonic or religion-based legal systems.

Thus, Poulter's approach is to oversell the capacity of the English legal system and that of international treaties (mainly the European Convention on Human Rights (ECHR)) to resolve legal pluralism in conflict. Note that, when he wrote, the ECHR had not been 'brought home' by the Human Rights Act 1998! In fact, his elitist prescriptions seem to be highly ethnocentric and in themselves likely to neglect, if not in themselves to perpetuate, conflict in a legally plural social environment. Indeed, Poulter's own studies, while not acknowledging this, show that there is massive evidence of unresolved conflict even in the official sphere, while other writers, notably Bradney (1993) and Hamilton (1995), although not adopting explicitly pluralist perspectives, are also showing similar evidence. Bradney (1993: 157), in particular, is critical of the sort of argument made by Graham Zellick, which mirrors Poulter's, that official recognition of religious diversity within certain limits is consistent with freedom of religion and showed, instead, that there is massive evidence of the *lack of* freedom of religion and that people are often compelled to act against the (official) law when seeking to conform to their religious beliefs.[8] Jones and Welhengama's (2000) study, taking an explicitly legal pluralist perspective, largely supports Bradney's conclusion, arguing that official law making and judicial interpretation, in particular, has relied too heavily on Anglo-focused values and taken far too little account of the ethnic and religious pluralism in Britain.

If the discussion in this section has taught me anything, it is to agree with Cohen (2000) about the 'incredible vagueness of being British/English'. His suggestion is that to find what British or English means we should look to its 'fuzzy edges' where it is in contact with its 'other'. This strategy provides a useful way of reading writings such as Poulter's as it seems to show more about how the issue of British/English ethnicity is resolving itself in conversation about the 'other', in this case Britain's ethnic minorities. Indeed, as Morgan (1985: 521) presciently observed a few years ago:

> ... there ought to be a recognition that we live in a society composed of a number of ethnic groups, one of which is the English. The latter may be expected to become more vociferous in the defence of their ethnicity, insofar as ethnicity becomes a more important organising principle in British politics.

Cohen (2000: 578) too observes 'the moderate but definite growth of internal expressions of English identity'. Therefore, the chapters that follow, recording some of the areas where British or English official laws conflict with those of Britain's ethnic minority population, can be seen as a further attempt to find clues about the identity postulate of the British/English legal order, and in the perhaps more ambitious project of reformulating a para-*mentalité* of Britishness along more inclusive and plurality conscious lines.

---

8   Later work is intended to develop Bradney's argument albeit through a legal pluralist analytical framework that also critiques Bradney's interpretation of religion as primarily determined by *belief*, which seems to be influenced by Protestant understandings of religion.

1.4   Scheme of the book

As stated above, the chief theoretical concern of this book is to pursue Chiba's identification of the relative lack of studies devoted to examining legal pluralism in conflictual situations which take into account the subjective aspect of pluralism. The conflict situations analysed in this book seem remarkably often to coalesce around basic differences in modes of social organisation that clash with each other. On the one hand, there are forms of communal organisation that are primarily based on kinship: in the South Asian case one might therefore talk in terms of caste, *jati, biraderi*[9]; or of various African concepts of kinship;[10] in Chinese terms one might speak of clans and *guanxi*; and so on. Such networks have been crucial to the process of reterritorialisation and legal reconstruction in the diaspora. As Ballard (1994b: 26) points out in the case of South Asians:

> While the hereditary allocation of occupational specialisation may have been swept away, the rules of endogamy are still just as strictly followed in the diaspora as in the subcontinent. As a result, all kinship networks remain caste specific. By itself this would be of little significance, were it not that kinship reciprocities still offer the most effective means of organising mutual support, especially in fiercely competitive urban environments. Thus whenever migrants have helped each other gain access to jobs, housing and other scare resources, and whenever they have sought to protect their gains (however limited) from encroachment, they have invariably found that kinship ties provided the most effective base for collective mobilisation. So although rapid economic change may indeed have eroded the caste system's traditional foundations, it has been reinvigorated by its role as a channel for kinship reciprocities, no less in Birmingham than in Bombay.

In legal terms, family and wider kin groups are the primary location of self-regulation, which also gives rise to conflict and negotiation in the wider British social order. Since Asian and African laws emphasise self-

---

9   The word *biraderi*, used in the northern part of the Indian sub-continent normally to signify one's agnatic relatives, seems to be borrowed from the same word in Persian, which itself derives from the word *biradar* meaning brother also in Persian. The Shorter Oxford English Dictionary further establishes a link with *bhrátá* in Sanskrit and brother in English, which is striking to say the least. On South Asian kinship see Uberoi (1993), and on how it has been operationalised among Pakistanis in Britain see Anwar (1979) and Shaw (2000).

10   The concept of 'tribe' seems increasingly contested by African intellectuals on the basis that it is imposed and used to portray Africans in a negative light. This does not mean that African concepts of kinship or ethnicity have become redundant but seem instead to offer the most viable safeguard against over-mighty states controlled by over-ambitious rulers, or as a survival mechanism, especially in situations where the post-colonial state has broken down altogether. See, for example, Hameso (1997).

regulated societies rather than positivist top-down regulation, as the British state law does, there is a fundamental clash of basic legal values or postulates in Chiba's terms. In practice it may be that many of the problems are 'sorted out' by the inherent flexibility of customs and thus officially much noise would never be made of clashes, while insults are often internalised as learning experiences. On the other hand, the official system is often and increasingly aware of self-regulatory and self-reliant modes of organisation amongst Afro-Asians and tacitly relies upon this to save state funds. Sometimes, as in the case of polygamous families (discussed in Chapter 5), it discriminates blatantly by denying recourse to state funding altogether.

Chapter 2 in this study is concerned with providing a semi-autobiographical account of my experiences of teaching about ethnic minorities in the law in a number of universities and some of the challenges that one is faced with in running such programmes. In teaching within British law schools, I am fortunate enough to be able to maintain what Kuang-Ming Wu (1998: 60–73) calls an 'insider-outsider' position, since I can identify myself as a member of an ethnic minority (or several) in a predominantly white European society, but have also had access to institutions of learning in a manner that few are in a position, or seem to want, to take advantage of. Thus, I can look in from outside and look out from inside our legal institutional systems in order to take forward our intercultural dialogue in legal studies. The account, however provisional, is I believe necessary because it gives air to experiences that would otherwise remain hidden and undebated in the academic environment, but also challenges the teacher continually to be reflective about what he or she is doing, or thinks he or she is doing! The chapter also provides reflections of interactions with students, and about addressing ethnic minority legal studies within a 'mainstream' curriculum which is largely colour and culture blind and thus suppressive of legal pluralism. I also emphasise the role and importance of ethnic minority legal studies in a rapidly pluralising environment, and make some modest suggestions for curricular development. Of course, much more could be said about the whole enterprise of teaching in this field as it provides a richness that only those who partake of it will appreciate, in terms of interaction with students, personal development, and the development of curricula that are more reflective of the law's social context.

Chapter 3, on the 'other incoming tide', examines the implications of the ethnic minority presence for the constitutional order. It looks, first, at how ideas of Britishness in nationality and immigration laws have been developing with an ethno-centric flavour since the imposition of major immigration controls on Commonwealth immigrants in 1962. It then goes on to examine how ethnic diversity is conceived of in official discourses with particular reference to the Census, but also the case law under the Race Relations Act 1976. The core of the chapter, however, is concerned to examine the extent to which the more subtle effects on the constitutional balance in the UK brought about by the ethnic minority presence have been integrated within writing on public law thinking. As Glenn (2000: 148) observes: 'The city has also emerged as a new field of inter-traditional activity, the result of massive population movement in the world, having possibly its greatest effect in Europe.' However, and perhaps not surprisingly, there is minimal coverage about this question among the public law writers, reflecting widespread assumptions that liberal democratic modes of governance are necessarily subscribed to by ethnic minority people. Here I also bring up the question of the different modes of governance present in traditional Hindu and Muslim legal systems as a way of reconceptualising the interaction of ethnic minorities with the elusive 'public' sphere in Britain. I would suggest that this discussion is highly relevant to emerging research that laments the lack of faith that ethnic minorities seem to have in existing official modes of governance in Britain.[11]

Chapter 4 deals with the fraught question of homicide and links to the widespread discussions taking place in Euro-American jurisdictions generally about the extent to which cultural defences should be admitted (for Britain see Phillips 2003). My 'take' is not to restrict the question of homicide by squeezing it within the cultural defence category but to introduce the issue as one of conflict of laws. So the question is: When South Asians kill are they not making their own choices under conditions of legal pluralism, as Chiba has it, rather than simply breaking English law? Thus, the problem becomes one of deciding on the justice of the case, given the conflict of laws and legal postulates involved, rather than deciding on when an *exception* to the general law should apply. We discuss the position of ethnic minorities under English criminal law and, in particular, the English framework on homicide. Then we examine some concepts relevant to homicide mainly under Hindu and Muslim law. Some case studies, chiefly those of Satpal Ram and Zoora Shah, are then introduced. I discuss, with respect to the *Zoora Shah* case, the intervention of expert anthropologist Roger Ballard, and how the vital socio-legal background to the case was dismissed by the Court of Appeal. Both case studies, it is argued, show how the official legal process

---

11 Some of this research is summarised in the Commission for Racial Equality's publication *Connections*, Spring 2004.

undermines the concept of the legal agency of individuals acting under conditions of legal pluralism. I suspect that we are not ready to face the conclusions drawn in this chapter, particularly given the rigidity of the concept of homicide in English law, but one hopes that it will take the debate in a much more pluralist direction than has been the case so far.

Case law relating to nullity has been dominated by Asians in Britain for many years now (Pearl and Menski 1998: 172–73), and recent case law on marriage solemnisation is also dominated by ethnic minorities, as seen in the cases of *Bath* ([2000] 1 FCR 419, [2000] 1 FLR 8, [2000] Fam Law 91 (Sikhs)), *A-M v A-M* ([2001] 2 FLR 6 (Arab Muslims)) and *Gandhi v Patel* ([2002] FLR 603 (Hindus)). It is far from clear that such cases have brought us any closer to resolution of the problems of recognition in the official sphere. Academic commentary meanwhile remains woefully inadequate, rather showing how family law discussions are dominated by majoritarian agendas about recognition of cohabitation, but thereby neglecting the importance of marriage solemnisation for many ethnic minority communities (Menski 1993: 260–61).

Chapter 5 focuses on one type of marriage form that has invited much opposition in the Western setting – polygamy. We examine the attitudes in English law as it has developed in various phases of the postwar settlement of different ethnic minority groups. I do this via an overview of how polygamy is managed by Asian and African legal systems, tracing the rather confusing developments in English conflicts of law (or private international law) from the 1970s, through the immigration restrictions imposed in the 1980s, and then discussing the wider question of polygamy as a problem that is illustrative of the status of ethnic minority laws. It is argued that polygamy remains a practice that some ethnic minority people wish to continue to observe despite the restrictions that English law has imposed, and quite complex patterns of avoidance are developing as a result. The official law refuses to recognise this practice, thereby driving it underground and penalising women and children. Contrary to Poulter's optimistic messages, this is one area where human rights law also fails to help the women and children affected, while the hypocritical silence of liberal and feminist academics, who otherwise argue for legal flexibility in recognising family forms, have also totally failed those who are penalised. Anne Phillips (2003: 520) recently suggested that in this area 'the current balance would seem to work largely to women's advantage'. I am afraid I have to disagree strongly. While there is no agreement either amongst members of ethnic minority communities about the wisdom of continuing to endorse polygamy solely on the basis that their traditional laws may allow for the practice, the evidence presented here shows that English law's response to the practice seems to be outrightly hostile, unnecessarily harsh and counter to the interests of the very women and children whom it allegedly seeks to protect.

Several writers have now addressed the broader processes of legal reconstruction in the diaspora, notably Menski (1993) on South Asians and Pearl and Menski (1998), Menski (2001b) and Yilmaz (2000) on Muslims. However, the broader picture needs sooner or later to be further refined by studies on smaller, micro-communities that attempt to discuss the specific issues that are arising within these groups, between members of these and other groups and between their members and the state. There are some studies taking explicitly legal pluralist perspectives on different communities (see Menski 1987, 1991 on Hindu marriage, Jones and Welhangama 2000: 213–42 on Sikhs, Yilmaz 2004 on Turks), and Poulter's study (1998) also contains case studies on various groups with much useful information. There is a whole mountain range to climb here, however, and we are somewhere very close to the foot. Chapter 6 on Bangladeshis in English law should be read very much in this context where our perspective may not be such that we have an overview of the entire gamut of different communities, but as an attempt to scale the foothills and to examine some of the key problems that are arising. Although it may seem to be an obvious fact to many observers, it is worth saying that we have much evidence of internal differentiation as between ethnic minority groups (Ballard 1994a, Mason 2003). As also seen in other chapters, the Bangladeshis have had their fair share, one might even argue *more* than their fair share, of conflicts between the communal sphere and the state's attempts at regulating it, often in sharp opposition as is evident in the area of polygamy. It seems that the state sought to restrict Bangladeshis early on in their efforts to form their version of *desh pardesh*, as Roger Ballard (1994a) has it, or the reterritorialisation of families, and thus reconstitution of legal structures in the diasporic setting.

While some of the discussion is devoted to charting the key points at which UK immigration law bore down to control Bangladeshi settlement, there is a noticeable amount of litigation in the official sphere which concerns other aspects of law among Bangladeshis, particularly in the family sphere. Unfortunately, we can observe that English law shows considerable ambivalence, if not outright hostility, in helping to sort out legal problems arising in various contexts, again often penalising women and children in the process. While one response to this lack of sensitivity will be the withdrawal of Bangladeshis from official fora, which was already in evidence some years ago, now among various South Asian minority groups (Menski 1993: 255) there is also a persisting impression that official law fails to correct mistakes where state agencies are being challenged for failure to show the proper appreciation of Bangladeshi norm systems, compounding feelings of resentment.

In his book, Bradney (1993: 160–61) was especially critical of the lazy processes which resulted in discrimination against different religious groups. He wrote:

> Legal rules are also often applied without thought of the difficulties they will cause for some faiths. This in turn happens because neither judges nor legislators are acquainted with much of the variety of religious experience. In some cases faith is devalued because its form runs counter to those religious traditions which have historically dominated Great Britain ... Judgments in some cases involving conflict between religions and laws suggest mutual incomprehension on both sides.

As with Chapter 4, where we see the intervention of an expert in the field of criminal law, in Chapter 6, we see a similar intervention in the family court. In Chapter 7, I examine the role of experts in the official legal setting in greater depth by focusing on the immigration field. Expert evidence constitutes one of the key means by which the official legal process 'receives' messages about what is going on at unofficial level. Thus, we may be in the initial stages of a sort of 'official legal pluralism', whereby the courts are being informed of varied practices and laws of the different ethnic minority communities. There is a sizeable number of 'country experts' with more or less detailed or specialised knowledge of the politics, laws, customs, religions, etc of the 'home' countries of immigrants, and Chapter 7 focuses on my personal experience of writing expert reports; on how knowledge of such 'translocal' communities' legal baggage can be brought to the attention of decision-makers; and on the problems that we as experts face in this context. However, this is not the only arena in which such 'mediation' takes place since, increasingly, lawyers in practice are consulting experts on legal arrangements, not in some 'foreign' jurisdiction, but on those which are firmly in place in Britain itself. The material produced in this way remains unreported (but see Cooper and Herman 1999: 361–63 on Jews), although it occasionally surfaces in fascinating cases such as *Re S* [2001] 2 FLR 1005, which is discussed in Chapter 6. Indeed, as Menski (2002a: 101), Europe's foremost authority on South Asian laws, observes:

> We are in a sense back to the methods of the late 18th and 19th century, when courts in British India employed *pandits* and *moulvis* to guide them on details of the respective personal law.

Crucially, it will be noted that the British authorities in India made the fateful decision to abandon the practice of consulting experts because of all the distortion and miscommunication that was inherent in such trial and error processes, before launching into the policy of attempting to turn India into a common law jurisdiction, and of codification and reform of the indigenous laws themselves, accompanied in this by spokesperson advocates from indigenous communities (see Menski 2000a: 174–84).

Whether the colonial example is one that will be followed here in Britain, after some steps to official acknowledgment of pluralism, remains to be seen, and this study provides evidence that at present there are counter-currents in different directions, and no clear discernable picture can be said to have been established; a typical example of British 'muddling through'? My view as an 'expert' would be that, at this stage, without a more definite commitment to official legal responsiveness, the intervention of experts remains a crucial, although far from systematic, component of knowledge that must go into making coherent decisions in the courts. It may well remain so in the longer term too, given current demographic developments. After all, it is now regarded as imperative that judges must be equipped with basic information about the various communities which they serve, the most concrete manifestation of which must be the *Equal Treatment Benchbook*, and the ethnic minority awareness training seminars that judges undergo. However, the ongoing suppression of ethnic minority legal cultures in legal education, official emphasis on assimilation, and the generally dismissive attitude to information about cultural, religious and legal background that experts do provide, means that the climate is far from conducive to a more progressive policy being formulated. A more recent trend among some judges seems to be to accommodate ethnic minority laws but to express the basis of decisions within a British/English legal idiom presumably to perpetuate the homogeneity of British/English law (Menski 2002a). Such developments cry out for further academic analysis.[12]

We have already noted the salience of kinship in the reconstitution of African and Asian communities in Britain. Indeed, elsewhere Ballard (1990, 2001b) has detailed the kinship-centred processes of immigration prevailing among people from the northern part of the Indian sub-continent, and there is much evidence to show that such processes are taking place across ethnic minority groups to a greater or lesser extent. Tamils from Sri Lanka have been arriving since the 1980s as refugees or asylum seekers in formal terms, but digging deeper shows that family and kinship are the main vehicles for organising asylum migration too, and the same could be said for Britain's growing Kurdish communities.

---

12 In *Singh v Entry Clearance Officer New Delhi* [2004] EWCA Civ 1075, *The Times*, 15 September 2004 the Court of Appeal struck down the long-standing non-recognition of inter-family adoptions for immigration law purposes which, incidentally, are valid in Indian law. It did so on human rights grounds, however, and did not refer to a report written by the present writer on the significance of such adoptions in Sikh and Hindu law.

However, in the effort of establishing trans-localisms, we again find the clash of basic principles of social organisation. Another illustration is provided by the story of British nationality as it evolved from its feudal to its decidedly modern form in the expansion to the Empire, but then again contracted to its more visibly nationalist, yet also very modern form, in the process of controlling immigration. As Paul (1997) tells us, Britain may well be unique among other Western countries in this respect. As British nationality contracted, so too did the rights that went along with it, cutting across trans-local communities, and often arbitrarily dividing families. The clash of principles that is involved here was put most starkly by Professor Arvind Sharma in a lecture on 'What is Hinduism?' delivered at SOAS on 8 October 2003. When asked about the linkage between Hinduism and the caste system, he responded by explaining that *jati*, the basic principle of Hindu social organisation, is like nationality in that both may be acquired at birth and lost with difficulty.[13] When these two principles are moving in opposite directions, often through deliberate targeting of kinship by legislation and other official practices, we have seen major cases of legal pluralism in conflict as exemplified in the British response to the reunification of families (Juss 1997, and Chapters 5 and 6 in this book) and family formation through marriage (Sachdeva 1993). All the while, officials have asserted the territorial principle, so linked to the nation-state (Parekh 2000a: 179–81) and to nationality, as the basis for unmaking private decisions taken along kinship lines, while the self-ordered societies that have been their targets have resiliently argued that their way of life deserves recognition by the state, although not without much human misery and suffering.

This problem was recently concretised by the *Manjit Kaur* litigation, discussed in Chapter 8, which brought in the European dimension, as the European Court of Justice (ECJ) had to rule on what classes of British citizen could be regarded as UK citizens for EU purposes. We see here one of Britain's fuzzy borders, that of its 'colonial past' (as the ECJ saw it) and the kinship structures that were built under its umbrella in East Africa on the one hand, and the Europeanising, new Britain on the other. It is as if the former belonged to a dark past the sooner to be distanced, than admitted to the white men's club of the European Union. Thus, it is argued that the creation of a European identity involves the suppression of the 'other', hardly an original realisation admittedly (see Ballard 1996d, Hansen 2004). The kinship aspect is not even mentioned; thus, Manjit Kaur is treated as being without a past or social context herself,

---

13   This comparison is discussed in more detail in Sharma (2003: 63–65).

but only as part of Britain's colonial past. This demonstrates the hegemonic and monolithic way in which being European is now constructed, even as Europe too rediscovers its own need for different speeds, overlapping circles and even legal pluralism. This is clearly seen recently when Slavic inclusion is accompanied by deep ambivalences, as nationality again breaks down in the face of Roma immigration.

Quite how we should conceptualise the challenges of finding an equitable balance among the various ethnic components of rapidly changing Euro-American societies is one of the key issues that this book attempts to address without, it must be said, providing any final answers to the predicaments raised. While a larger work involving a more diverse range of theoretical perspectives and substantive issues is long overdue, this book emerges out of a perceived urgency to provide students with accessible material and to continue the debate among the wider communities of ethnic minorities, scholars, policy makers, legal professionals and others working within and outside the legal field. Thus, questions of what we think 'law' is, of power differentials, outright racism and the problems of knowledge about the 'other' are all implicated, while it is clear that legal study cannot avoid being a part of the solution to building successful multicultural societies. Otherwise, we as legal academics will continue to be part of the problem of transmission and perpetuation of majoritarian biases that act as hegemonic devices to marginalise the 'other'.

Chapter 2
Ethnic Minority Legal Studies: Towards a Jurisprudence of Difference

I have been teaching Ethnic Minorities and the Law at undergraduate and masters level for some 10 years now. It is my conviction that the subject has achieved certain maturity and that it is high time that it was taken serious notice of in legal education circles at all levels. This chapter therefore dwells on some of those experiences and briefly charts a way through the approaches that have been adopted to the study of ethnic minorities in law. I also suggest some ways in which our teaching about ethnic minorities in Britain could be developed out of the straitjacketing and assimilationist effects of dominant legal studies to reflect the living legal experience of ethnic minorities in Britain.

2.1   Student and academic perceptions

I started off co-teaching Ethnic Minorities and the Law in the early 1990s as a timid postgraduate student at the School of Oriental and African Studies (SOAS), University of London, where Werner Menski had broken the mould, a few years previously, by introducing the first such course in the UK. I had actually been a student on the same course two years prior to that, a sort of refugee from a not-far-from-typical-law programme elsewhere in the University of London. As I continued with my doctorate, I began to be more and more immersed in teaching this course, together with an assortment of other offerings on undergraduate and postgraduate programmes. In 2001, I started to teach a similar undergraduate course at the University of Kent at Canterbury, and now teach the same subject at both levels at Queen Mary, University of London.

The questions that we were asking on our courses were also reflected in wider European debates, as I saw while teaching for five years in the 1990s on an inter-university course on migration and 'inter-culturalité' hosted annually by the Institute National de Langues et Culture Orientale (INALCO) in Paris. While at Kent I therefore began to build on this experience and to think about how the question of ethnic minorities and the law could be taught and discussed in a postgraduate course focusing on migration issues in Europe. I was struck and heartened by the level of interest for my tentative introduction of the topic of the legal situation of

Muslims in Western Europe.[1] These were experimental baby steps in a discipline that offers much potential interest in terms of research and teaching.

Indeed, it is remarkable that student interest for courses tackling these topics has generally tended to be quite high. Although I am convinced about this, we have noticed that a number of reservations also preoccupy students when considering taking up such courses. Not least among these are worries about being marginalised or penalised in the job market. In our experience, this is largely not the case in actual practice and there is evidence that older lawyers are rewarding students who have studied areas that they themselves never had the opportunity of studying. The ever increasing emphasis on diversity-aware workers provides an added incentive in this context.[2]

Another reservation, often unexpressed, tends to come from white English students that such courses are simply not for them, or they react angrily to the issues that they are presented with, and this applies particularly to white male students. The result is that almost all the students who end up staying on the courses tend to be of Asian or African origin themselves. An ever present worry for us is therefore the possible 'ghettoisation' of the discipline. More worrying is the assumption that white English law students do not need to know about the legal implications of increasing cultural pluralisation within British or European societies. I say specifically 'white English' because my experiences at SOAS, Kent and Queen Mary have proved to me that there is a lively interest in these topics among students from Scotland and continental Europe, as well as from North America. Many students are pleasantly surprised about such innovations in legal education in Britain, as compared with their own jurisdictions, while being aware that demographic changes in their home countries pose similar questions there too. In this larger context, one may legitimately question who is being ghettoised, or rather is self-ghettoising. Another important trend has been that the overwhelming majority of students are tending to be female, and there is cause for thinking about whether and why ethnic minority studies in law are also gender-coded in students' minds. There appear to be parallels here with Family Law and Women and the Law courses which attract mainly female students.

---

1 On the salience of this issue Europe-wide see, for example, Ferrari and Bradney (2000).

2 Gidoomal *et al* (2001) recently made the point even more explicit and compelling, arguing that lack of awareness of ethnic diversity and a lack of intercultural competence results in huge loses to the UK economy, and this would include intercultural competence in law.

There is, predictably, reluctance about the topics taught or approaches taken within law departments too where fellow academics can often be dismissive due to prevailing orthodoxies or latent fears. On the other hand, my appointments at Kent and Queen Mary were made specifically because I had had experience teaching ethnic minorities and law as well as immigration law. This may tell us something about the slow but sure recognition of the subject as universities increasingly come under pressures to make their offerings more market-friendly, but also that some law departments genuinely wish to broaden their focus in the post-Macpherson era by taking diversity issues more seriously.[3] There are inevitably also implications flowing from the fact that someone like myself, coming from an East African Gujarati background, teaches such a course. It may mean further ghettoisation, combined ironically with a perception of greater legitimacy. Both results carry their own dangers.[4]

2.2   Ethnic diversity in the UK

In teaching about ethnic minorities and law one cannot avoid some analysis of the demographic character of British society and how it is conceptualised. In our courses the minorities of key interest are those from Asia, Africa and the Caribbean (or 'Afro-Asian', as I sometimes say in short form). This approach inherently poses problems and might provoke accusatory responses on several grounds. Are we not excluding concerns about 'white' ethnic minorities? Do we not consequently problematise the presence of non-white ethnic minorities? Do we not thereby legitimate skin colour distinctions, and thus outmoded social Darwinist notions of 'race', as a point of departure? What these criticisms point to is that the whole notion of ethnicity has to be problematised in a way that takes it beyond narrow notions of racial dualism. In that sense, the question of 'white' ethnicities is one of the central issues that needs to be confronted. It is entirely defensible, and in fact necessary, that white ethnicities in Britain be discussed in the context of debates on ethnic plurality and law (see further section 3.3). Our concentration is, nevertheless, accounted for partly because of our linkage to an institution

---

3   Many British readers will already be familiar with the unresolved murder of the black teenager, Stephen Lawrence, in 1993 and the major government-initiated inquiry under the chairmanship of Lord Macpherson, a former judge, which concluded in 1999 that the London Metropolitan police were 'institutionally racist'. The inquiry's effects have rippled through the British legal system in many ways.

4   Menski (1997a: 72) critically observes: 'If the experience of schools is a pointer, it could be disastrous to expect non-white colleagues to shoulder 'ethnic' subjects – the point is precisely that ethnic minority legal issues concern us all.'

that is primarily focused on Asian and African studies. Teaching about ethnic minorities as part of a law curriculum was thus pioneered as a response to the diasporic establishment of Asian and African cultures in Britain in a radical way since the end of the Second World War, and the myriad legal issues that this was throwing up.[5]

Since then a major challenge for policy makers in Britain has been to find an adequate conceptual mechanism to capture the character of the ethnic minority presence. Social science and policy understandings came to be dominated by discourses on racial exclusion and deprivation as the so called 'race relations' industry flourished. Roger Ballard (1992) and Tariq Modood (1996) have both observed how racial discrimination was diagnosed as the key problem, which was then seen as reinforcing the well known phenomenon of class inequality, within which framework the problems of the new minorities, it was advocated, had to be understood. However, this approach typecast their situation within a 'deprivationist' frame that neglected the varied goals of the groups and individuals concerned. It was nevertheless one into which many ethnic minority 'spokespersons' were co-opted. Under its influence the salience of ethnicity, culture or religion as operational characteristics was hardly investigated. While it is certain that skin colour is constantly used as a marker to discriminate, to concentrate one's analytical efforts solely on this marker was to neglect how the minorities' agency is harnessed, not only for resistance to discrimination and penalisation for non-conformity, but to pursue self-determined goals. As Ballard remarks (1992: 487, 490):

> It is precisely through their rejection of the conventions of the dominant majority, together with their skilled and creative redeployment – both individually and collectively – of the alternative resources of their imported cultural traditions that the new minorities are not only beginning to circumvent racial exclusionism, but to do so with ever increasing success. Although great care must be taken not to romanticise these processes, their force is self-evident at least for those with eyes to see. The ethnic colonies which are now such a salient feature of inner-urban life, and whose very foundation lies in vigorous networks of mutual support and solidarity, provides clearest possible evidence of their vitality ... Indeed the very

---

5   Derrett (1976: vii) had hinted that practical concern about Hindu law outside South Asia, South-East Asia and East Africa was revived by the arrival of 'the massive immigrations of Hindus and Sikhs into Britain'. Derrett was then Professor of Oriental Laws at SOAS. The reference to Hindus and Sikhs under the umbrella of Hindu law is probably accounted for by the subsumption of Sikhs, as well as Jains and Buddhists, under some statutory provisions in India and East Africa referring to Hindus, a cause of some consternation, especially among Sikhs (see Menski 2003: 293).

power of ethnic resistance is its ideological autonomy: if there is one set of values around which one can confidently predict that vigorously resistant minorities will *not* predicate their activities, it is those which underpin their excluders' taken-for-granted cultural presuppositions.

Menski (1997a: 64) similarly outlined the underlying methodological implications for legal studies: 'What if the critical element in the legal analysis of race is not in fact 'race', as much of Britain's sociological writing continues to argue, but rather something like 'ethnicity' or 'culture'?' However, there are signs that the deprivationist model is now being applied in the case of Muslims as an underprivileged religious group, a mode of discourse with which many Muslim spokespersons are colluding, with eerie echoes of earlier decades. On the other hand, indicators such as educational performance, employment and the more worrying prison figures for Pakistani and Bangladeshi origin males would seem to bear out the worries that Muslim scholars have themselves expressed (Modood *et al* 1997: 60–147, Ansari 2002, Bunglawala 2004). But the question remains whether we ought to treat this as evidence of deprivation or as part of the increasing pattern of differentiation among Britain's ethnic communities (Mason 2003).

Nevertheless, it is the inner dynamics and value systems of the ethnic minority groups which are crucial to analysing the character of legal reconstruction that they have pursued on British soil. This also implies that expectations of assimilation – that is, the abandonment of one's inherited cultural traditions, and conformism to a dominant British legal culture, whatever that was – were also based upon false assumptions (Ballard 1994b). I will need to discuss further below the impact that this realisation is having within legal scholarship. At the same time, we should not delude ourselves that the British education system has necessarily assisted in the smooth reproduction of community values, with disastrous results in many cases (Sewell 1996, Mehmet Ali 2001). Students are thus constantly being (mis-)educated to underplay their multiple cultural heritages and this can constitute a formidable pedagogical hurdle. Menski (2002a: 89) has pointedly remarked that:

> I am sure that the contributions of young Asians to scholarship on their own communities are less prominent than they might have been if the climate had been more supportive for an open exchange of views.

As argued further in this chapter, the dominant positivist orientation of legal study hardly helps but, rather, serves further to suppress ethnic minority value systems. In this respect, the duties placed upon educational institutions in the Race Relations (Amendment) Act 2000 focus too much, in my view, on performance, but leave educators guessing as to how truly intercultural education could be initiated.

2.3 Problematising prevailing paradigms

In analysing the response of scholarship, and hence approaches to teaching about ethnic minorities in law, we need to start by underlining the profound ambivalence that the British (and Western) legal tradition has about the reconstruction of Asian and African legal orders in the diaspora. Of necessity, therefore, we have to begin with a deconstructive exercise, by questioning the assumptions and limitations of the prevailing jurisprudence, before engaging with alternative, agency-oriented perspectives and the more substantive issues.

As already outlined in Chapter 1, the tradition of legal responses to the presence of Afro-Asian minorities in Britain has been through the prism of the Race Relations Acts, while the initial focus for ethnic minority legal studies in Britain tended to be in the anti-discrimination and immigration law fields (Poulter 1986: vi, Menski 1997a: 65–66). As Lester and Bindman (1972: 13–15) pointed out some 30 years ago, this involved confronting a fundamental contradiction, since immigration laws were most often targeting the very same people whom the anti-discrimination laws seemingly sought to protect. The recent extension of the Race Relations Act to the exercise of public powers, including immigration control, can still co-exist with racist immigration policies. Indeed, we have seen in recent case law that judges have ratified discrimination against Roma people coming to Britain (*R v Immigration Officer at Prague Airport and Others* [2003] IRLR 577 EWCA), while authorisations that allow discriminatory practices to continue are extremely widely drafted.[6] The Race Relations Acts were also consistent with the privileging of 'race' that otherwise expected conformism to the equal citizenship model, which was itself premised on assimilation in cultural terms. Further, the legislation is predicated on the processing of individual grievances, and I would suggest that this sort of response has been seen as appropriate precisely because more generalised exclusionary patterns can thereby be individualised, and largely made containable, than if they were treated as group phenomena. We know through successive studies that discrimination against ethnic minorities remains widespread (Mason 1995: 58–61).[7]

The recent amendment to the 1976 Act is itself remarkable for the extent to which it minimises the impact of the Macpherson inquiry report

---

6   For the latest, see the Race Relations (Immigration and Asylum) Authorisation 2004.

7   The appeals system in immigration law since the Immigration (Appeals) Act 1969 is also subject to the problem of individuation, and also presupposes individualism in migration decisions.

into the death of Stephen Lawrence. The inquiry's radical definition of institutional racism, which should have provoked serious consideration about how to deliver services to British people appropriate to their culture and ethnicity is significantly diluted in the Race Relations (Amendment) Act 2000, which only imposes on public authorities the need to have 'due regard' to the need (a) to eliminate unlawful racial discrimination and (b) to promote equality of opportunity and good relations between persons of different racial groups. Given that local authorities, who had been under this duty since the 1976 Act was first enacted, were never quite sure about what it implied, and it certainly has not resulted in comprehensive reformulation of service delivery at local level, it is hardly surprising that other institutions have not sought radical solutions à la Macpherson either (Kenyon and Hill 2004).

We also see that when group issues arise through this legislation the legal system begins to appear unable to handle their implications. It is possible that when framing the definition of 'racial groups' the draftsmen of the 1976 Act had not realised the difficulties that the courts would face, and that they would in turn create. The definition of 'racial groups' includes 'ethnic groups' and it is ethnic group status which has come, in recent years, to be much more significantly contested in official terms. As a result, it seems that patterns of differential treatment within the operation of the anti-discrimination law have now been created as people who claim protected status as members of ethnic groups have approached the courts (Jones and Welhengama 2000: 27–57). Sikhs may therefore legitimately complain about discrimination against those who wear turbans to cover uncut hair, but Rastas cannot claim that they too regard maintenance of long hair as a sacred duty. On the one hand, the law accords racial group status without much fuss to whites, including Jews and Welsh as well as Japanese, while Muslims and Hindus, on the other hand, have found it an uphill struggle to be recognised. This implicates the legal system in a complex politics of recognition whereby admission to membership of a protected category is made to look more like a favour (Menski 1997a: 67–68).[8] Would it not be far simpler for the

---

8   Council Directive 2000/78/EC now allows individuals to claim protected status on the basis of their 'religion or belief' as of 2 December 2003, albeit only as concerns discrimination within the employment field. Why religion has merited treatment separately from 'race' and 'ethnicity', as provided for by Council Directive 2000/43/EC, would be an important question to investigate. One may speculate that traditions of secularism and Christian pre-dominance throughout the EU may have been behind reservations about members of minority religious groups claiming protection in fields other than employment. The fuss over Muslim women wearing the *hijab* in several EU Member States, not just France, is a case in point.

legal system to start with the premise that everyone is different? It is possible that current discussions about diversity, and value pluralism (Gray 2000, Melissaris 2004), might result eventually in such a societal ethos. It would, however, seem that the key legal postulate of Western legal systems, that at least rhetorically promises equality, but which is often aimed at assimilation and homogenisation, is a significant hurdle in this respect.

By the mid-1980s, the focus on immigration and discrimination was beginning to give way to more diverse coverage with the surfacing of some key writing. Sebastian Poulter's *English Law and Ethnic Minority Customs* and David Pearl's *Family Law and the Immigrant Communities*, both published in 1986, discussed a whole range of legal issues raised by the settlement and increasing presence of Afro-Asians. The focus remained very much on the conflicts of law (or private international law) perspective, however, which typecast ethnic minority issues as involving 'foreign' legal rules within an English (or UK) context. It was not conceded that recently settled ethnic minorities would have to, sooner or later, be seen as further pluralising (even Orientalising!) the English legal system. We were, at that stage, probably still at the point where it was thought that the loosening of links abroad, and therefore reliance on overseas domicile, would inevitably result in large-scale recourse to English legal norms. This was particularly so for the English born or raised generations with their exposure to the British education system.

Indeed, it remains vitally important to discuss how the conflicts of law approach has changed since the signs of acceptance of plurality in the early 1970s. There is evidence that the official approach was considerably tightened to curb signs of judicial independence in this area that would have allowed widespread recourse to non-English laws. Early cases, such as *Qureshi v Qureshi* ([1971] 1 All ER 325), showing considerable receptivity to ethnic minority laws were reversed through legislation that attempted to enforce assimilationist agendas in fields such as divorce within family law (Pearl and Menski 1998: 382–98, Jones and Welhengama 2000: 118–32, Mayss 2000). (We see further strong evidence of this in Chapter 5 where we discuss polygamous marriages.) An over-concentration on the conflicts approach therefore carries the implication that ethnic minority legal issues continue to be seen as 'foreign' – therefore what further is there to discuss about those who have adopted Europe as their home – surely the *lex loci* will and should prevail! In *A-M v A-M* [2001] 2 FLR 6, Hughes J argued that to hold that a *nikah* contracted in London was valid under English law would mean that:

> ... the same would no doubt apply to all manner of self-derived rituals intended to be binding in conscience by those forsaking civil forms of marriage, as well as to 'marriages' according to *foreign religions*, and to other

ceremonies which make no attempt to be English marriages within the Marriage Acts. (emphasis added)

Thus, the state legal system assumes that it can territorially delimit the scope of ethnic minority laws so that they are given no legal recognition officially, and if this approach continues in teaching then we are in danger of ratifying such marginalisation processes by following the tradition of consigning ethnic minority laws to the 'extra-legal' sphere.

There is, however, an increasing consciousness that this approach is no longer adequate, as some of our European colleagues have also been telling us (Foblets 1999, Ferrari 2000: 6–8). It is no coincidence that Ferrari (2000: 6) poignantly argues for the reintroduction of the teaching of the laws of religions as a way of bridging the knowledge gap about the legal issues of importance to the Muslims of Europe. To be sure, Poulter's prolific contributions offered one way of conceptualising the Afro-Asian presence beyond the traditional conflicts of law approach. He argued that the state had to tolerate ethnic diversity at the very least in the interests of social peace, albeit within limits. However, one indicator of Poulter's ambivalent approach was his choice of terminology, which carried significant policy implications. He spoke of 'ethnic minority customs' (Poulter 1986: 3–4) and later also of 'Asian traditions' (Poulter 1990a) rather than 'laws'. As he stated (Poulter 1986: v–vi):

Legal recognition must be afforded to many ethnic minority customs on grounds of practicality, common sense, individual liberty, religious tolerance and the promotion of racial harmony. However, a few restrictions and limitations must equally be imposed, in the interests of public policy, to protect certain core values in English society and to obviate any genuine and reasonable claim by the majority that ethnic minorities are obtaining preferential treatment or special dispensations which cannot be justified by reference to established legal principles. In drawing a suitable dividing line, reference may usefully be made to the provisions of those international treaties to which the UK is a contracting party which are designed to protect human rights and fundamental freedoms.

More recently, Poulter (1998: 391) wrote:

While English law should broadly approach other cultures in a charitable spirit of tolerance and, when in doubt, lean in favour of allowing members of minority communities to observe their diverse traditions here, there will inevitably be certain key areas where minimum standards, derived from shared core values, must of necessity be maintained if the cohesiveness and unity of English society is to be preserved intact.

Suggesting that minority traditions should be viewed as *customs*, rather than anything specifically *legal*, therefore allows Poulter to posit that English law may retain the freedom to choose between those elements that it wishes to see continue and those which it does not. In this respect, the difficulty of establishing the existence of customs generally under English law is instructive (Allen 1964, Zander 1989: 375–84). The treatment of ethnic minority customs as disposable may also overstate the prospects of enforcing uniformity given our observations above about the unrealism of expecting assimilation.

Poulter also tries to drive home the message that conformity to English norms is demanded as a condition of acceptance. In that case it is difficult to resist the conclusion that English law remains very much culture-bound and really quite ethnocentric, or as Santos (2002: 247–51) might say, 'ethno-cratic'. The invocation of human rights treaties as a means of finding a minimum set of agreed-upon values is an unfortunate resort to a legitimating device that disregards the contested environment in which such purportedly universalising treaties exist (Shah 2000a and section 1.3.2 below). This reinforces the ethnocentrism of Poulter's analysis, although it can be expected that an emphasis on human rights will discourage all but the most critical and confident students from raising concerns about this problem.

Another writer, Lucy Carroll (1997: 105), who has taken on the challenge of analysing the status of Muslim laws in the context of the growth of a parallel set of Muslim tribunals in Britain, writes:

> It is important to realise that in the modern world Islamic law, *as law*, does not exist as some disembodied entity floating in the stratosphere, overreaching national boundaries and superseding national law. In the modern world, Islamic law exists only within the context of a nation-state; and within the boundaries of any particular state it is only enforced and enforceable to the extent that, and subject to the reforms and modifications that, the nation-state decrees.

Carroll here tries to reinforce the message that, whatever the feelings of Muslims, they cannot expect to follow Islamic law in Britain, except in so far as decreed by the state. This underlines the persistence of 'legal centralism' (Griffiths 1986: 3) in that the state and its court system assume all power territorially to delimit the recognition and application of ethnic minority legal orders, thereby denying the existence of the unofficial trans-state and transplanted laws that Chiba identified (see section 1.1 above). These writers therefore reflect types of dominant, state-focused perspectives that continue to destatus ethnic minority laws in Britain (but see critically Menski 1993, Menski 1997a: 70, Jones and Welhengama 2000: 97–106). A by-product of such approaches is precisely to advantage those members of ethnic minority communities who can or are willing to navigate between legal orders and who will try to fool lawyers and judges by effectively abusing 'tradition'. On the other hand, those who do not have these means are penalised and often exploited by those in the former group, and there is growing evidence that unofficial abuses and their official non-recognition is affecting women and children in particular (Menski 1993, Pearl and Menski 1998, Shah-Kazemi 2001). Politically correct claims to be seeking gender justice thus seem to ring hollow in the case of ethnic minority women who find themselves doubly disenfranchised under English law. I look at much evidence of such destatusing and penalisation in the following chapters.

2.4 Teaching and doing legal pluralism

If the British legal order largely expects conformity, refuses fully to recognise diversity, and penalises people for cultural and legal hybridity, is there a framework of inquiry that can help us to approach things more positively? Our response has inevitably had to involve a departure from the way in which law was being taught elsewhere and as it was (and is) generally presented in the leading textbooks. This appears to be the case regardless of which subject is being dealt with in particular. Indeed, it has been essential to start from 'basics' and pose questions about how we conceptualise 'law'. We therefore question the fundamental premises of Western 'model jurisprudence' (Chiba 1986: 1) as a way of eventually understanding that the legal situation of Asian and African (and indeed any other) ethnic minorities (or majorities) cannot be adequately analysed within traditionally accepted 'black-letter' renderings, which still dominate the academy (Hutchinson 1999). Further, we try also to decentre 'legal centralist' presuppositions by showing that the claims of modernist legal thought are far from realisable in practice. Official state-based legal systems simply cannot control everything, and ontological and epistemological space is also necessary for other types of ordering.

For critiques most relevant to a study of ethnic minorities in Western legal systems we turn to legal-pluralist writers, most of whom have actually been concerned with the nature of non-Euro-American legal systems (for example, Hooker 1975, Moore 1978, Chiba 1986, 1989, Griffiths 1986, Menski 2000a). Chiba (1998), on the other hand, suggests that the concept of 'legal culture' tends to perform the function in Western societies that legal pluralism does for others. At a general level, legal pluralist theories argue that 'law' can be generated by different sources, whether recognised by the state or not. This idea is often shocking to people schooled only in Western law, possibly because it concedes too much to 'the people' who would then also have to be viewed as law making agents in their own right. In this context, the observations made about the blinkers that legal education seems to put onto students' vision made by Conaghan (2002: 319–21) are especially apposite. In that sense, one of the challenges for ethnic minority legal studies, as for feminist legal studies, is precisely to try to enable critical thinking about law to take place. Some pluralist writing also argues that the state and lawyers end up obtaining too much power by overemphasising top-down structures that undermine the power of self-regulation within the society or societies concerned, by denying that such self-regulation actually occurs and is a legitimate concern for study. Others have sought to highlight that an approach to legal study that ignores social, cultural or religious fields neglects an important component of the 'law' itself, how it operates and its effectiveness and relevance. Pluralist theories therefore also open up avenues for arguing that 'law' is very much determined by one's cultural presuppositions. Immediately, strongly-held beliefs about pursuance of legal uniformity as a mark of a developed and modern legal system are also put into doubt, especially when one is working within a polyethnic context. For students at SOAS, this material has been largely palatable and digestible since they are exposed to an explicitly comparative curriculum. It encounters resistance elsewhere, however. There is an interplay of several factors here. Schooling in non-Euro-American legal systems is just not available widely enough; theorising in that field also suffers from the homogenising claims of development- or globalisation-oriented scholarship; and it is wrongly assumed that personal law systems were simply a colonial by-product or a British invention and therefore to be viewed as a mark of submission in the post-colonial era (Menski 2000a: 131–32). The prevalence of caricatures and stereotypes of Asian and African legal systems can then easily be used to discredit attempts at deeper analysis.

However, an emerging literature taking an agency-oriented approach to the situation of migrants and their offspring has now begun to discuss the implications of the diversity of legal cultures in Britain (Menski 1993, 2001, Pearl and Menski 1998, Jones and Welhengama 2000, Yilmaz 2000, 2001, 2002a, 2004). From legal pluralist perspectives, ethnic minorities are themselves seen as navigating among different legal orders, thereby reconstructing Asian and African laws in hybrid forms. This means that their traditional obligation systems are still understood by members of these communities as paramount, while they are seen to build in the requirements of official law as necessary or expedient. A specifically Muslim variant of this is termed *angrezi shariat* (Pearl and Menski 1998), an Urdu term simply meaning British-Muslim law, and there is discussion now of *angrezi dharma* (Menski 2003: 592), the equivalent emerging legal order in diaspora for Hindus. That discerning these elements of legal behaviour involves taking account of 'unofficial' (Chiba 1986: 6, 1989: 136) practices means that our book-based laws are of much less relevance; an examination of the law reports or a textbook on any key area of English law will still not yield much information about the operation of *angrezi dharma* or British-Yoruba laws, precisely because they are relegated to unofficial status, and therefore considered irrelevant to dispute resolution in the courts.[9]

The publication by the Lord Chancellor's Department of the *Equal Treatment Benchbook* and its vigorous promotion by Lord Justice Brooke, as well as ethnic minority awareness training for magistrates and judges, is certainly to be welcomed in this regard, although students have immediately questioned whether this approach is really not tokenism or simply too little. All this does, however, mean that people with field knowledge become especially important in providing information about reconstruction of Asian and African, and the already emerging, Latin American laws. Given that there are very few persons with such training, and that few law departments have seriously acknowledged its relevance, means that we may have to rely on anthropologically inclined colleagues, who are specifically interested in bottom-up field observations, to supply the necessary skills and knowledge.

Such persons are increasingly sought by lawyers in practice to provide expert background information in order to shed further light on cases they are handling. Both Menski (1993: 251, 253) and Ballard have argued that the common law system, with its case-by-case approach, may potentially be suited to meeting the demands of justice in such disputes, provided that courts are brought up to speed on the ethnic minority issues involved. However, Menski has observed that the lack of adequate information and appropriate training for lawyers, who act as key gatekeepers, means that by the time a dispute reaches the courts the 'ethnic' elements in it will have been twisted out of recognition if not altogether eliminated. Ballard, on the other hand, has expressed some disappointment with the higher judiciary after crucial information in criminal cases has been dismissed as irrelevant. Leading experts have therefore tested the common law system and concluded that it may, in fact, not be a suitable vehicle through which to seek justice without its acknowledgment of plurality on a much more fundamental level.

I have found, however, that such material produced by experts, now growing in various private collections, is a very useful supplement to our existing teaching tools. While students often find intuitive appeal in reading legal pluralist perspectives, they are often uncertain about their practical value. The use of expert reports therefore enables students to see how field knowledge can be applied in real casework contexts, thereby opening the door to discussions about how legal pluralism could work in

---

9   On Yoruba settlement in London, see Oyètádé (1993).

practice or, as one colleague recently remarked, how one can *do* legal pluralism. I am convinced, despite what may be apparent from our law reports, that a huge market exists out there for such work as long as we are able to train people with the right sort of skills. While this should also open up a more lively debate about the role of experts within the legal system, it is beginning to appear that, for the moment, and despite official reluctance to admit that we are moving towards a sort of Afro-Asian personal law system in Britain, this role is vital in ensuring ethno-sensitive service provision. We revisit the issue of expert reports in Chapters 4, 6 and 7.

2.5   Curricular concerns

We have seen then that there are considerable conceptual hurdles that need to be confronted and discussed as a necessary precondition to engagement with the more substantive aspects of teaching about ethnic minorities in law. Here, one will most likely be developing on one's own areas of strength and research interest. Immigration and anti-discrimination law continue to be of relevance. From a relatively marginal position, they have indeed risen to prominence in practice in recent years.[10] However, the potential range of other topics that can be covered is huge. Besides immigration and anti-discrimination law and the conceptual issues that have been discussed above, we have tended to focus on the following legal areas: family law, criminal law, racial harassment and violence, mental health, blasphemy and education. There is certainly room for (and in theory no limit to!) further diversification and various other issues such as business, planning, housing, legal education, the legal professions and dispute resolution could be included.

One key issue will be that of teaching materials. Using law reports as a teaching tool is, of course, indispensable. However, law reporting remains fraught with its own politics that have ensured the systematic non-appearance of cases of crucial relevance to ethnic minority laws. We can be sure that reports represent merely the tip of the iceberg when it comes to ethnic minority legal disputes, many of which will never be presented before official fora as traditional avoidance mechanisms come into play (Menski 1993: 255). We have also noted above how the 'ethnic' elements in disputes may be engineered out of the hearing by lawyers or claims about 'tradition' may even be raised to the unfair advantage of

---

10   Complementing the Immigration Law Practitioners' Association there is also now the Discrimination Law Association. Both organisations offer multiple advantages and, for academics, a way of keeping in regular touch with practice issues.

one party. With cases that do appear in the reports, there will be issues as to precisely how to interpret the background as well as the result as presented by judges. Discussing the various 'visible' and 'invisible' elements in judgments provides a fascinating area of critical legal education in itself.[11]

Articles derived largely from the minority press have been a key source of information showing how the social basis of the legal order is changing ethnically, and in ways which are barely discussed in the academic literature. Although matters are improving, reliance on 'unorthodox' sources is still necessary; academic writing has simply not caught up in this respect. Besides, there are some types of issue that would seldom be brought to light in textbook form. The Stephen Lawrence case that led to some incisive questioning of the criminal justice system by Macpherson's team, or the trial of the Leeds footballers charged for crimes against an Asian youngster, Sarfraz Najeib, I have found, can be fruitfully discussed through the press reporting that they received. Another valuable source of information has been non-legal academic writing, particularly by social science colleagues. Again, it is here that many issues are being addressed that are not being built into legal writing, because they are dismissed from legal-centralist perspectives as 'extra-legal'. Teaching in this area therefore necessarily requires some inter-disciplinary navigation (Menski 1997a: 71). This may result in complaints from law librarians, but there may be ways in which inter-departmental resources can be pooled, thus making the most of existing material.

A more general curricular concern is whether one should teach a course on Ethnic Minorities and the Law as a separate optional offering, or whether an ethnic minority focus ought to be integrated into all areas of teaching. In principle, I am certainly in favour of the latter approach. Indeed, if it is now accepted that the police, magistrates, judges and other officials are prone to institutional racism, and that training is essential to mitigate its effects, then it would seem impossible to argue that law students should not be taught about the implications ethnic diversity in Britain has for all areas of law. Indeed, on this basis, one ought to be able to argue for resources dedicated to building diversity programmes in all law departments. However, I do not yet see a movement in this direction – 'mainstream' legal writing, and therefore also education, continues to

---

11   A good 'test case' here is *Kaur v Singh* [1972] 1 All ER 292 where the court accepted the claim that it is normally the duty of the groom's side to make the arrangements for a Sikh wedding. I am constantly amazed by how many students, even those of South Asian background, fail to spot how the judge was misled about this.

remain overwhelmingly 'culture blind', which really means a white, Euro-focused approach. I recently argued (see Chapter 3), and was criticised for doing so, that post-war writing on public law has taken virtually no account of Britain's changed ethnic character, and it is certain that the same can be said of all 'mainstream' areas of law teaching in Britain. Building in plurality-conscious approaches into every area of law would have implications for the underpinnings of every course as one would be forced to recognise the cultural specificity even of the 'majority' areas, and their claims to ideological dominance would thereby be severely compromised.[12] A real danger still exists that separate optional courses on ethnic minorities can be pushed further into an 'ethnic niche', so that other academics can comfortably avoid taking the need for changes in their own curricula seriously. This should not, in any case, deter committed individual teachers from being more adventurous in their own repertoires.

---

12 This does not mean that there are no changes at all in response to ethnic diversity. A new edition of Hoggett *et al* (2002), a leading family law undergraduate course book has, in its first chapter, a sizeable extract from the *Equal Treatment Benchbook* discussing the diversity of family structures in Britain today. Unfortunately, this has allowed the rest of the book to maintain a 'culture blind' perspective, with the strong suggestion that official English law remains the dominant ordering system among ethnic minorities too. In comparison, Probert (2003), while containing discussion and extracts of many reported ethnic minority court cases, maintains a modernist, Euro-focus, showing the persistence of dominant attitudes. European discussions now coalescing around the idea of a uniform European family law system (see Boele-Woelki 2003) remain woefully inadequate, while emphasising a modernist, 'white' focus, and ignoring growing evidence of ethnic minority input. Such ideas would be subject to the same sort of criticisms that Legrand (1997) so powerfully spelt out against a European civil code.

Chapter 3
The other Incoming Tide:
The Diasporic Challenge to the
British Constitutional Order

If constitutions and constitutionalism are about the normative regulation of the relationship between the governed and the governors of any particular polity, as well as about notions of propriety among the governors, then the immigration of people from outside that polity may have a tendency to disrupt a pre-existing constitutional system, and force the asking of hard questions about how new subjects or citizens are to be accommodated, and whether their arrival and settlement is to require a change of approach in the hitherto accepted forms of governance. Where the new arrivals are used to notions and norms of governance premised on a fundamentally different conceptual order, then finding answers to those questions may not be an easy task. In this scenario, their presence, or simply the prospect of their presence, may provoke defensive reactions on the part of the existing polity on grounds of racial or cultural dilution or contamination, perceptions of threats to the existing way of life, or loss of control. Crucially, this reaction can then translate into a denial of the significance of the changed normative character of a society, and consequent refusal to discuss the constitutional implications flowing from this.

In this chapter the focus is on some key themes. It looks first at how the self-concept of the British polity has been transformed through defensiveness about race and culture as a result of immigration into a recognisably ethno-centric vision of belongingness that effectively tries to exclude or limit access to citizenship as well as other forms of legal status and recognition to 'others'. Indeed, we will see that the possibility of migration itself comes to determine the shape of citizenship in an arguably unique development, even as new categories of belonging, notably European citizenship, are accommodated. We then explore the extent to which, when confronted with a *de facto* multicultural social base, the British state has come to terms with the constitutional implications of this altered scenario. We will have to examine how far the new picture of increased cultural pluralism is accounted for in official terms, and how this state of affairs is recognised in the writing of constitutionalists. We will see that much of the existing scholarship has been largely unwilling or unable to grasp the nettle. Then, taking a socio-legal perspective that views immigration as also involving the arrival and establishment of different legal cultures, and migrants and their descendants as having the *agency* to reconstruct these cultures *on their own terms*,[1] I examine some alternative readings that account for the cultural specificity of recent developments and outline some potential implications for the constitutional order.

3.1   Defining Britishness

While the African and Asian presence has been evident in Britain for centuries, as a number of historical works have demonstrated (Fryer 1984, Ramdin 1999, Lahiri 1999, Visram 2002), it is the post-war history of immigration that has left lasting and long-term implications for the British social order. Ballard (1994b: 1–3) prognosticates that the change wrought by post-war immigration to Britain may prove to have as much of a profound impact in the longer term, as did the Norman irruption. If the impact on the British legal order initiated by the Normans is anything to go by, then we may indeed be looking at significant implications that have hardly been worked through yet.

It appears that policy makers in top government circles were discussing the potential implications, in terms of social peace, of the immigration of people from various parts of the British Empire and Commonwealth in the Caribbean, Asia and Africa from the late 1940s. Given the continued need to overcome post-war labour shortages, recruitment on a large scale in far-flung territories continued, despite concerns about the gradually increasing presence of non-Europeans in Britain. The earlier sponsored immigration of European Volunteer Workers in hundreds of thousands was never to provoke such hidden resentment. Once hostility against non-European workers had been openly expressed in racist violence in the late 1950s in places such as Nottingham and Notting Hill (Pilkington 1996, Phillips and Phillips 1998: 158–88), it seemed also to become acceptable overtly to advocate the limitation of their presence in Britain.[2]

---

1   This phrase is borrowed from Roger Ballard's (1994b: 5) characterisation of Britain's South Asian communities in which, far from following the assimilationist models, 'both the older generation of settlers and their British born offspring are continuing to find substantial inspiration in the resources of their own particular cultural, religious and linguistic inheritance, which they are creatively reinterpreting to rebuild their lives *on their own terms*'.

2   A number of studies cover the history and development of immigration controls in the UK, notably Evans (1983), Bevan (1986), Dummett and Nicol (1990), Juss (1993) and Sachdeva (1993).

Thus, the imperial norm of citizenship, encoded in the British Nationality Act of 1948, that still meant that all nominally British subjects whether from existing colonies or the expanding Commonwealth were free from immigration control, began to be redefined. The Commonwealth Immigrants Act 1962 predicated control on the place of issue of passport rather than stress the implied racism. Nevertheless, the first major step to redefine citizenship of the UK on a racial basis, and importantly in terms of immigration rights, had been taken. Britishness was moving away from the imperial ideal of an expansive and inclusive, although still hegemonic notion, in reaction to the immigration of non-European people. It also therefore said something about who then remained 'British' (Paul 1997, Spencer 1997).

This pattern was repeated with alarming frequency and continuity with every significant piece of immigration legislation since 1962. That Act had itself indirectly begun to affect the character of migration patterns in the UK as worker migration began to give way to large-scale family reunion, which continues in different ways to this day. It is this shift that has led to the raising of extremely important questions about the changing ethnic nature of the British social order. For the moment, however, we can note that continuing immigration, particularly from South Asia, also ensured its continued politicisation and the advocacy of greater control.

The Kenyan Asians exodus in late 1967 and early 1968 therefore led to the curtailment of immigration rights of a large group of British passport holders, many of whom did not enjoy access to another citizenship status, or who, in reliance on assurances made in the transition to independence by leading members of the British government, did not wish to access it in an atmosphere of growing political hostility in East Africa. Thus, the Commonwealth Immigrants Act 1968 led to a redefinition of those free from immigration control in the UK. The 1968 Act added to the requirement that a qualifying passport must be a UK-issued passport by stipulating that such a passport must also be held by someone having a connection with Britain (birth, naturalisation, etc in the UK), at the very least, through a grandparental link. This move emboldened other states to limit entry to East African Asian British passport holders, and the harsh consequences of such a strategy really came to the fore during the Ugandan Asians crisis when Britain was forced to accept the Asian people expelled by the Amin regime.[3]

---

3   The treatment of Asian British nationals from East Africa under UK law is dealt with in detail in Shah (2000b: 69–99) and, for cabinet discussions at the time, see Lester (2002).

The distancing strategies enacted through legislation were also finding echoes in judicial decisions. The case of *Thakrar* concerned a British-protected person expelled from Uganda. In response to the claim on his behalf that, being a British national, he ought to be admitted to Britain, Lord Denning (*R v Immigration Officer ex p Thakrar* [1974] QB 684, at 702B–D) stated:

> They are said to be British nationals but they are not British subjects. These number, or used to number, many millions. They were not born here. They have never lived here. They live thousands of miles away in countries which have no connection with England except that they were once British protectorates. Is it to be said that by international law every one of them has a right if expelled to come into these small islands? Surely not. This country would not have room for them. It is not as if only one or two were coming. They come not in single files 'but in battalions'.

This is one of the better known examples of the disdain shown by British judges against non-European British nationals, as they have regularly failed to address problems faced by claimants coming to the courts.[4]

The concern of policy makers to continue with the programme of ethnically driven controls was consolidated by the Immigration Act of 1971, essentially still effective through its distinction between 'patrials' and 'non-patrials'. These later determined the nationality categories and the immigration status that went with each one in the British Nationality Act 1981. British nationality was thus divided into several groups along typically Aristotelian lines (Gray 2000), one of which, the British citizens, came out on top with full rights of abode. These strategies of inclusion and exclusion though nationality law were also evident in the responses to the regrouping of Bangladeshi families in the UK (on which see Chapter 6), in the case of Hong Kong's transfer (Menski 1995), and they have continued to be manifest in various ways right down to the present day.

There is, of course, a European angle to all of this. Around the time of the passing of the 1971 Act the precise terms of membership of the then European Economic Community were being negotiated. No definition of British nationality was incorporated in the 1971 Act, nor in the European Communities Act 1972 that gave effect to European law in the UK legal order. The definition, effectively excluding all non-patrials (except Gibraltarians), was rather incorporated in a Declaration of 1972 appended to the Treaty of Accession. It is certain that the narrow definition of British nationals was, at least in part, triggered by concerns of existing Member

---

4   See, for other examples, *Amin v Entry Clearance Office, Bombay* [1983] 2 All ER 864; *R v Secretary of State for the Home Department ex p Patel* [1993] Imm AR 392; *R v Immigration Appeal Tribunal ex p Nargis Sunsara and Others* [1995] Imm AR 15.

States about the free movement of non-European British nationals. However, the precise legal character of the Declaration, as well as its more updated version of 1982, remained uncertain until the ECJ's decision in the *Manjit Kaur* case (C–192/99, judgment of 20 February 2001). This case concerned the status of a Sikh woman from Kenya who had lost her right to enter the UK under the 1968 Act, although she still held a British passport. The exclusionary motives behind the Declarations were obscured in the *Manjit Kaur* litigation, at the conclusion of which the ECJ upheld their validity. While it looks as if the ethnically exclusive definitions of citizenship are being reinforced with Europeanisation, I examine this background in greater detail in Chapter 8.

So what does this brief and rather selective excursus through some key points in the history of British nationality and citizenship law tell us? For this we can turn to an excellent study by Kathleen Paul who draws two key conclusions. First, she notices the salience of an observation made by Roger Brubaker that in much of the contemporary literature on citizenship, which has been inspired by the plight of guestworker populations in Europe and illegal aliens in the United States, the central question has been whether rights of citizenship should be extended to all residents, regardless of whether they are formally citizens of the country in which they live, or whether access to citizenship should be opened up in order to provide access to these rights. She notices, however, that: 'In all these debates Britain remains a little apart because ... while other countries debated the admission of immigrants to citizenship, Britain alone was discussing the admission of citizens as immigrants' (Paul 1997: xiv).[5] Secondly, she observes (*ibid*):

> And most unhappily of all, modern Britain is still plagued by past perspectives that categorised some Britons as more British than others. Facing the fact that successive governments did not want them and tried to reclassify them as something other than British, British subjects of color still have to fight to identify themselves as British. They do so within a domestic community many of whose members, thanks to successive legislative acts, have come to understand race as a natural divider and nationality as an accidental commonality.

She further observes that this pattern suggests that a resolution of the 'immigrant and refugee problem' across Europe, including Britain, consequently relies less on legislative change and the institution of

---

5   The high profile example in respect of the former is Germany (Joppke 1998, Marshall 2000), where there remains a great ambivalence on the question. Other EU States have also tended, since the 1990s, to adjust legislation in order to prevent access to citizenship to recent non-European settlers. See Simmons (1994) on France and Biondi (1995) on Italy.

formally expansive nationality policies and more on a concerted effort to redefine the national identity as more inclusive (Paul 1997: xv). In this context, it is instructive to note that the recent extension of British citizen status to the inhabitants of Britain's Overseas Territories and the stateless British passport holders (see further Chapter 8) has been accompanied by ministers underlining the small numbers that can be expected to migrate to the UK as a result. Furthermore, the Nationality, Immigration and Asylum Act 2002 premises acquisition of nationality upon knowledge of English or Welsh and 'sufficient knowledge of life in the UK' (Shah, R 2003a), again sending assimilationist messages to ethnic minorities, since no concomitant obligations are placed on the 'host' society having to learn about the minority communities. We will see shortly that other areas of the British social and legal order have continued to reinforce messages about exclusivity and exclusion.

3.2   Avoiding pluralism

Apart from skin colour, which obviously constitutes a crucial dividing line in the games of exclusion and inclusion, what has come to the fore since the 1960s is the question of assimilation to dominant modes of behaviour and minimisation of cultural difference. And immigration control has played a central role in this. We have observed how migrants switched their strategy in the aftermath of the 1962 Act to family reunification and formation, a pattern that was also witnessed some years later in other parts of northern Europe with the 'immigration stops' of the 1970s (Castles *et al* 1993, Collinson 1993). For Britain, there had been significant immigration since the 1950s from the South Asian regions of the Punjab in both India and Pakistan, Azad Kashmir governed by Pakistan, Gujarat in India and Sylhet in Bangladesh (formerly East Pakistan). Predominantly male, these 'rotating' migrants realised that in order to attain secure immigration status and continue to take advantage of economic opportunities, the best option was to remain and reconstitute their families in Britain. Thus, as with the Caribbeans before them, Britain began to witness the establishment of South Asian colonies in industrialised urban centres. The migrations from East Africa also added significantly to the Gujarati and Punjabi populations.[6] Impressions began to form quite early

---

6   Ballard (1990) writes interestingly about the variations of decisions to reconstitute families among South Asian groups. On the South Asian presence more generally, see Ballard (1994a). Of the groups of South Asian men who had worked in Britain in the early part of the post-war period, it seems that the Bangladeshis were the last to make moves towards family reunification, a process that continues today. As a result, their families came to be caught up in some draconian restrictions applied to South Asians – see Chapter 6.

on about how, while the Caribbeans could be expected to assimilate to British norms (were they not Christians and did they not speak English after all?), the South Asians whose numbers were increasing fast could not possibly adopt British (predominantly English?) norms of behaviour (Rose *et al* 1969: 417–75).[7] As a consequence, the job of immigration control came to be defined in terms of preventing significant cultural or ethnic pluralism in Britain.

Public records released in early 2002 of cabinet discussions that took place prior to the passing of the Immigration Act 1971 show this quite clearly. The 1971 Act and accompanying Immigration Rules would substantially improve the standing of potential migrants from the white Commonwealth. At the time, different systems of control were applied to so called aliens and Commonwealth citizens. While the Prime Minister, Edward Heath, favoured one single regime with work permits to be issued to anyone wishing to qualify for entry, his Home Secretary Reginald Maulding opposed this. In a paper sent to the Prime Minister (*The Guardian*, 1 January 2002) he stated:

> The difficulties lie in the nature of the people concerned. Of the (non-Commonwealth) aliens coming here to work the great majority wish only to stay for a short time and return home. The number who want to settle permanently are relatively few and, for this reason and because they come from a cultural background generally fairly akin to our own, it is not difficult to assimilate them. But of those wishing to come from the Commonwealth, particularly the new Commonwealth, the majority would want to settle permanently and, by reason both of this factor and of the fact that generally they come from a different cultural background, the task of assimilation, as experience so bitterly shows, is all but impossible. Here is the fundamental dilemma that faces us. If we put the Commonwealth citizen on the same basis as what at present is the practice for aliens, and abolish the quota which applies only to Commonwealth citizens, the result would be a great increase in coloured immigration.

The problem of assimilation was therefore identified as a key issue at that time, and also explains the subsequently overwhelming focus on controlling family-based migration particularly from South Asia. At its most vulgar, the preoccupation with South Asian immigration led to virginity tests being carried out on women culminating in a British

---

7   To be sure, Rose *et al* were far from being naively assimilationist and were acutely aware of the differences among Caribbean migrants. They noted (1969: 424): 'But it was only those who aspired to be 'white' in the special West Indian sense who adopted European values and followed European culture patterns. The rest of the population remained within an Afro-West Indian culture.' Sadly, since immigration, the African elements of the Caribbeans' culture have continued to be suppressed.

apology to the UN Human Rights Commission after a complaint was lodged by the Indian government (Malik 1997: 45–47). All manner of other exclusionary mechanisms have been devised to refuse applicants, including the development, refinement and judicial endorsement of the 'primary purpose rule', mainly designed to exclude incoming male spouses, through which thousands of South Asian families remained divided across continents (Sachdeva 1993, Menski 1999); the introduction of visa requirements (JCWI 1987, Drabu and Bowen 1989); and derecognition of family relationships more generally (Sondhi 1987, Juss 1997), that is also leading to the creation of a very negative, ethnocentric approach to private international law (Mortimore 1994, Pearl and Menski 1998, Mayss 2000, and see Chapters 5, 6 and 7 below).

3.3   Representing ethnic diversity

If the immigration control system, supported by the law, was designed to avoid pluralism, then it has not fully succeeded. As noted above, the post-war history of the Britain's urban industrial centres has been characterised by a changing cultural landscape with the formation of ethnic minority colonies. However, knowledge of the extent and nature of the ethnic minority presence had for long been limited by lack of access to clear data.[8] The 1991 Census, for the first time, measured ethnic affiliation, although this attempt to do so has been rightly criticised on several grounds (Ballard 1996c, Aspinall 2000: 588–92). It looked for the self-identification of non-white groups through the use of ethno-national labels (Pakistani, etc), but failed to capture identifiers that might make sense in terms of minority communities' multiple internal realities (region of origin, religion, or *jati* (caste), for example).[9] It failed to represent some, such as the Greek and Turkish Cypriots, Yemenis and Arabs altogether, perhaps prompting the option to tick 'white'.[10] The 'white' category was itself presented as uncontested and internally undifferentiated, representing the continued denial of the ethnicity of and within white majority groups – 'whiteness' is widely assumed to be the norm after all. The Census categorisation could thus be rightly criticised

---

8   Earlier, statistics were collected on the basis of the country of birth, not ethnicity as such, causing considerable problems of estimation. On implications for socio-legal research in light of the growth of South Asian communities, see Menski (1993: 239–43).

9   Nesbitt (1997) points out the persisting salience of *jati* among younger South Asians. See also Chapter 1 for other observations about *jati* and kinship.

10   Mehmet Ali (2001) observes that the 'invisibility' of Turkish-speaking communities in official statistics leaves a yawning gap in information around educational performance, thus preventing the devising of strategies to tackle problems.

as a form of official racism in that it impliedly problematised the non-white presence. In line with Kathleen's Paul's observations (above at 3.1) about citizenship law, others (Jacobson 1997, Parekh 2000b, Hoge 2002), have also reported unease with the use of 'British' as an identifier among many ethnic minorities, precisely because the concept is still too heavily perceived as racially or ethnically coded, as already prefigured in the title of Professor Tariq Modood's (1992) book: *Not Easy Being British*.

By conflating many different groups into the 'white' category, the Census also obscured the fact that the UK, like many other countries in Western Europe, has at least two different sorts of history with white ethnic (or religious or linguistic) minorities. There are, on the one hand, the older so called national minority groups such as Scots, Welsh, Cornish and Irish (if one takes the UK as a whole), each also being internally diverse (Protestant and Catholic Scots and so on). Although they are no strangers to ethnic conflict, the state system as a whole has allowed for the legal specificity of these groups for reasons that include their historical association with a territorial base and campaigns for concessions gained over a longer time period. However, they too are exposed to centralising norms when 'deterritorialised', at which point they can also be regarded as ethnic minority groups vis-à-vis the English majority. On the other hand, it can be expected that non-belongers are expected to conform to group norms – what, for example, is the legal position of the Chinese of Ulster or Pakistani-Scots?[11]

In addition, we also have white immigrant minorities and their descendants through different periods of history such as Normans, Huguenots, Jews, Irish Catholics, Italians, Poles, etc. Catholics and Jews (Hamilton 1995: 5–8), for example, have gained concessions (even a right to exist) under British laws over a long period of time. Nowadays, their presence may hardly seem to be problematic and therefore, rather uncritically, they are not perceived as posing a major challenge to dominant norms. Rather than simply assimilating to these norms, it is much more likely that members of these populations have learnt over time, at least publicly, to minimise their differences vis-à-vis the majority, naturally being helped in this by their skin colour. After all, state-enforced conformism has a long history in Britain. This may explain the ease with which unrestricted migration is accepted for European Union nationals in the UK, while non-Europeans are perceived as threatening (and not necessarily because of their skin-colour) to what is assumed to

---

11 See Hussain (2001) on South Asians in Glasgow under immigration law. Recent reports indicate that English minorities in Scotland have begun to highlight and win cases of discrimination, as have Scots and Welsh people in England.

be a shared national character. However, one can also see that freedom of movement is not extended willingly to the nationals of all the new Member States as of 1 May 2004, partly because of the fear of Roma immigration. On the other hand, Englishness, against which others have tended to be defined, is itself not disentangled nor challenged, and this reluctance possibly explains the choice of the Census designers to leave that particular stone unturned by opting for a 'racial' classification: 'white'. The official compilations then certainly did not share the view that everyone is 'ethnic', again reinforcing the image of the homogeneity and the normality of a white majority.[12]

Some of these criticisms have been addressed by the way in which the 2001 Census included religion and broke down the 'white' category further to include options for White-British or White-Irish. It also responded to the development of hybrid identifications amongst other ethnic minority groups by widening rubrics to include including options on Asian-British, or Black-British, etc. However, if ethnicity has posed difficulties for Census designers, the new question on religion is bound to be even more problematic. Aspinall (2000: 586) observed that the initial motivation for including a question on religion was to find out about the religious affiliations of South Asians in Britain, and only later was the category widened to take account of other religious groups in the UK. While the public policy case for knowing about religious diversity can be made (Aspinall 2000: 592–94), representing South Asians as Muslims, Hindus or Sikhs severely underestimates the internal diversities within each in terms of sect and non-exclusivity or pluralism of practice, thereby essentialising such categories (see Ballard 1996b, McLeod 1989, Elst 2001). An even more radical problem is raised by Staal (1996) who argues that the very notion of 'religion' is itself Western in origin and at most applicable to the three Abrahamic traditions of Judaism, Christianity and Islam.[13] For 'religions' in Asia, he argues, what is more central is not the formal denomination with its identifiable belief system, but ritual practice. Staal's suggestion, if taken seriously, would have the effect of an inclusive approach and would thus account for Chinese, Japanese and other traditions of Asia, as well as traditional African practices, at present totally suppressed by the Census.

---

12 For a poignant account of the 'invisibility' of Irish ethnicity, see Mac an Ghaill (2000).

13 Aspinall (2000: 591), however, cites research in which it is found that among Jews ritual practice is found to be less clearly linked to strength of belief, but far more closely related to ethnic identity.

Both Censuses, at the same time, show some interesting trends.[14] Statistically, the non-European ethnic minority population is of more and more significance. The 1991 count showed that it had reached some 5.5% of the UK population, while the 2001 figure is 8% in the UK and 9% in England. Significantly, the ethnic minority population is concentrated in particular urban areas of Britain. Some of the more striking statistics would include: Bangladeshis make up 33.4% of London's Tower Hamlets Borough; Indians make up 25.7% of Leicester; over 10% of Southwark, Newham, Lambeth and Hackney Boroughs in London are black Africans, as with Lewisham, Lambeth, Brent and Hackney for black Caribbeans. 3.1% in England stated their religion as Muslim, with 8.5% of Londoners being Muslim, with 36% Muslims in Tower Hamlets and 24% in Newham. 4.1% of Londoners are Hindus, as are one in seven people of Leicester, while Harrow is 19.6% Hindu. Barnet in London is 14.8% Jewish, and over 8 % in Hounslow and Ealing are Sikh.

Thus, in the larger conurbations of Greater London, Greater Manchester, the cities of the east and west Midlands, Sheffield, Scunthorpe and the textile towns in the Pennines, we find this presence to have more visibly affected the environment, local norms and cultures. Adding ethnographic information to the statistical picture, we also find that particular ethnic groups are concentrated in certain localities *within* these conurbations. Migration patterns based on kinship and local connections in areas of origin have often significantly influenced subsequent residential choices (Werbner 1979, Robinson 1986).

Clearly, there is no simple picture here, but how geographical concentration determines certain legal developments remains a fascinating though under-explored area of study (although see Menski 1988: 11–12, Pearl and Menski 1998: 59–61, Nielsen 1988, 1992).[15] A recent case concerning Bangladeshis in East London strikingly illustrates that such developments altering the legal nature of local environments have not escaped the notice of alert judges.[16] Current official and institutionalised emphasis on 'dispersal' (Harvey 2000: 195–96, Shah

---

14 See Peach (1996) in detail, and Mason (1995: 32–35) briefly, on the 1991 Census. The 5.5% figure, broken down further, shows 2.7% as South Asian, 1.6% as 'black' (including African, Caribbean and 'other' categories) and 0.7% as being Chinese and 'other-Asian' people. For the 2001 figures see the National Statistics website: www.statistics.gov.uk.

15 Saggar (1996) argues, more ominously, that policy decisions were taken in top government circles earlier in the post-war period to ensure that debates on the pluralisation of British society would remain concentrated at local levels, thereby avoiding wider, national debates on policy taking place.

16 We discuss this case: *Re S (Change of Names: Cultural Factors)* [2001] FLR 1005 *per* Wilson J in Chapter 6.

2000b: 199–200, Stevens 2004: 251–54), not in itself a new idea, is a direct and, I believe, deliberate attack on the potential development of the same patterns for newer migrant communities. The frequent use, and expansion of, reporting requirements for asylum seekers, as well as residence restrictions, can then be seen as bolt-on mechanisms for dispersal, to keep people in their place, so to speak.

3.4 The limits of dominant perspectives on constitutional law

The conceptual confusion and uncertainty about ethnic diversity at the official level fundamentally affects legal approaches too, and we have seen some of the confusing signals that the case law under the Race Relations Act 1976 gives to members of different minority communities (see section 2.3). It would appear that in Anglo-American (even Western) jurisprudence there is a general reluctance to accommodate ethnicity within legal and policy frameworks, as Hameso (1997: 5, 10) shows, from an African perspective. In official terms, therefore, recognition of ethnic diversity has led to hardly any acknowledgment of its manifold legal implications, with minimal impact at the teaching and academic levels also (Menski 1997a, and see Chapter 2). Diversionary strategies are regularly deployed in the legal field, despite overwhelming evidence of diversity from other social sciences; law is seen and taught still very much within the Western positivist tradition, and that position of dominance seems to suit power brokers. On the other hand, there is considerable evidence that legal writers who confront this field retreat into Eurocentric evaluations. Thus, English or UK law is ultimately treated as 'ethnicised' property to be controlled and to control 'others'. Prominently, the prolific responses by the late Sebastian Poulter fall, as we saw in Chapters 1 and 2, into this category, although he is hardly an exception. Today, trendy universalistic pontification about human rights offers much potential to level abuse and disparagement at Asian and African cultural and legal orders. It is notable, on the other hand, that human rights law, with its roots in liberal humanist political philosophy, has been unable to handle pluralism and the related problem of minority protection, leaving a gap to be filled by widespread conflicts between existing nation-states and those who would lead postmodern tribal states.[17]

---

17 For a general appraisal of liberal political philosophy in relation to cultural pluralism, see Parekh (2000a), and for value pluralism, see Gray (2000). For a globally-focused legal analysis on the status of minorities, see Welhengama (2000).

If the general picture of ethnic minorities under UK law, despite the endeavours of writers coming from legal pluralist perspectives to inject some socio-legal realism into academic debates, remains relatively dismal, then how have writers on constitutional law coped with the changing social scenario? Ivor Jennings (1966) wrote that:

> Great Britain is a small island with a very homogeneous population. Few think of themselves primarily as English, Scots or Welsh. The sting has long ago been taken out of religious controversy ... There is always a common public opinion which has agreed about principles, and the divergences are more often about methods than about objects.

Jennings was arguably unable to reflect the state of affairs existing at the time, but it would certainly be difficult to maintain this view today. But to what extent is it evident that the immigration of legal cultures in the post-war period has influenced perceptions of change within constitutional law? My answer would be 'not much at all', particularly when it comes to attitudinal or paradigm shifts. I came to this conclusion after a sample survey of books on constitutional law as to whether, how and to what extent each book contained discussions of the change introduced in the British social order by migration from Asia, Africa and the Caribbean.[18] It would appear that, apart from a few, relatively minor references, there has been virtually no discussion about this impact. The references to the presence of immigrants or new ethnic minorities basically fall into two main categories: the existence and operation of powers under immigration law and the representation of ethnic minorities in legislative structures.

In the first category there are odd, usually minimalist references to the existence of immigration legislation, as well as to the putative power of the Crown to exclude aliens (Yardley 1978: 103).[19] There are also some passing references to immigration control within the context of the growth of administrative functions of the state (Harden and Lewis 1986: 65), or as part of a wider discussion on the curtailment of freedoms (Foley 1999: 50–51). One prominent concern is with the peculiarity of Immigration Rules as a legislative form since they are not seen as either statutes or secondary legislation, but yet somewhat stronger in legal weight than mere departmental instructions (Turpin 1995: 400–01,

---

18 Apart from those cited further below, the following were also consulted but were generally not found to contain relevant discussions to any significant degree: Blackburn and Plant (1999), Brazier (1991), Burrows (2000), Ganz (2001), Hartley and Griffith (1981) and Pollard et al (1997). I have not taken into account specialist works focusing on immigration law here.

19 This coverage had hardly changed by the 7th edition, Yardley (1990: 115–16).

Baldwin 1995: 87–91). These discussions are very technical, involving exercises in reconciling obviously contradictory judgments by the higher courts. Surprisingly, the only reference that I found to immigration-related judicial review applications, which have been one of the largest categories of cases for around the past two decades, comes in a rather defensive tone from Lord Nolan (1997: 74) who argues that the balance of cases that are decided against the government is about right. Exceptionally, there are chapter length treatments of immigration law issues within texts on public or constitutional law. These are either in very technical form with minimal contextual information (Hood Phillips *et al* 2001) or try to raise wider problems about control and accountability of powers in this field in some detail (Harlow and Rawlings 1984).[20]

In the second category, the discussions centre on the representative nature of voting systems, either at parliamentary or sub-national levels. This is particularly so when speaking of the question of reform towards a type of proportional voting system. To guarantee representation for racial or religious minorities it is argued that some form of proportional representation may be necessary (Harvey and Bather 1977: 74–75).[21] As Bognador points out, this is especially the case as female or black candidates are noticed because of their presence in the first-past-the-post system, and noticed because of their absence in the proportional system. In 1992, six members from ethnic minorities were returned, although they were nearly 10% of the population, while with a million Muslims in Britain, no MPs were of that faith (Bognador 1997: 63). Striking gaps have similarly been noticed about the London elections more recently (Tomaney 2000: 260). While valid in their own right, these observations and arguments do not question the fact that the issue of political representation is being viewed from a majoritarian framework, which cannot ultimately prevent the subjection of the minority to majority wishes. Nor can such a framework account for the political behaviour of minorities not subscribing exclusively to liberal democratic notions of governance.

---

20 The two chapters on the theme in the 1984 edition are left out, however, in the 1997 edition – was it because of the impending change of government? See also Vincenzi (1998), who is more focused on the question of the Royal Prerogative to exclude 'aliens', and argues, rightly in my view, that the understanding of the ambit of this power today is based on relatively recent and badly founded judicial statements.

21 While not acknowledged as such, could an earlier *avatar* of this idea have been the separate electorate systems that were widely in use as a mode of representation in legislative assemblies in polyethnic territories, such as Kenya, South Africa or India, where they arguably exacerbated interethnic tensions and rivalries?

Besides this minimalist coverage, we hardly find material that examines the implications of the changed ethnic character of British social order at any deeper level, and no consideration about how our perspective should be affected because of the presence of Africans, Asians and Caribbeans in significant numbers in Britain. If Jennings had found the putatively homogenous nature of the British population to have been significant, is it not surprising that more recent writing has tended to assume that intervening demographic shifts have been inconsequential? Conversely, if we were to go by what the public law writers tell us, we would be forgiven for thinking that migrants and their descendants have really had a minimal impact on the reshaping of the constitutional system in Britain. But I would suggest that this is more of a problem of approach, and of taken for granted assumptions, which effectively deny agency to migrants and their descendants, and constitute part of the system of suppression of their value systems. The current scenario, it seems to me, is a formula for disempowerment and breeding frustration. How can we look at things differently? We need to dig deeper.

3.5   Overcoming hegemonic ideology

Before we can go on to chart a way out of the prevailing, limited perspective, we need to consider some of the reasons why existing problems have failed to be analysed with sufficient depth or clarity. Let us look more closely at what happens when the putatively strong state contends for ascendancy over competing legal orders. Indeed, we are now in a position to reflect on some theoretical material which helps to conceptualise the ordering processes within the concept of state law as it is understood in modernity.

From a political theory perspective, Gray (2000) argues that when faced with conflicting values, the response of the dominant strands of Western philosophy, from Aristotle to Mill, has been to rank them in order of value. He argues, however, that such ranking ignores the incommensurability of value as between different goods, and advocates instead recognition of value pluralism that allows a modus vivendi among different conceptions of the good life. Gray argues further that inherent in the ranking process there is a suppression of some values over others. This reading of the dominant liberal Western political theory comes very close to the analysis by Parekh (2000a) whose concern is specifically to discuss the prospects of multiculturalism within the liberal state. Parekh sees the liberal state as a homogenising institution that seeks to replace modes of allegiance based on cultural communities that compete with itself and the abstract polity of its citizens, again leading to injustice and oppression.

Similarly, Melissaris (2004), who argues in legal pluralist terms, but equates the ultimate form of legal pluralism to value pluralism, also delineates the spectrum of responses in dominant modes of legal ideology. He points out that even in 'pluralist' responses to legal theory, there is either an outright suppression of alternative concepts of law as these are regarded as too imprecise or as not conforming to criteria set by the dominant order, or they propose a ranking. Both forms of response have the effect of suppressing alternative traditions of law. Indeed, Melissaris's outline corresponds well to Griffiths's (1986) categories of 'legal centralism' and 'weak pluralism', both of which are opposite ends of a spectrum whereby the positivist state-led model prevails. In the theories and legal systems that Griffiths refers to as exhibiting weak legal pluralism there is the sort of ranking of value to which Gray and Mellisaris also point, and consequent suppression of the totality of legal pluralism by failure to acknowledge what Griffiths terms 'strong legal pluralism', which, for Griffiths, is simply a *fact*. This echoes what Chiba observes for the various components of law, which simply *exist* and do not ultimately depend on each other for validation.

H Patrick Glenn, in a hard-hitting comparative analysis of legal traditions globally, focuses the issue in terms of constitutional law itself. Significantly, he does so under the heading, 'The state and the New Diasporas'. He states (2000: 51):

> ... the state's internal instrument of rationality, constitutional law, becomes the arbiter of other forms of rationality which may continue to exist or emerge within it. There are increasingly expressed opinions that western constitutional law, as it has existed until now, is unable to do so. The exclusivity of its sources, the logic at its disposal, would make it more an instrument of repression of other traditions than an adequate means of reconciling them. This would be in no way the fault of constitutional lawyers, who sometimes accomplish near miracles, but the fault of elevating one tradition into a position of institutional dominance over others. The system of the state cannot tolerate the possibility of other systems within it; this is the nature of systemic thinking. The system necessarily controls the inter-acting elements which compose it.

If we go by Glenn's analysis here then we can locate the problem at the very heart – that is, within the Western conceptualisation of constitutional law itself. He seems to imply that the system will therefore have to be adjusted out of its exclusivist posture. If, on the other hand, it does not remain open to other influences, sources or traditions, and other forms of rationality that arise, then we might be looking at their repression, as is already happening in practice.

It seems that there are several problems that overlay each other to form a complex series of silences or suppressions. These have been perpetuated for such a long period of time that we find that recent assessments of the past view the matter rather uncritically. For example, Harvey and Bather (1977: 517) tell us:

> Wherever they went, English settlers took with them the principles of common law. Hence, apart from the province of Quebec, which has French law, there is a fundamental similarity in law throughout the Commonwealth.[22]

This world view, which is constantly ratified by much of comparative law writing today, is of course deeply Eurocentric with its implication that legal traditions that already existed in colonised territories were extinguished upon the establishment of the common law system. In fact, we know that colonial powers had no choice but to recognise the existence of indigenous legal systems wherever they went, even though this was often accompanied by distortion as well as denial. Nevertheless, colonialism has left lasting psychological impressions about the place of indigenous Asian, African and American legal traditions extending to the post-colonial era, even though we have witnessed the rejection or collapse of the Westminster model almost everywhere. It has therefore become much harder to conceptualise the place and functioning of indigenous legal orders in the non-Western world. As we saw Kakar (1982: 5) pointing out in Chapter 1, the West is no longer a geographical region but a state of mind now.

This is particularly so in the area of constitutional law because colonial legal regimes tended to push indigenous legal systems into an 'ethnic niche',[23] thus allowing them to operate officially at the level of *personal* laws, in the areas of family, property and religion.[24] Therefore, despite the minimal acknowledgment of the functioning of indigenous legal orders under colonialism, there remains a strong perception that the export of common law from England, meant its dominant if not exclusive

---

22 On assertions by South Asian informants that 'we follow English law also in India' and that 'we follow English law in Britain', and for a critique of such views, see Menski (1993: 255).

23 See Menski (2000a: 178, 2003: 156–63) for Hindu law, and (Menski 2000a: 292–93) for Muslim law in India. Of course, in the parts of the world that escaped European colonialism such as Afghanistan, China, Ethiopia, Iran, Japan, the Ottoman Empire (and later Turkey) and Thailand, Western paradigms have influenced legal developments at least in terms of code-making. The impact of this at the level of socio-legal reality, and consequent forms of hybridity, is another question altogether. See Chiba (1989) on Japan and Yilmaz (2002b) on Turkey.

24 For Hindu law, this happens in some form at the time of Muslim rule in India: Menski (2000a: 172, 2003: 152–56). This may explain its relative inarticulation in explicitly constitutional terms since. Although in official abeyance it remains relevant, as with Islamic concepts, through the colonial period and today.

reign. If we want to argue for the operation of Asian and African constitutional norms within the putatively strong Western state with its ideology of 'legal centralism', which seemingly displaces all other legal orders, our task is that much harder. But if we grant that British settlers at least took their own legal systems with them to other territories, is it not reasonable to think that the reverse process of colonisation that is occurring today carries similar implications? It is precisely this phenomenon, or the realisation that this has in fact been taking place for years, that is much resented officially. A report (see Wainwright 2001) on the summer 2001 riots in the northern English city of Bradford claimed:

> Immigrants ... can and often do maintain key elements of their culture for generations, but in many other ways they accept the dominant, host culture. Colonists do not. They come into a country to displace the existing culture and establish their own. From colonist to immigrant is the dominant pattern historically. However, this process seems to have been thrown into reverse in Bradford.[25]

The fact that a new type of cohabitation of cultures is portrayed as the unwarranted dominance of one reveals, it seems to me, more about the persistence of dominant attitudes according to which there is a refusal to see such coexistence outside of a position of hegemony of one or the other. However, the phenomenon observed also inevitably implies that it is hardly the case that Afro-Asian legal cultures *do not* bring their own of perceptions about correct modes of behaviour, and they may indeed also bring their notions of propriety of relations between rulers and ruled. It is this very process of legal reconstruction in the diaspora that poses a challenge to prevailing paradigms.

3.6   Legal postulates of the centre-locale relation

If we are to dig any deeper we already begin to run into problems because the phenomena we are dealing with generally remain unaccounted for in the understandings of Western social sciences, or at

---

25   The quoted statement is reminiscent of statements by Margaret Thatcher to the effect that immigrants were swamping local cultures in the late 1970s. Similar statements are to be found echoed through different periods, and seem to continue on a greater frequency as Britain becomes more culturally pluralised. Ballard (for example, 1994b) has consistently, and perhaps provocatively, used the term 'colonies' to describe geographically concentrated settlements of ethnic minority communities in Britain. Recently, Menski (2002a: 94) has observed that 'many Asians in Britain now behave as though Britain were an extended part of the subcontinent', adding that they are thereby drawing on their own cultural resources, although this has hardly been appreciated by modernity-obsessed research.

best remain a minority, marginalised occupation, given the predominance of modernity-focused research.[26] Stepping out of such conceptual straitjacketing, Menski (2000a: 286–87) points out that chthonic and religiously founded systems are generally:

> ... starting from the conceptual premise that there is a universal world order in which such divisions of the public and private may well exist at the visible level. But at the invisible level of the higher order, all these divisions are immaterial, because everything humans do is subject to one and the same overarching legal authority that is not man made, and which lawyers therefore refuse to analyse.

It appears therefore that positivism, and the related universalist and homogenising assumptions of much of our social sciences, may not be useful here. Rather, a deeper understanding of non-Western cosmologies and obligation systems is needed, although we can proceed by hypothesising that, being deeply internalised, they operate as cognitive structures. Given the prominent presence of South Asian migrants in Britain we may look, in very general terms, at key Hindu and Muslim 'legal postulates' (Chiba 1986: 6–7, 1989: 139).

Under the Hindu concept of *rajdharma* (Menski 2000a: 163–64, 2003: 107–11), the ruler takes on the role of the guardian of his subjects' *dharma*, in which his or her primary function is to support modes of self-control already expected of Hindus at large. It is thus viewed as a form of assisted self-control, but not a positivist legitimation of power. Thus, self-control is the key element, and the *raja*, wielding the proverbial *danda* (punishing rod) might step in with harsh and gruesome punishments, but only when order breaks down. On the other hand, the ruler remains the servant of the cosmic system of order, *rta*, and its manifestation in individual behaviour, *dharma*. He never becomes an Austinian ruler unless he oversteps his limits and begins to abuse his powers, in which case he may be killed. The implications of this for the relationship between the political centre and the locality are extremely important for us.

Menski (2000a: 164, 2003: 122) quotes from the ancient Indian text of *Manusmriti* which provides (at 8.41–42):

> A ruler who knows (his duties according to) *dharma* must inquire into the customary laws of castes, of districts, of guilds, and of families, and thus settle the law peculiar to each. For men who follow their respective

---

26 See, for example, the observation by Spalek (2002: 2) that criminology has by-passed religion as a subject of analysis, given its modernity-oriented focus. See, further, Chapter 4.

occupations and who abide by their respective duties become dear to the people, even though they may live at a distance.[27]

Several things follow from this. Custom remains the major source of law in social reality and that the ruler's *dharma* must be to guard his subjects' *dharma*, rather than usurping it through top-down regulation as a modern state might do.[28] Far from customary law being a *creation* of colonial authorities, as is often claimed, we see that ancient principles already operated along lines that took account of this socio-legal reality, and that colonial regimes only attempted to apply those principles in their own peculiar ways.[29]

This also implies a kind of 'soft' state that is hardly exclusive to Hindu legal theory but which can be seen all over the Asian and African world. Echoing Burton Stein's (1980: esp. 264–85) work on political state-society relations in Southern India,[30] Menski (2000a: 11) observes that the 'formal superiority but actual remoteness of the state's legal system appears to be a remarkably common element of all traditional legal systems in Asia and Africa.' This means that the role of the state is based around a norm of non-interference in local and family affairs, thus allowing, and even depending on, self-regulation, although circumstances may in extremity require certain rules of the centre to be enforced. For us the norm of non-interference is also important in a wider, comparative sense, in that it suggests a strategy to allow for the management of a plural society with lots of internal diversities.[31]

When we are talking of the South Asian context, we may hypothesise that the above Hindu cognitive structure will have had a syncretic

---

27   Menski (2000a: 156, 2003: 128) cites another passage of Manusmriti 8.46 where it is stated: 'What may have been practised by the virtuous, by such twice-born people who are devoted to *dharma*, that he shall establish as the rule, unless it is opposed to the customs of countries, families and castes.' Again, this shows not only that customs at local level were to be respected, but to even take precedence over other elements of law, again underlining the non-positivistic approach of post-classical Hindu law.

28   It would seem that this vision of the ancients has not lost its relevance in India, either in the context of debates on a Uniform Civil Code, see Menski (2001a: 345–402). The same issues are now cropping up in the EU context as Legrand (1997) discussed critically.

29   See Derrett (1968: 53–55) for models that may have influenced the British to be more receptive to the idea of a personal law system In India.

30   Burton Stein's adaptation of the political model of the 'segmented state', that draws on work done earlier on Africa by Aidan Southall, and is applied to Southern India by Stein (1980) himself, offers a very useful framework for conceptualising State-society relations in the Asian and African world.

31   In this respect, it is worth citing an article by Copland (2000), where he argues that by the early 20th century, while Hindu-Muslim communalism was becoming more endemic in British India, it was relatively infrequent in India's Princely States, which tended to pursue policies of 'managed pluralism'.

influence for Muslim communities, thus introducing another case of legal pluralism.[32] On the other hand, the divine law of Islam, the *shari'a*, provides its own framework within which the *fiqh*, defined here as the doctrinal writings of scholar-jurists exercising their judgment in accordance with defined principles, became a reference point mainly for legal relations among Muslims. It is evident that, given its concern constantly to ascertain God's will, this doctrinal material treated law making by human agency in sceptical terms. Nevertheless, it later also accounted for the position of rulers who were engaged in law making and administration from a 'secular' viewpoint, and for the public interest. Muslim legal scholarship thus evolved to account for the role of ruler in the doctrine of *siyasa shari'a* – 'government in accordance with the revealed law', a concept covering areas much wider than the doctrinal *shari'a* itself (Coulson 1964: 120–34, Menski 2000a: 288–91).

As with Hindu thought, rulers retained a large measure of discretion, to be used according to the individual conscience of the *caliph* or *sultan*, who could also act in a tyrannical manner. On the other hand, Muslims are said to have been given to a tradition of political quietism, possibly along lines of the Qur'anic injunction to submit to the 'head of affairs' (Brown 2000: 189).[33] These certainly look like accountability gaps, compounded by the fear of the possibility of no ruler at all, at which point a general state of disorder could set in. But the ultimate sanction of Hindus is to remove legitimation from a *raja* who abuses power, and we have seen that the *raja* may well be killed too. In Muslim thought, idealistic as it seems to be, a bad ruler's punishment is reserved for the time of his death. Crucial for our purposes is that Muslim rulers, unlike their Christian counterparts, were not in a position to enforce religious orthodoxy through the state in premodern times, and the question of the separation of church and state never arose as it did in the Christian world (Mayer 1987: 130–35, Brown 2000: 31–42). Further, although Muslim states and empires engaged in building administrative and court systems, positivist law making was not on the menu when it came to that area of law governed by the *shari'a*. Modernist experiments along those lines by states such as Pakistan can therefore be viewed as out of sync

---

32 For an anti-essentialist account emphasising common elements of popular religious beliefs and practice among Punjabis, see Ballard (1996b).

33 Brown (2000: 189) cites a *hadith* of the Prophet Mohammed in which he is reported to have said: 'There will be leaders who will not be led by my guidance and who will not adopt my ways. There will be among them men who will have the heart of the devil in bodies of human beings.' When asked what should the believers then do, the prophet answered: 'You will listen to the amir and carry out his orders, even if your back is flogged and your wealth is snatched you should listen and obey.'

with the classical legal situation, although Euro-American states with their emphasis on the same, purportedly uniformising model are hardly in a position to complain. In the premodern Muslim context, we also, importantly, have a tradition of distance between the state and local communities, whereby the *shari'a* is left to engage in its own dialectic with existing customary norms among Muslim communities, with widely differing and syncretic results.[34]

What then is the relevance of this material concerning Asian and African modes of governance to the British scene? As already noted in Chapter 2, and in this chapter, from a socio-legal perspective, there is much evidence of the recreation of Asian and African legal orders in Britain. On the other hand, there is also the potential for misunderstanding, mutual avoidance, conflict or – as both Glenn, Parekh and others pointed out – repression. Contrary to what much of the literature on public and constitutional law assumes Asian and African legal orders are not irrelevant in the British scenario, but have themselves been reconstructed in the diasporic setting. What may also need to be built into this picture is the process of absorption of Western value systems and norms of governance that may tell us important things about the developing picture of legal pluralism and, in particular, of legal pluralism in conflict. On the basis of available information, we can already begin to chart some of the key issues at this stage.

In the British scene, therefore, we have an uneasy coexistence of at least two models of legal regulation. One is the positivist, modernist, top-down model of state regulation, with a territorial emphasis, either throughout the country or in its subdivisions. On the other hand, we have a series of cultural communities which overlap territorially and residentially, with their varying values effectively forming zones of *self-regulation*. This is very much along the lines of what Menski (1993) proposed in an article more than 10 years ago, although it has been almost totally ignored by other legal academics. This silence is not justified by the fact that there is an absence of contact and conflict of legal orders as between the minority communities and the state's agencies. On the contrary, in my research and teaching so far, apart from the area of

---

34 On the 'unorthodoxy' of states attempting to enforce *shari'a* rules through modernist legislative mechanisms, see Mayer (1987, 1990). Indeed, Islamisation though legislation appears to be a 'modern' phenomenon initiated by the British in India (Pearl and Menski 1998: 38), although the Ottomans too experimented with introducing legislation as a way of modernisation prior to the setting up of the Turkish Republic (Menski 2000a: 298–303). I am not saying here that Muslims do not have disagreements amongst themselves about the ambit of the *shari'a* or even about who is and is not entitled to call himself a Muslim, often leading to a climate of persecution.

immigration, Asian and African communities have been seen in litigation in the fields of education, blasphemy, criminal law, mental health, housing, social welfare and planning – almost every major area of public law.

Still, we can see a systematic silence or highly selective perspectives adopted by constitutional writers because they have internalised the elevation, as Glenn (2000: 51) states, of one tradition over others. In the litigation mentioned above, we find two dominant modes of interaction between the state and the communities: suppression of ethnic minority values or their ratification when they meet the stereotyped expectations of the dominating system, often expressed through self-appointed spokespersons. In either case, we get a distorted picture of how ethnic minorities are coping with a purportedly culture-blind state system. Thirdly, because the state pushes people away, it is effectively a means by which funds can be saved as they are not spent on meeting their needs. This does not mean, however, that state bureaucracies may not be reinforced with a view to ruling the ethnic minorities 'better', as recently seen in the 'dispersal' system and in the systematic detention and criminalisation of asylum seekers. However, in each of the cases there is a failure to analyse, in Chiba's terms, the destiny of the transplanted legal order and how it is internalised in the legal orders of the communities concerned.

Here too there are varied effects. On the one hand, suppression has led to avoidance reactions so that many ethnic minorities seek to avoid contact altogether.[35] On the other hand, it leads to violent reactions in extreme cases, as seen in the 'urban disturbances' through the 1980s (Cashmore and Troyna 1991) and, most recently, in the northern English 'textile' towns in the summer of 2001. It appears that they have all been reactions to heavy policing or the authorities' allowing far right activity in the respective areas, but one cannot exclude the drip-drip effect of the lack of ethnically appropriate public services. Indeed, such patterns of interaction continue to operate – it is no comfort to black people in Britain today to know that their men have consistently been shown to be several

---

35 This is in addition to the preference for self-regulation which effectively means that many problems are never brought to the courts. Menski (1993: 253) noted that 'thousands of important disputes among Asians, as among all communities, never come before the official courts.' The recent high-profile *Patak* litigation in 2004, involving the makers of the famous pickles, also came to a settlement after initial recourse to litigation. I am tempted to see in this a resort to Hindu modes of self-regulation winning out over expensive and embarrassing resort to the official courts, although modern Afro-Asian elites often carry on with court battles as part of a settling of scores which extends beyond the official law.

times more likely to be stopped and searched by a police force (Bowling and Phillips 2002: 139–48) composed overwhelmingly of white men and women who are frequently rude, aggressive or even worse. A further sort of reaction is the gradual undermining of the self-regulatory value systems of the ethnic minority communities. Thus, the youth in particular are exposed to the potential of falling outside of their parental value system, retention of which is seen as leading to penalties in the external environment, while they are ultimately never accepted by the dominant group(s). Thirdly, ethnic minorities are pushed into a state of ideological insecurity which does not normally lead to the adoption of the dominant value system, but to the recasting of 'traditions' into a modernist frame. While, it is hard to estimate how widespread this tendency is, this is often what lies behind dreams of a Khalistan, or a 'pure' Islamic state, or forms of Hindu fundamentalism – all models admittedly quite far from their lived reality, but with all the dangers of authoritarianism which has the potential to haunt us for years to come.

Thus, instead of the kind of self-regulation envisaged in the premodern Indian setting, we have a conflict of values and principles between the state and the self-regulatory orders of ethnic minorities, leading to different sorts of 'deviant' behaviours, both within the state and among the minority communities. The premodern Indians were therefore very *postmodern* in ways that we still find it hard to recreate in our supposed age of diversity. This may be what Menski (2003: xx) means when he argues that:

> ... in light of ancient Indian evidence ... it is worth considering whether postmodernism is not all that new and represents a reinvention of ancient wheels, with a few new elements, rather than the pinnacle of sophistication of human development and understanding.

How different at the end of the day are the exhortation to rulers by the ancient Hindu scholars that they must ensure the observance of their subjects' *dharma*, and the Macpherson team's advocacy of the necessity for the modern British state to provide services appropriate to race, ethnicity and cultural background of members of the public?

Chapter 4
Criminal (in)Justice in a Plural Society: South Asians and the English Law on Homicide

As discussed in the preceding chapters, the presence of ethnic minority communities in Britain has given rise to myriad questions for the official legal sphere – from immigration, discrimination and racial violence to family law, but also, increasingly and worryingly, the field of crime. Old concerns about fairness and justice become overlain with new questions about the underpinnings of those concepts, and whether assumptions about the definition and nature of crime still hold in a social context exhibiting radical cultural and legal pluralism.

To be sure, Euro-American societies have never been homogeneous but the spectre of modernity, built on Judeo-Christian and Hellenistic foundations, has reinforced notions about uniformity of morality and therefore also about the legal controls to be applied when the social order is threatened. The Afghan writer Idries Shah (1999: 13) recounts a rule of law that now seems far from the prevailing legal consciousness: 'Under the Normans, if you killed someone and could prove that the deceased was fair-haired and thus presumed to be (only) English, and not a Norman, the customary penalty for murder could be avoided.' At least formally, the racial order implied in this quote has eclipsed with the slide into modernity, whereby presuppositions centred on homogeneity have been transplanted into the common law as reformed by statutes.[1] The assumption now powerfully holds that basically everybody is equal under the law, and therefore to be treated uniformly when breaches of that law occur.

In a period that was only just being stirred by the scale of the post-war migration, Radzinowicz (1966: 12–13) outlines well the dominant liberal attitudes to crime – that criminals be punished for what they have done, not who they are or likely to become, nor whether they might be socially or individually conditioned, and punished according to the same type of punishment on the assumption that they would react in the same

---

1   For the manner in which Anglo-Saxon laws on homicide, in particular forms of emendation for homicide, gradually came to be replaced by the crown's courts' exclusive competence, see Hurnard (1969: 1–30).

way to that punishment. Some years later, and with specific reference to the Asian presence in Britain, Sebastian Poulter (1990a: 129) pointed out:

> For a long time the general approach of the English courts has been to apply a uniform and consistent standard to all those who are accused of criminal offences, regardless of whether or not they have foreign origins. The purpose of the criminal law is to impose certain minimum standards of behaviour which the community as a whole regards as necessary for the peaceful order of society. It is therefore logical to apply, in the vast majority of circumstances, a universal set of principles to determine who is guilty and who is innocent.[2]

There would seem to be little difficulty on the face of such cherished axioms, but once we unpack their consequences, they begin to look like a recipe for injustice.

In this chapter we explore the deep cultural and legal conflicts that come to the fore in the context of the English law on homicide. Ethnic and cultural diversity present particular problems for the 'official', that is, the state made or state sanctioned, law (Chiba 1986: 5–6, 1989: 139). This is partly because the view that uniformity is the ideal mode of legal development (Menski 1993: 239) runs so deep in Euro-American states that it in fact masks incidents and patterns of discrimination that all members of society routinely engage in, while it is still less able to accommodate diversity. Some discriminatory patterns within the criminal justice system, which disproportionately criminalises Afro-Caribbeans, have been established (Hood 1992) and are accompanied by many accusations of abuses of official power and miscarriages of justice. Rarely, however, are voices heard against the homogenising and assimilationist underpinnings of the legal system. There are several and interrelated reasons for this state of affairs.

First, according to some writers, criminal law represents an expression of 'public' values or interests (Smith 1996: 17–18, Wilson 2003: 4–6) with the connotation that they are generally non-negotiable, that their accommodation to suit specific groups might jeopardise their

---

2 Elsewhere Poulter (1989: 122) pointed out: 'In determining the question of guilt English judges have decided to apply a uniform standard to all-comers, regardless of their origins, their cultural mores or their ignorance of English law.' In a finding that related to post-conviction stage McConville and Baldwin (1982: 652) stated: 'There appears to be no evidence of direct systematic bias on racial lines in sentencing in the Crown Court. The implication is that defendants are treated equally once they attain the status of convicted persons: not necessarily fairly or appropriately, but equally.' The statement was subsequently said to have acquired a mantra-like quality (Hudson 1989: 25), despite the limited nature of the research upon which it was based. One wonders whether the axiomatic assumption of equality tends to act as a wish-fulfilment device here.

integrity, and that linguistic, cultural, or religious diversity can be enjoyed so long as it does not offend against public policy as directed by the state.[3] The criminal law is after all an expression of the fact that it is the modern state that enjoys a monopoly of violence, displacing forms of 'private' legal ordering, a classic case of 'legal centralism' (Griffiths 1986: 3). Secondly, an overwhelming amount of criminological writing about ethnic minorities adopts assimilationist and deprivationist perspectives. Given its close affinity to the 'race and class' paradigm (Ballard 1992), such writing discusses discrimination (see, for example, Cook and Hudson 1993), but has not adopted a culturally-grounded framework that takes the analysis of the problem much further. In addition, while the Afro-Caribbean population has remained the main dubious beneficiary of high levels of imprisonment (Bowling and Phillips 2002: 192–212), the widespread application of assimilationist presuppositions vis-à-vis its presence in Britain ensured that the debate remained centred on establishing the existence of discrimination.[4] Thirdly, the increasing presence of South Asians within the prison system now presents questions that the earlier literature, with its culture-blind, religion-blind underpinnings simply cannot supply answers to. Thus, in a recent book on *Islam, Crime and Criminal Justice*, the first of its kind in Britain, Spalek (2002: 2) observes that:

> It seems that the issue of religion has rarely featured in criminological work. This may be partly attributed to the modern roots of the academic discipline of criminology, which means that the values adhered to under modernity have also underpinned much criminological work.

---

3   We remind ourselves, at this stage, that the division between 'public' and 'private', presupposed by concepts such as the 'state' or 'public policy' (see Pearl 1972: 120, Poulter 1986: vi), is nevertheless rather difficult to defend in the British/English context – see Dyson (1980: 115), Poulter (1998: 26-29), Parekh (1998) and Chapter 1 of this book.

4   Goulbourne (2002) asks whether there will be a distinct British Afro-Caribbean population to speak of in 50 years, such have been the pressures on members of this group against the retention of a sense of distinct cultural identity. Another indicator of assimilation pressure upon Afro-Caribbeans is the penalisation of Rastafarians who avowedly refuse to accept the values of white society. While Poulter argued that English law is flexible enough to accommodate diversity, he also discusses (1998: 358–63) decisions from the higher criminal courts concerning convictions of Rastas for possession and supply of *ganja*, which hardly demonstrate signs of accommodating the concerns of this ethnic minority group. For expression of judicial doubt that such convictions constitute a breach of the European Convention on Human Rights (ECHR), see 'Judge advises Rastas over drug challenge', BBC News, Monday 18 December 2000, http://news.bbc.co.uk. We know, of course, that Rastas have been refused recognition as an 'ethnic' group under the Race Relations Act 1976, while their status as a 'religious' group is also often denied.

The modernist antipathy, if not hostility, to religion underscores its lack of analytical inclusivity since any discussion of South Asian laws in their diasporic setting could hardly avoid reference to it. Lastly, and closely linked to state-centrism and ethno-centrism, is the fact that the criminal law sphere is hardly analysed as involving an interaction of a 'dominant' (Hooker 1975) legal order with various diasporic legal cultures with the potential for various outcomes in the spectrum of possibilities, including clashes and conflicts, inherent in such cases of legal pluralism.[5]

4.1 The English law framework

Since the Murder (Abolition of Death Penalty) Act 1965 conviction for murder entails imprisonment for life in English law. Although judges can recommend a minimum term to be spent 'inside', they are still bound formally to pronounce life sentences for those convicted. However, release can follow a recommendation by judges and by the parole authorities, although Home Secretaries have often intervened to keep prisoners locked up (see Cavadino and Dignam 2002: 274). This fact has led to continued disputes between judges and Home Secretaries for the last few decades about the extent to which 'life means life' (van Zyl Smit 2002: 117–24, 128–31). Prior to 1965, a conviction for murder of course meant the death penalty.[6] Here, the discrimination faced by ethnic minority defendants could have severe consequences as in the case of Mahmood Mattan, a Somali who lived in Cardiff, whose conviction was declared to have been 'demonstrably flawed' by three Court of Appeal judges in 1998, some 46 years too late (Tibballs: 279–86).

The lack of a flexible sentencing capacity in English law still makes the consequences of a finding of murder particularly harsh in some cases, and its reform has been considered several times in the last few decades (van Zyl Smit 2002: 97–104). It is possible, however, that a total defence can result in acquittal or that a partial defence can result in the reduction of the conviction to that of manslaughter, allowing flexibility in sentencing. Total defences include self-defence and duress, while provocation has also been available at common law as a partial defence. Since the Homicide Act 1957, defendants can also plead diminished responsibility or homicide pursuant to a suicide pact as partial defences.

---

5   Another area with similar problems in need of investigation is that of mental health law.
6   I have been unable to find any studies that link the death penalty and the concept of human sacrifice, which is certainly known of, if not practised, in many of the world's cultures.

Despite reform attempts and legislative changes in recent decades, including the Human Rights Act 1998, it appears as though the notion of murder has retained an essential stability within the English legal consciousness. As van Zyl Smit (2002: 97) recently observed, the 'crime of murder remains a common law offence, although statute has nibbled at its edges'.

As already noted, the English courts have generally tended to assume a homogenised and idealised idea of criminality purportedly without regard to the cultural or ethnic background of the individual concerned. Indeed, the most basic ideas of crime in English law stem from a particular ethico-religious conceptual framework. As the late Professor Antony Allott (1990: 212) stated in one of his lesser known essays: 'the very fabric of criminal liability traces back to a Christian analysis of guilt, with its notion that criminal liability is not created merely by a wrongful act but must be accompanied by a guilty mind (*mens rea*).' It may also be that the moral absolutism inherent in the Judeo-Christian formulation of homicide – 'thou shalt not kill' – constitutes a significant hurdle to flexibility, although it now operates at an invisible level – one would be very hard put to find a reference to the roots of modern criminal law in Judeo-Christian concepts in any recent textbook.

Furthermore, there is some evidence to suggest that judges can and do discriminate against ethnic minority defendants where they have discretionary powers, and South Asians appear to be penalised at a higher level when it comes to incidents of violence (Hood 1992). Additional evidence indicates that other actors in the criminal process – the police, the Crown Prosecution Service, the probation service and the prisons – are all liable to act in ways that discriminate against ethnic minorities (Bowling and Phillips 2002). Lawyers are rarely trained about issues of culture and ethnicity that go beyond narrowly framed problems of discrimination (see Chapter 2), although the increasing number of ethnic minority lawyers in the legal profession can sometimes bring their inherited knowledge to bear in actual cases. It is all a bit 'hit-and-miss', however, and unfriendly judicial benches, as some of the case studies below show, might not give encouraging signals to lawyers to plead for an ethnically informed approach.

The one key factor in serious criminal trials is the role of juries. Due to legal restrictions on revealing their deliberations, there is hardly any research that casts a light on what takes place in decision-making by juries. We do know that over the last two decades the rights of defendants to object to jury members without cause (the so called 'peremptory challenge') has been progressively reduced to the point of elimination and at least one writer (Gordon 1988: 303) argues that this was done specifically in response to trials in which ethnic minority defendants had been acquitted by juries. This links to the more tricky issue of the ethnic composition of juries, and here too we are back to the possible influence a person's cultural background (of the accused and the juror) can have on the outcome of a case. After some signs of liberality in the early 1980s, the Court of Appeal has closed off the option of objecting to jurors on the basis of ethnicity, and insisted that jury selection must be random.[7] This institutionalises a majoritarian moral/ethical bias in jury decisions that is liable to skew the outcome of many a trial. English judges have also occasionally shown a remarkable unwillingness to handle clear evidence of racism amongst jury members, with the conduct of at least two such trials having been challenged in the European Court of Human Rights (ECtHR).[8]

All this merely scratches the surface, however. The different culturally-grounded experiences of South Asians within the English criminal process can only be addressed seriously after an appraisal of their traditional South Asian legal inheritance. This would provide us with a clearer idea of the possible zones of conflict that are likely to arise. One would then want to inquire about cultural and legal transplantation in the diasporic setting, and concretise the discussion with an analysis of some available case studies. Our reading of the emerging issues as a clash of legal cultures thereby implicates English law not only as a result of its demand for homogeneity but, crucially, also because of its state-centred presuppositions.

4.2   Homicide under traditional South Asian laws

It is no easy matter to summarise the way in which homicide has been seen under the traditional laws of South Asians. There are several overlapping factors that contribute to the complexity. An obvious issue is the diverse origins of the South Asian diaspora in Britain, ranging from

---

7   *R v Ford* [1989] 3 All ER 445, and Enright (1991).
8   See factual situations in *Gregory v UK* (1998) 25 EHRR 577 and *Sander v UK* (2001) 31 EHRR 44. In *R v Mirza* [2004] 2 WLR 201 the House of Lords, Lord Steyn dissenting, refused to allow an appeal against conviction despite the evidence that the deliberations by the jury involved questioning the defendant's use of an interpreter as he had lived in the UK for a number of years, and after conviction there was evidence provided to the court that the deliberations had been prejudiced on racial grounds. The Court of Appeal in the same case had considered itself bound by the decision in the prior case of *R v Qureshi* [2002] 1 WLR 518, where the appeal had been unsuccessful although there was an allegation of overt racism in the jury room. In both cases human rights arguments were raised and considered, but eventually thought insufficient to shift the balance in favour of the appellants.

Indo-Caribbeans of Guyana and Trinidad, Punjabis (Muslim, Sikh and Hindu), Kashmiris (mainly Muslim), Gujaratis (Hindu, Muslim and Jain) many of whom, like Punjabis and Goans, have an East African connection, Sylhetis (predominantly Muslim), Mauritians (mainly Hindu), Malaysian and more recently Sri Lankan Tamils (mainly Hindu, and some Muslims) and Sinhalese (Buddhist and Christian). These are among the larger communities, but there are an innumerable number of smaller groups from other parts of South Asia and beyond. While this lends a potential richness to any discussion about South Asians, it also adds immense difficulties of generalisation, especially when it comes to the analysis of the multiple and highly syncretic legal influences to which all groups have been exposed, and the particular histories of the micro-legal systems of each one.[9] An important factor here might be the extent of ties maintained with the region of origin and the extent and types of ties developed in areas of settlement. I therefore focus only on some key issues within Hindu and Muslim jurisprudence that might help to shed light on the potential for cultural conflict in the English setting.

Both the Hindu and Muslim 'families of law' (Menski 2000a) are inherently plural in that they account for the active role of individuals, their immediate communities and the state in the formulation of legal concepts, and in the maintenance of social and cosmic order. This also holds for the manner in which homicide specifically is perceived. The active role assigned to each level is especially important in the bearing it has on the potential for cultural conflict as state-centred English law, and Western legal systems generally, ascribe minimal legal agency to the other two levels of legal regulation. At the individual level, both Hindus and Muslims are expected to maintain self-control, where necessary, with the assistance of the wider community and the state. This order indicates *reducing* influence as one moves outwards from the individual, therefore challenging the positivist thesis of 'model jurisprudence' (Chiba 1986: 1–2). In both Hindu and Muslim jurisprudence it is also difficult to maintain a strict separation between the notions of 'sin' and 'crime' (Thakur 1978: 70–72, Day 1982: 91–101, Doongaji 1986: 3–4, Menski 2003: 110), which is reflective of the non-separation of the 'religious' and 'secular' at the macrocosmic level, thus adding an extra dimension of plurality and fluidity. The linkage between 'sin' and 'crime' is also familiar to, and has also greatly influenced, English law (Devlin 1965), although officially its influence may be regarded as of marginal significance.

---

9   On the difficulties of research in this field see Menski (1993: 239–42).

For Hindus much of the evidence for premodern legal thinking is drawn from the long history of production of the *shaastric* literature, as it might be referred to in the collective (and includes the *dharmasutras* and *dharmashaastras*), which is supplemented by the later compilation of commentaries and digests (Menski 2003: 93–152). While this material, as important cultural documents, does provide clues to conceptual underpinnings about crime and punishment, it has, very much like the Muslim, Sikh and other material, to be read as not directly representative of the huge variety of local traditions that indeed have a primary role in determining crucial questions, nor as legislation or 'codes', as they have frequently been misrepresented. There is a marked reluctance, again unlike the modern Western models, to specify exhaustively the types of occurrences that can be considered crimes; nor was there agreement in the number and manner of punishments that can be prescribed (Menski 2002c: 830). This may be due to the general Hindu legal principle, as also with Muslim law (Rosen 2000: 79), that no two cases are really the same. Some of the ancient writers did attempt to specify crime-like behaviour but, as indicated, there was not ultimately a strict separation between the notions of sin and other socially harmful acts. This may actually be indicative of a more general indeterminacy about the nature of right and wrong itself.[10]

However, each transgression is perceived as affecting the invisible macrocosmic order, *rita*, and the microcosmic level of order, *dharma*, and the key aim of any punishment is to repair this breach in order. The chief agent in this process is the individual, whose self-control is informed by the theory of *karma* or self-enacting retribution in present or future lives (Menski 2002c: 829), also expressed in Jain, Buddhist and Sikh teaching, and reinforced by local custom.[11] If a transgression *does* occur, the duty of expiation, or *praayaschitta*, lies with the individual. This might involve the performance of any number of rituals or penances to restore order.[12] Communities too, starting with the most immediate, kinship and local authorities were also able to inflict punishments, including excommunication where appropriate rituals

---

10 Thakur (1978: 12–13) observes that in the *dharmashaastra* it is 'freely acknowledged that *why* a particular act, or course of action is *dharma* or right and *why* the contrary act, or course of action is *adharma* or wrong, cannot ever be explained either by means of physical demonstration or by logic'.

11 The notion of *karma* does differ somewhat as between Hindu (which itself shows variations), and Jain and Buddhist teachings. See, for example, Mahony (1987) and Kogen (1987).

12 Attention to expiation is given to several books on crime in the Indian traditions: Day (1982: 202–40) who also discusses the extent of treatment of the issue in the traditional texts; Doongaji (1986: 188–241).

have not been performed (Thakur 1978: 89). Ultimately, so could rulers under the traditional, ever-present, and sometimes actualised, concept of *danda* (literally, 'the punishment rod'). As already indicated, the traditional order of precedence is from the individual outwards with the kingly courts deferring to the rulings of the locally-constituted fora, thus indicating a residual role for the king and central state as law maker or enforcer (Day 1982: 166, Menski 2000a: 160–72, Menski 2002c: 829, Menski 2003: 107–11).[13]

Acts of revenge for killing and monetary compensation to the family of the slain were both approved of as the working out of the principle of retribution (Thakur 1978: 29–30, Day 1982: 121). Indeed, punishment at all the different levels outlined can be summarised as the outworkings of acquired demerit, thus freeing a person from guilt (Day 1982: 242–43). Thus, there was no clean dividing line between the retributive aspect and the reformative aspect of punishment, with the focus being on the transformation of the individual's conscience, setting him or her on the right track again.[14] This element of personal freedom from guilt has also been addressed in modern European thought, if relatively marginalised, given its state-centred presuppositions that under-acknowledge individual legal agency.[15]

Unlike the English law scenario, intentionality is not the determinant of guilt in the Hindu conceptualisations, affecting rather the degree of guilt not the substance of it (Day 1982: 101–05, 214). Killing in self-defence, in defence of women and other weak people who cannot defend themselves against a murderous and violent attack, may result in no punishment and a light penance (Thakur 1978: 65–66). Imprisonment is not in itself regarded as a penalty in Hindu terms, but only as a means to enable the establishment of guilt or the infliction of punishment (Day 1982: 152). This aspect obviously represents a stark contrast to punishment as it develops in modernity.

The killing of children was prohibited by the Qur'an, while some of the Hindu texts spoke against female infanticide, as did the 10th guru of

---

13 Having said this, kings occasionally took it upon themselves to protect animal lives also, in contrast to the anthropocentric nature of the Western tradition: Thakur (1978: 90). The reputed English fondness for defending animal lives, and the relatively high number of vegetarians in the country, may represent an exception to the dominant Western tradition.

14 Could this be one message of the following verse in *Manusmriti* 7.18 (as quoted in Menski 2000a: 162): 'Punishment alone governs all creatures, punishment alone protects them, punishment watches over them while they sleep; the wise declare punishment to be identical with *dharma*'?

15 Nargolkar (1974: 237–42) attributes awareness of the expiatory function of punishment in relation to the human conscience to Dostoyevsky in his *Crime and Punishment*, as well as to Shaw in *The Crime of Punishment*.

the Sikhs, Guru Gobind Singh (Thakur 1978: 58, 61).[16] In a striking contrast to the Western notion of equality, the Hindu texts openly acknowledged that punishment for murder also depended on the station of a person in society. Thus, the penalty for killing a Brahman was higher than if a person from other sections of society were killed and the same if a man rather than woman was killed, unless she was with child (Thakur 1978: 43–49, 73–76). On the other hand, a person of higher standing was said to merit a heavier punishment than one belonging to a lower caste for a similar offence (Thakur 1978: 77). The parallels with the Chinese Confucian tradition are striking, to say the least, in such cases of differential punishing (Menski 2000a: 498–503).

Under Islamic law, killings do not come within the purview of the *hadd* (pl *hudud*) punishments, ie, acts (such as unlawful sexual intercourse, theft, etc) for which severe Qur'anic punishments are prescribed (Mansour 1982, Lippman *et al* 1988: 45–49). Killing itself is classified as a *qisaas* offence (Anderson 1951 in detail, Bassiouni 1982, Lippman *et al* 1988: 49–52), and a variety of degrees of culpability are recognised, based, not exactly on ascertaining what was in the mind of the perpetrator but, more objectively, on what weapon or method of killing is used or how the causation chain leading to death is set off. These then require different degrees of punishment. The main remedies are *qisaas* (revenge killing) and *diyaa* (compensation in its stead) payable by the clan and/or forgiveness. Similar to the Hindu notion of *praayashchitta*, a *kaffaara* or atoning sacrifice may also be performed, through fasting or feeding people (Thakur 1978: 34).[17] At the higher, divine level retribution is meted out, not through the working out of *karma* as in the Hindu perspective, but on the Day of Judgment, which nevertheless functions as a primary mechanism of order maintenance.

Islamic law also allows for punishment for killing at the three levels outlined for Hindu law, by the individual, by the community and by the state, although an ambiguous role is outlined for the state. The role of the individual in Islamic law has unfortunately also been somewhat occluded given the predominant emphasis of the juristic legal texts – the *fiqh* literature – that focus on compliance with God's will, and the

---

16 The *Qur'an* VI: 152 reads: 'Do not kill your children for fear of poverty; for we supply them or you with food. Verily the killing of children is a most heinous crime.' Thakur (1978: 58–60) points out that the killing of children in Arab society prior to Islam was prevalent, as was (and continues to be) the killing of girl children or female foetuses in South Asian communities.

17 Ideally one would want to build here on the insights offered by Shaw (2000: 204–12) and Ballard (2001a) about popular religious practices amongst Pakistani Muslims and the role of intercessors, such as *pirs*, to examine the extent to which they assist in expiatory performance.

ambivalent place accorded to individual discretion in ascertaining that will. Nevertheless, it must be the case that it is first and foremost the duty of the individual to decide how to conform to the divine will. The place of the community, whether family, clan (or in South Asia, *biraderi, jati or zat*) or the wider Muslim community (the *ummah*) is, of course, important. Despite the formal marginalisation of custom in the juristic texts, in practice, custom (*rivaz, urf* or *adat*) is a key 'source' of Muslim law (Rosen 2000, Menski 2000a: 272–77). As with the Hindu position, the state takes third place, given the rejection of the positivist model under classical Muslim law. In this connection, one could cite Coulson (1964: 18), who reduces the Islamic concept in terms more familiar to a Western audience, when he states:

> Homicide remains an offence which falls into the category of civil injuries rather than that of public offences or crimes, for it is the relatives of the victim who have the right to demand retaliation, accept compensation or pardon the offence altogether.

This rather seems like the approach that prevailed in England prior to the Norman reforms.

As with Hindu law, certain specificities arose depending on whom one killed. Thus, the killing of a slave might result in less punishment than that for a free man; likewise, that for killing a woman. Killing an unbeliever did not require vengeance by blood, except when a promise of protection of life had been given; a lesser *diyaa* may be payable for killing a non-believer than for the killing of a Muslim (Thakur 1978: 32–33). Retaliation is not inflicted against a father or a teacher who kills a child in the course of correction, and Lippman *et al* (1988: 50–51) argue that it is this provision that 'allows a father or other male guardian to kill a female relative who, through an act of unchastity, has marred family or tribal honour'. While one could qualify such textual assertions by recourse to the study of social practice, it is evident from Kanwar's (1989) study of homicide in Pakistan that the family relational system and considerations of honour constitute key reasons for acts of homicide, even when penalised by the modern state law of Pakistan. There are lessons here for attempts to curb 'honour killings' taking place not just among Muslims, and which are now also well publicised in Western countries (Rosen 2000: 202–05, Phillips 2003).[18]

---

18 Since Kanwar's study, the Pakistan Penal Code has again been revised in 1992 with notions such as *diyaa* and *qisaas* being incorporated in a detailed way. This shows, *inter alia*, the State moving towards Islamic models of punishment for injuries to the person. We still await an academic analysis of the operation of the revised provisions which is a matter of some urgency not least because of the frequency of immigration and asylum cases in Britain that appear to depend on such information.

In the conclusion to his study on homicide in India, Thakur (1978: 97–98) observes that:

> The only striking difference between the ancient and modern laws is that while the ancients showed special favour and made distinction between different communities and cared more for sanctity of life while prescribing punishments, in the eyes of the modern law there is no such distinction between man and man and the punishments are applicable to all committing a particular crime or offence.

While Thakur rightly identifies the tension between tradition and modernity here, and in particular between situation specificity and universality, one also finds that the courts in modern India have not forgotten the need to adapt mechanisms of punishment to the needs of a diverse society. As Menski (2003) shows, the 'traditional' legal elements constantly resurface and show their capacity for reconstruction into postmodern forms.

This is evident from Australian academic, Stanley Yeo's (1998) fascinating study where he interrogates the problem of defences to murder in England, Australia and India. One of the key issues that Yeo examines is the extent to which, in each of his three chosen jurisdictions, the ethnic, cultural or class background of a person can be taken into account in assessing reliance upon defences to the charge of murder. He finds that, while the UK courts have insisted on excluding such considerations, thereby assuming a homogenised notion of criminality, the Australian courts have increasingly had doubts about whether one size can be made to fit all. The most 'radical' approach has been adopted by the Indian courts, which explicitly allow for the various background features of the accused person to be taken into account. As an illustration, he cites Justice Subba Rao, giving the judgment of the Indian Supreme Court in the now prominent case of *Nanavati v State* (AIR 1962 SC 605, at pp 629–30) with reference to the defence of provocation:

> Is there any standard of a reasonable man for the application of 'grave and sudden' provocation? No abstract standard of reasonableness can be laid down. What a reasonable man will do in certain circumstances depends upon the customs, manners, way of life, traditional values etc; in short the cultural, social and emotional background of the society to which the accused belongs. In our vast country there are social groups ranging from the lowest to the highest state of civilisation. It is neither possible nor desirable to lay down any standard with precision: it is for the court to decide in each case, having regard to the relevant circumstances.

I read this as a reflection of the Indian courts silently acknowledging and drawing on thousands of years of thought within Indic philosophical systems about uniformity and diversity. The main point here is that

Indian notions of justice are premised on context sensitivity, thus accommodating difference and diversity in society. Uniformity was and, it seems, continues to be, seen as conducive to injustice, and the crisis now perceived in the Indian criminal justice system might to some degree be a consequence of the ill-fitting British legal inheritance in the form of Macaulay's Indian Criminal Code (Menski 2002c: 830–31).[19]

Rosen (2000: 12), observing the way *qadis* in Morocco operate in applying Muslim legal principles, also draws attention to the continued link between official adjudicative mechanisms and societal norms, as well as the perceived necessity for context sensitivity in justice, when he states:

> ... it is assumed that, within certain broad limits, it is only fair to gauge the standard of conduct to which an individual should be held according to what sort of person he is. To hold an educated man to the same standards as one who is unlettered, or a woman to the same standards as a man, would, most qadis insist, be grossly unjust.

Such statements concerning judicial behaviour in the modern setting therefore not only show the persistence of traditional norms and values, and the way they are allowed to penetrate the official sphere, but also the extent to which the situation of a defendant or litigant comes to be relevant, as part of the overall context, in assessing the demands of justice. I turn next to examining how the application of a culture-blind approach, and following a formal equality model, potentially lead to clashes of legal culture in the British setting.

4.3   South Asians and English homicide law

Up to the mid-1980s, there was little by way of literature regarding the position of South Asians under English law, but since then we have witnessed the steady build-up of material that establishes the outline of

---

19 Thakur (1978: 41) notes with some concern that: 'The philosophy and main guidelines in the matter of organising individual and common life, which have moved Hindu thinkers from the earliest times right up to the end of the eighteenth century, are so radically different from those which have been, and are, influencing us in our present endeavour to build our national life that it may need a high degree of patience and objective to appreciate the true significance of principles and norms developed in this system. The growing criminality of our present day society depends to a large extent on the proper appreciation of the causes of this radical difference between the two sets of principles and approaches.' See, however, Menski (2000a: 161) on the continuation of the 'old order' in dispensation of punishment and, more critically, on the failure to analyse the problem of the role of traditional self-control mechanisms in light of imposed positivist notions see Menski (2003: 111). For Pakistan, Kanwar (1989) more than confirms the persistence of the 'old order' which is arguably even reflected officially since the 1992 revisions to the Pakistan Penal Code (see note above).

certain key processes that are taking place. One issue must be the significant growth in the South Asian population and, as already mentioned, the sheer diversity amongst South Asians (see Ballard 1994a). This leads to problems of establishing any pattern with certainty, but it also means that a diversity of micro-legal systems, bringing particular portions of their South Asian legal inheritance, in their interaction with English law, must be studied (Menski 1993: 249–51).

What is sure is that South Asian laws have firmly established themselves onto British soil; what is less certain is what approach ought to be adopted to their study, and what recognition can be given to them in the official sphere. The general approach in English law has been to grant recognition on specific issues such as burial, slaughter and crash helmet laws, but to relegate other forms of legal practice amongst ethnic minorities to the unofficial sphere, as 'customs' or 'traditions' (Poulter 1986, 1990a). On the other hand, minorities have themselves concentrated on several types of negotiations between what English law demands and the freedom it provides to continue or adapt their own practices (Menski 1993, 2001b) thereby, and largely quietly, reconstructing their norms on their own terms.

One consequence of pushing ethnic minority laws systematically to the unofficial sphere is that there is little awareness of the background to the sorts of culture-specific issues that can lead to homicide. One stark example is that of dowry-related deaths, already a significant phenomenon in South Asia, but also a feature of South Asian communities in Britain. However, the leading study about this problem (Menski 1998) reports that there is little awareness of it amongst legal personnel in the official sphere and no specific machinery to protect Asian women. There is bound to be some hidden evidence of dowry-related deaths in official statistics that record Asian women as four times more likely to have committed suicide. On the other hand, English law seems very much concerned to control the increasing phenomenon of so called 'honour killings'. Generally, these are cases of young women who are killed by members of their own family, for suspicion of engaging in what are regarded as illicit sexual relations outside of marriage, or sometimes for going against the family's choice of marriage partner. One can see a progressive tightening of penalties in such cases where judges have moved from initially admitting a plea of provocation to finding murder in more recent cases (Edwards and Welstead 1999, Phillips 2003). While one can therefore see some campaigning, press outrages and murder convictions there is no thorough evaluation of the prospects of English law being able to bring this phenomenon under control. Indeed, according to Kanwar's (1989) results from Pakistan, persons who kill for 'honour' feel justified enough to bear the punishments meted out by the state.

Let us examine more closely two cases that have become somewhat well known, within Asian circles at any rate, to illustrate and concretise the complex reality of South Asians under English homicide law. Both cases involve convictions for murder. Both, in their own way, could also be described as 'honour killings', although I have not seen any coverage that uses this term for them, probably because they do not fit the stereotype scenario outlined above.

The first is the case of Satpal Ram,[20] released from prison in 2002 after 16 years inside. He was convicted in 1987 aged 20 for the murder of Clarke Pearce, one of a party of six in a Birmingham 'Indian' restaurant. Pearce had been urging that the music in the restaurant be turned down, which resulted in an argument with Satpal, who in turn urged for the music to be turned up. Pearce then started abusing both him and the restaurant waiters racially. Having received two cuts with broken glass, Satpal retaliated by stabbing Pearce with a knife that he carried for work at his warehouse job. Pearce later died in hospital from the wounds after he refused treatment.

At the trial at Birmingham Crown Court, the judge himself acted as the translator for one Bengali waiter (or was he Sylheti?) who gave evidence. This seems very odd, given that the judge did not speak Bengali. Satpal claims that his lawyers let him down, failing to submit a written statement from the same key witness. His barrister, a Queen's Counsel, also pursued the defence of provocation (a partial defence) rather than self-defence (a total defence). The case went to the Court of Appeal, which refused leave to appeal against the conviction in 1989, partly on the basis that it could not reopen the case on account of Satpal's lawyer's failure to pursue the defence in any particular way, and partly on the basis that the evidence would have made no difference to the outcome. The Criminal Cases Review Commission decided in 2001 that it would not refer the matter back to the Court of Appeal.

Satpal was kept inside five years longer than the trial judge had recommended as he refused to admit guilt, and was released only two years after the Parole Board's recommendation for release. That recommendation had been overturned by Jack Straw, the Home Secretary, and he might still have been in prison were it not for a ECtHR's ruling in another case that found the Home Secretary's practice of overruling the Parole Board as being a violation of human rights. Even

---

20 Some information is gleaned from the following judgments in the case *R v Satpal Ram*, Court of Appeal, 6 March 1989, *R v Satpal Ram*, *The Times*, 7 December 1995, CA.

the Parole Board's decision-making has been critically evaluated in more general terms by Cavadino and Dignam (2002: 274):

> Although there is no blanket Parole Board policy against granting parole to 'offence deniers' (which would be unlawful) denial is often a potent factor working against a prisoner since it is seen as an indication of poor attitude and unwillingness to address one's offending behaviour ... This, of course, places genuinely innocent prisoners in a cruel 'catch-22' dilemma – should they continue to honestly deny the offence and jeopardise their parole chances, or lie and admit the offence, crushing their chances of ever having their miscarriage of justice righted? Given the number of such miscarriages which have come to light in recent years and the likelihood that many more have not, there is no saying how many people, wrongly in prison to start with, have to be kept in prison because they honestly assert their innocence.

It has been suggested that the authorities are here applying a concept of expiation, but in a sense recognised in Christian doctrine, ie, that of confession to a sin or crime.[21] His treatment, as a consequence, could be read here as penalisation for non-conformity. Satpal also suffered much abuse in prison, where prison officers regularly taunted him to kill himself.[22] He spent much time in isolation and was refused permission to attend his mother's funeral. Satpal, regretting the loss of life, maintains that he had only defended himself and, were the tables turned, Pearce would have received merely a slap on the wrist.

There are several levels at which one can discuss this case. It should be of concern that the trial was so badly mishandled, and that written evidence from the waiter, which would have backed up Satpal's story, was not submitted. Also, provocation is a very narrow defence requiring a reasonable person temporarily to lose self-control. In cases of racial harassment it may well be difficult to put across to a wholly or mainly white jury how provocative racial taunts might be for some ethnic minority defendants. There can hardly be only one standard of measuring what is reasonably strong provocation in this context. In this case we have a Sikh man who refuses to tolerate racial abuse and stands up for himself and others. In the larger context, I interpret Satpal as not only challenging the abuse itself but also the expectation of a white supremacist society that ethnic minorities should take such treatment as a matter of course since they are 'newcomers' to the society. When ethnic minorities stand up for themselves in this way they doubly defy the

---

21   I am grateful to Roger Ballard for this suggestion in an interview on 13 November 2003.

22   Recent reports indicate that the practice of taunting and bullying may be quite widespread in prisons, Statewatch, Vol 13, No 3/4 (May–July 2003), pp 15–16.

position that white society wishes to allocate to them. I suspect that, at least at a subliminal level, this perception of defiance is what determined Satpal's treatment in the criminal justice system. Furthermore, from a South Asian or Sikh cultural perspective, standing up against insults to oneself or others is commendable, even expected, even though not all South Asians are good at standing up in this manner. This element did not figure in the case nor in any of the reports that I have seen of it. It can however be argued that Satpal's continuing to maintain that he was merely attempting to defend himself could be seen in this context.

Satpal's treatment, while unacceptable, is not unique in this respect, and continues to figure in the criminalisation of minorities. It is quite common to find ethnic minority complainants of racial harassment and violence receiving short shrift from official agencies, and they may in turn have action being taken against them. I have even seen a report of a member of a minority community being convicted for a racially aggravated offence for standing up to harassment by a police officer. In a bizarre reading of the Crime and Disorder Act 1998 we find that defiance of white authority figures is interpreted as a racist crime![23]

Another powerful case is that of Zoora Shah, a Mirpuri woman, who came to Bradford in the early 1970s, illiterate and having limited knowledge of English. Zoora was convicted in 1992 of murder, attempted murder and solicitation to murder, to all of which she pleaded not guilty. She had killed by poisoning her long-time abuser Azam Mohammed, a Pathan with whom she had taken up after having been abandoned by her husband. Zoora's married life was full of torment. She was forced into having abortions in order to avoid the birth of girls, and her husband was violent, which caused her to lose another baby. When he left she was also told to leave by his family. She was then befriended by Azam, whom she later described as a *goonda*, underlining his close links with the Bradford underworld. Azam initially helped her to obtain a mortgage while retaining the title to her house for which she made repayments. He demanded sexual favours in return, often forcing Zoora to have sex with him. He also threatened her with violence if she did not follow his instructions to become a drugs courier. When Zoora refused to do this he again forced himself upon her.

This cycle of oppression worsened when Zoora attempted to obtain the help of others within the Bradford community. She sought the help of Azam's brother Sher Azam, who was one of the leaders behind the *Satanic Verses* protests, but he refused help. Zoora then attempted to have

23   *Statewatch*, Vol 9, No. 6 (November–December 1999), p 9.

Azam killed through the help of another man, who turned out to know Azam and his brothers. He let Azam know about Zoora's plot, which led to attacks on her house. In April 1992, when she discovered that Azam had sexual designs on her older daughter, she sent her to Pakistan and arranged her marriage there. While in Pakistan, Zoora obtained some arsenic on the advice of a *hakim* in order to control Azam's sexual demands, and a *taweez* from a *pir* for her own ritual protection. When she later found out that he was also interested in her other daughter she gave him a larger dose of arsenic and he died on the same day in hospital.

None of this information came out during her trial in December 1993. Indeed, she had not spoken of her experiences to her general practitioner, her friends, nor to her lawyers. As she was to explain later:

> … the shame and the insult to me … I could do nothing. I was a mattress for men in Bradford. Disgrace for me … it was my sons and my daughters. I was frightened and my children in danger … How could I tell them the truth? (Edwards 1998: 667)

The prosecution depicted Zoora as a scheming woman whose main intention was to obtain the house in Bradford. Zoora was found guilty on all the charges and sentenced to life imprisonment for murder, and to serve concurrent sentences for the other offences. Zoora later appealed to the Court of Appeal which refused to quash her conviction in 1998. In particular, that court had before it an expert opinion by anthropologist Roger Ballard who had interviewed Zoora in prison and revealed the information presented here, and much else besides, about Zoora's life in Britain. The crucial point that he sought to get across to the court was that there were sound reasons why Zoora had been in no position to mount a defence in her trial. But given the information he was able to elicit from her, and placing it in the cultural context of Bradford's Muslim community, it was entirely explicable that Zoora had her justifications for doing as she did, while not revealing any of it in court. He explained that the basic principles that govern life within such communities were the twin considerations of *izzat* and *sharam* (honour and shame). Within this context, Zoora was justified in keeping her degradation through the years under wraps as a way of not jeopardising the social position of her daughters, as underpinned by the concept of *izzat*. She was furthermore justified, from her own viewpoint, in doing as much as she could to protect her daughters from harm, and she was pursuing this aim when she gave Azam the arsenic overdose.

Ballard has subsequently written of the way in which his evidence was treated by the Court of Appeal. He writes that Lord Justice Kennedy did not openly acknowledge his detailed report, but went on to pick on each of the points that Ballard had highlighted only to reach the very opposite conclusions. The court referred to the fact that there was no bruising, that she did not share her troubles when her own liberty was at stake, that her behaviour had been inconsistent – she shared her problems with a holy man in Pakistan but concealed them in Bradford. The evidence adduced did not provide a reasonable explanation since, in the court's view, she had little honour left to salvage (Edwards 1998: 668)! This despite Lord Justice Kennedy's avowed allowance for the 'difficulty of giving evidence through an interpreter to English judges whose knowledge of Asian culture is bound to be limited'. The court here appears to insist upon some recourse to official, state-recognised agencies as a condition for legitimating her difficulties. It did not seem to matter that, from Zoora's point of view, she had indeed approached the persons that mattered, including seeking counsel of a *pir*, before taking the final step of giving an overdose to Azam. The court meanwhile seems to expect her to conform to a pattern of behaviour that had no intrinsic meaning for her.

One may of course wonder why it is that such a case is prosecuted at all, since the Crown Prosecution Service presumably needs to account for the prosecution as being in the public interest. One may also wonder why it is that crucial evidence, as that eventually prepared by Roger Ballard, was not introduced by Zoora's lawyers at the outset. There is a parallel here with cases such as that of Kiranjit Ahluwalia, whose appeal against conviction for murder of her husband was at least allowed in 1992, some three years later (*R v Kiranjit Ahluwalia* [1992] 4 All ER 889). It was accepted that Kiranjit had suffered from years of abuse and thus could rely on the partial defence of diminished responsibility, although I am not convinced that this reflects Kiranjit's actual position. While there was much abuse and torture in the case, it may be worth considering whether the 'trigger' for Kiranjit's killing of her husband was the fact that he had threatened to leave her for another woman. Such an assertion of sexual and marital agency seems not to have been discussed in the official report of the case at all. In Zoora's case too, while the threat to her daughter was clear, the 'trigger' could well have been Azam's forcing her to cook for his wife – the 'other' woman. These readings would of course have been officially unpalatable and of no help to the women concerned in their defence or appeals, and are perhaps therefore totally silenced in the official version of events. There may be much truth therefore in Susan Edwards's (1998: 667) dubbing of Zoora as the woman 'who could not speak and when she spoke she could not be heard'. At the time of writing she still awaits release although Jack Straw, when he was Home Secretary, had eventually reduced her tariff by eight years. We may wonder what interest is being served in Zoora's still serving time in prison.

Both Satpal's and Zoora's cases illustrate several of the issues as discussed above. Like most of us, neither had a totally unblemished record, but it is their very human frailties that have in part provided justification for actors within the official legal system not seriously to (re)consider their cases. We might deplore the prosecutions and the resulting suffering caused to women in the position of Kiranjit Ahluwalia and, more recently, Trupti Patel. Unlike them, however, neither Satpal nor Zoora was able to furnish evidence that was so 'scientific' as to take their cases above cultural specificity. In the Ahluwalia case the appeal lawyers in fact pleaded *against* the direction of the trial judge who had said that the jury might wish to bear in mind that she was an Asian woman. Trupti was received as the model of a middle class professional woman, and therefore able to navigate through the codes of the dominant society. One can only speculate what her fate would have been were she able to speak hardly any English. Further, in both their cases the issues being contested (domestic violence and cot death respectively) were also espoused by a broader range of people within white society.

On the basis of these cases it appears that the official criminal law process is not prepared to take a culturally informed approach in cases concerning South Asians or members of other ethnic minorities. This is partly attributable to the fact that English lawyers have avoided having a healthy debate about the idea of 'cultural defence', a notion that has lurked in the background because we have not wanted to face certain hard issues about diversity and justice (but see Phillips 2003). Personally, I have reservations about the bells that the 'cultural defence' label rings, not least because there is an implication that only (some) ethnic minorities somehow possess a culture that needs to be accommodated, and white (and black) people do not. Taking cultural issues into account in evaluating defences is not necessarily asking for preferential treatment but fair treatment. However, the issues go beyond legalistic questions of this or that particular legal defence being accepted, or whether adjustment to doctrine or process is the key to solving the problem. That is because underneath there lies a systemic problem about the lack of understanding of the different ways in which members of minority groups appreciate the moral significance of what they do, and the legal presuppositions with which they are acting.

I somehow also suspect that Satpal and Zoora were over-penalised because they went against one of the central presuppositions of English and Western criminal law. This is that the individual has, if at all, a marginal role as a legal agent. Here then are two individuals who are seen as literally 'taking the law into their own hands', and that too in an area so closely attached to the principle of 'public interest'. While it might be considered morally right, even obligatory to act, even to kill, for certain principles under the cultural codes that each lived by, this appears to have been unacceptable to the legal centralist ideology of English law.

The lack of debate about these issues has meant an acquiescence in the fact that the process of criminal law is loaded in favour of white, middle and upper class men who indeed receive preferential treatment because they do not have to face additional barriers to explain the cultural codes that they live by – these are simply taken for granted. Admittedly, these are not simple problems and I fully acknowledge that minority groups too are changing internally. There are powerful assimilationist pressures operating on them, with complex intergenerational negotiations taking place, all of which make for a shifting canvass against which to judge characters and events. Yet the existing processes mean that some people come out empowered vis-à-vis 'the system' at large, while others remain disempowered precisely because they cannot navigate through it.

Chapter 5
Attitudes to Polygamy in English Law

This chapter documents and discusses recent developments in English law towards polygamy.[1] Selective and Eurocentric perceptions of non-Western legal orders have often coloured the treatment of polygamy in the British context. Indeed, the issue of polygamy seems to be a crucial site in contemporary conflicts of the legal postulates of Western, historically Christian states and liberal states and those of Afro-Asian legal orders, and this largely underlies and explains the strong reaction in the West against this system of family formation in the face of the evidence of family break-up or avoidance of official law such as is presented in this chapter. In the first section of this chapter, we therefore put into perspective legal developments in overseas legal systems, showing that while, officially, certain controls may have been introduced for the regulation of polygamy, this may have little bearing on the 'living laws' followed by most people or, for that matter, on the 'legal baggage' of migrants.

The chapter then turns to the examination of English developments in response to different phases of non-European immigration. The British case differs from Afro-Asian systems in the extent to which strong anti-polygamy messages have been sent by the state. In the post-war period the issue of polygamy initially became linked to the arrival and the different legal arrangements of Asian and African migrants who came to Britain. At this time, the courts reacted by trying to reconcile their historic disdain for the practice of polygamy with the demands of justice that the new migrants were making. In the early 1970s, however, the UK legal system took a restrictive turn by introducing statutory reform in a bid to force migrants to conform to English behavioural patterns, while disregarding the consequences for South Asians who potentially faced large-scale derecognition of their marital unions. Although judges reacted by mitigating the worst effects of the legislation, the situation remained

---

1   'Polygamy' denotes the practice of either women or men taking more than one spouse – known as 'polyandry' and 'polygyny' respectively. In this chapter polygamy is used to mean polygyny. This chapter does not attempt to address the issue of concubinage that is also familiar to Asian and African legal systems.

unsatisfactory, as the ability of South Asian men to enter into plural marriage could still be limited, or so it seemed, by the manipulation of the concept of domicile.

This became apparent especially when immigration officials took advantage of official legal ambiguities by deciding to refuse South Asian women who sought entry under the family reunion provisions. From the late 1970s, therefore, with the onset of family reunion among Pakistanis and, later, Bangladeshis, a considerable body of case law developed that raised the problem of the validity of polygamous marriages, particularly when the admission of second wives was at issue. With the peaking of family reunion among Bangladeshi migrants, the official law reacted again with the attempted ban on the admission of second wives under the Immigration Act of 1988.

This case study of polygamy also provides a more general lesson of how a dominant legal system is ill-advised to attempt to impose a monocultural and ethnocentric regime upon a legally pluralist social base. It also reads as another instance of English law acting in direct conflict with legal arrangements arrived at by ethnic minorities themselves. It is argued here that English law has not achieved the aim of eliminating polygamy as ethnic minorities continue to navigate among various legal levels to circumvent official laws. We see, therefore, that cases of polygamy constantly emerge, showing the 'limits of law' (Allott 1980), but also the capacity of the legal system to tolerate and even cause the penalisation of women and their children in this sphere. The chapter ends by drawing out certain lessons from this case of conflict in legal pluralism for the situation of ethnic minority laws generally.

5.1   The comparative law context

An important feature of Asian and African legal systems has been the continuing maintenance of systems of personal law since premodern times. Modern states have therefore tended to operate on the premise that, particularly in the realm of family law, the customary and religious law of the group concerned prevails, and should generally govern the relations among members of that group. While state laws have often intervened to regulate elements of these 'personal laws' during the colonial and post-colonial periods, the latter still largely form the basis of the social and, therefore, legal order.[2] In such systems a larger zone of self-regulation among variously constituted ethnic communities is

2   For a definition of 'personal law' see Derrett (1968: 39–41). For the argument that personal law systems predate the colonial impact, see Menski (2000a: 131–32).

therefore presupposed. In this scenario, the state claims formal superiority through what Chiba (1986: 5–6) would call the 'official law', while allowing the maintenance of, and recognising the consequences produced by, subordinate legal orders. This approach is quite different to that prevailing in most Western unitary states that are characterised by state legal systems that generally claim an exclusive space for legal ordering, thus acknowledging a minimal, if any, space for non-state ordering systems. They also tend to emphasise uniformity as a desired goal of legal development. This goal, as we see below, is ill-suited to the plural nature of Asian and African societies. It is also causing major problems and conflicts with Asian and African legal cultures that have been reconstituting in Western societies, as we have begun to trace through the preceding chapters. The above characteristics of Asian and African legal systems, as fundamentally different from Western legal systems (see also sections 1.1 and 3.6), have had a crucial bearing on the former's approach to the regulation of family systems that allow for polygamy, despite apparent modernisation.

In many Asian and African societies polygamy has been a long-standing practice which has generally received recognition by the official legal sphere. Different states have adopted various approaches to its legal control, however, although few can be said to have achieved its outright abolition despite the modernisation euphoria that attended post-independence family law reforms. Among South Asian states, from which a large proportion of ethnic minorities in Britain originate, various approaches to legal regulation have been attempted. Modern Hindu law in India, which also covers Buddhists, Sikhs and Janis, goes furthest in this respect and potentially criminalises it. Under the Hindu Marriage Act 1955 a second marriage may also be declared void. This has not prevented Indian courts from recognising the legal consequences of polygamy, however, as the full enforcement of the statute law is seen as often leading to injustice for the women and children concerned. In Pakistan and Bangladesh, Hindus continue to be regulated by Hindu personal law, which allows polygamy. The Indian Hindu legal provisions were also applied in similar form in Kenya and Uganda (although not in Tanzania) immediately prior to independence, with as yet unascertained consequences. On the other hand, the Muslim *sharia* is recognised in India, permitting Muslim men to marry up to four wives, although the absence of statutory regulation in this area has not meant the absence of any control on polygamy and its consequences by the courts. In Pakistan and Bangladesh, observance of certain statutory conditions prior to contracting a second marriage are stipulated by the Muslim Family Laws Ordinance of 1961. Non-compliance with these conditions does not result in voiding of the marriage, however, and judges have still had to grapple with the difficult position of first or second wives who reluctantly find themselves in polygamous situations.[3]

In all these South Asian countries polygamy continues to be observed as a social practice among Hindus, Muslims and others, although there appear to be a very small percentage of the population who adopt the practice. It is notable, however, that no state law, and arguably no customary, personal or religious law recognises the untrammelled power of men to take as many wives as possible and that there are some norms or simply practical limitations regulating the practice at the different levels. This is especially so when the first wife objects to a second marriage, or is effectively deserted without being accorded the rights of a wife or the dues owed to her consequent to divorce, or when a second wife is duped into believing that no prior marital relationship exists. On the other hand, despite the views of many commentators that an outright ban is the right or obvious course for South Asian countries, this may not in fact be the right approach. Although such legislation has been passed as a means of modernising Hindu law in India, and Muslim law in Turkey and Tunisia, it has not absolved official fora from finding appropriate solutions to the plight of women and children and results rather in the practice 'going underground'.[4] The uncritical acceptance of the view that polygamy has been legislatively 'abolished' in the countries of origin may be part of the explanation as to why there are so few recently reported cases in Britain on such issues concerning Hindus or Sikhs or migrants from Turkey. Further below (at section 5.2) we look at

---

3   See in detail Menski (2001a: 139–230) on India and Menski (2003: 374–426) specifically on Hindu law there; Hinchcliffe (1970), Pearl and Menski (1998: 237–73) and Serajuddin (2001: 124–94) on Muslim law in South Asia and elsewhere; and Derrett (1963: 535–56) on Hindu law in East Africa. In Kenya the applicable statutory law is found in the Hindu Marriage and Divorce Ordinance 1960 and in Uganda in the Hindu Marriage and Divorce Ordinance 1961. Mole (1987: 44) observes that: 'The form of Hindu and Muslim marriage is broadly the same amongst the East African Asian communities as in the Indian subcontinent except that polygamy is rare amongst East African Asian Muslims and is not condoned by most communities.' For South Asian Muslims, see similarly Salvadori (1989: 186n) and Hinchcliffe (1970: 27–28), who notes the rarity of polygamy among Ismaili Khojas in Africa, and points to a holy *firman* issued by the Aga Khan in 1962, contained within Part 7 of the Constitution, that forbade the practice.

4   Menski (2001a: 201–02) on Turkey and Tunisia and Yilmaz (1999: 228–34) on Turkey. In the case of *Hassen v Director of Public Prosecutions* (CO/182/97), 30 July 1997, QBD (unreported) a conviction of a Tunisian defendant for 'bigamy' was quashed ultimately on the basis that the prosecution had not been based on firm evidence about the legal position in Tunisia, where the defendant had contracted a first marriage. He, however, appeared to maintain that under Tunisian law he was allowed to enter into plural marriage. While not conclusive, this background to the case at least raises the question of the disjunction between the official Tunisian law and unofficial, personal law.

some more evidence of how overseas laws have been reinterpreted in English courts to suit their agenda.

These as well as some alternative explanations may have to be sought for the relative absence of recent case law relating to sub-Saharan Africans settling or settled in Britain.[5] As in other areas of concern to Africans in Britain, research on polygamy lags behind that concerning other groups. Earlier research on African jurisdictions, particularly on the colonial period, indicates that polygamy was identified as one of the practices most obviously opposed by the missionary zeal displayed by Christian churches anxious to gain conversions to their tenets (Phillips and Morris 1971, Morris 1972). While Muslim law was generally recognised, the colonial states were, at the same time, faced with having to make uneasy compromises as between the churches' positions and the political imperative of minimising interference in ancestral African practices.[6] The balance was inevitably found somewhere in the middle and colonial practice varied a great deal from region to region, from denying Christian converts or those who had registered their marriages with the state the capacity to marry polygamously to criminalising the practice. However, the various statutory enactments by colonial states combined with missionary exhortations, whether strictly enforced or not, did have a destatusing effect on African practices such as polygamy. Phillips's observation that 'there has seldom been any dispute as to the inconsistency of polygamous customs with civilised standards of life...' (Phillips and Morris 1971: 86) is an academic reflection of the one-sidedness with which autochthonous perspectives were marginalised. While there has not been much emphasis on amending offensive legislative postures in the post-independence era, it does appear that the strictures that had previously been put into place have quietly been allowed to lapse.[7] How this history affects present day African attitudes,

---

5   For earlier potential polygamy cases, see *Ohochuku v Ohochuku* [1960] 1 All ER 253, concerning Nigerian Christians and *Sowa v Sowa* [1961] 1 All ER 687, concerning Ghanaians.

6   Anderson (1954) is a useful source for Islamic law in British-dominated Africa. Phillips (in Phillips and Morris 1971: 86) explains the 'softer' attitude adopted by the colonial states in Africa with respect to polygamy: 'It may be that the policies of the British and French governments have been to some extent influenced by their experience and commitments in other parts of the world (eg, India and North Africa) where Muslim law prevails.'

7   For confirmation of this view in light of social realities in Nigeria, see Iwuji (1983) and in Ghana, see Yeboa (1993–95). On the other hand, in African countries where non-Orthodox Christianity has been accepted, a vigorous debate continues about the compatibility of Christian (Catholic) doctrine and traditional African customs including polygamy, particularly since Vatican II in the 1960s: see Kanyadago (1991).

particularly of migrants navigating among various legal levels, obviously requires further exploration, although there is much anecdotal evidence that polygamous practices are simply not being communicated to British officialdom. This mutual stand-off is not going to be sustainable for long as sub-Saharan Africans are rapidly re-emerging as a significant component of the UK's ethnic minority population.[8]

5.2 Control through choice of law rules

In this section, we examine how it was that English law reacted to the increasing presence of Afro-Asian immigrants in the post-war years. While we see that in the early post-war case law judges attempted to overcome their historical reluctance to recognise polygamous marriages, whether they were actually so or not, by 'converting' marriages to monogamous form whenever they could. There was an attempt to override this judicial discretion by special legislative provision from the early 1970s. The aim, it seems, was to restrict polygamy further, although, in its targeting of this practice, it appears that many people in *de facto* monogamous marriages also risked derecognition of their marriages because they had taken place abroad in a legal system that recognised polygamy. The Court of Appeal eventually came in to resolve this issue partially. Therefore, while the higher profile debate centred around such problems, we also see that actual polygamy also came to be of increasing concern, particularly in the context of immigration control. I therefore trace the development of trends in family reunion and link this to the case law that began to emerge, as a significant number of marriages were not being recognised for immigration purposes. I examine in some detail the approach of the Immigration Appeal Tribunal (IAT) and the courts, although this case law was eventually to be superseded by a more draconian form of control, which is examined in turn in the subsequent section.

5.2.1 English private international law and the refusal to see personal law

Since at least the late 19th century, English law has found the concept of polygamy difficult to deal with, and even to recognise, for the purposes of disputes within its courts, which upheld an avowedly Christian

---

8   The 2001 Census figures indicate that 'Black Africans' are now some 0.8% of Britain's population, and some 0.9% of England's, while constituting 10.5% of the ethnic minority population. Also refer to the discussion in Chapter 3.3.

viewpoint. This meant that the likelihood of non-recognition was extended to marriages that, even though actually monogamous, took place under a legal system that allowed polygamy – hence the frequent encounter with *potential polygamy* in the reported English case law. The reluctance to accord recognition or award relief in polygamy cases was in large measure due to the long shadow cast by the decision in *Hyde v Hyde* (1886) LR 1, P&D 130, in which Lord Penzance had declared that 'marriage, as understood in Christendom, may for this purpose be defined as the voluntary union for life of one man and one woman, to the exclusion of others' (*ibid* at 133; see further Poulter 1986: 47–51, Jones and Welhengama 2000: 109–18). Such attitudes lingered on well into the 1960s. Lord Devlin (1965: 9) argued in his famous tract that:

> In England we believe in the Christian idea of marriage and therefore adopt monogamy as a moral principle. Consequently the Christian institution of marriage has become the basis of family life and so part of the structure of our society. It is there not because it is Christian. It has got there because it is Christian, but it remains there because it is built into the house in which we live and would not be removed without bringing it down. The great majority of those who live in this country accept it because it is the Christian idea of marriage and for them the only true one. But a non-Christian is bound by it, not because it is part of Christianity but because, rightly or wrongly, it has been adopted by the society in which he lives. It would be useless for him to stage debate designed to prove that polygamy was theologically more correct and socially more preferable; if he wants to live in the house, he must accept it as built in the way in which it is.

It will be remembered that the main purpose of Lord Devlin's book was to mount an attack against the decriminalisation of homosexual activity. Legislation in force from November 2005 allows registration for gay couples entailing rights and obligations on a par with married couples, but the restrictions on polygamy have remained and have been strengthened during the intervening period as we shall see.

The generally inhospitable attitude to polygamy since *Hyde* is described by Parashar (1982: 206) as 'influenced by the rather condescending and intolerant attitude that was prevalent at that time towards Afro-Asian culture'. However, as a result of the altered political status in the countries concerned, British courts were compelled to recognise the existence and the effectiveness of other states and their laws. The key factor precipitating a change in the attitude of the courts, as Parashar (1982: 206–07) points out, was the:

> … ever-increasing number of immigrants from Asian and African countries. These people who had come from countries which had cultures entirely different from England brought their customs and traditions with them. They were validly married in their countries and could not be expected to

go back to their countries for getting matrimonial relief. Hence the English judges found a way out by holding that [the] nature of marriage could change. The change in attitude was from a complete denial of validity to the position that a potentially polygamous marriage could actually become monogamous.

Besides drawing attention to the link with the increased presence of Asian and African migrants (see similarly, Carroll 1984: 63, Hamilton 1995: 69), Parashar's key observation here is that, as a way of conferring recognition, these 'potentially polygamous' marriages had first to be *converted* by English law to monogamous ones before any application for relief could be entertained. This was an early portent of things that were to follow in that the reaction to increased migration was not to recognise 'alien' customs according to their own terms but rather to make them undergo a process of conversion first.

In the English case of *Prakasho v Singh* ([1967] All ER 737) the neglected wife's right of recourse to the court was resisted by the husband on the basis that their Sikh marriage celebrated in India had been entered into on the basis that it was potentially polygamous. In order to provide a remedy, however, the Divisional Court found it necessary to hold that the Hindu Marriage Act 1955, which had been enacted since the marriage took place, had converted the marriage into a monogamous one. While the judge's action is understandable, in that he clearly saw that the potential polygamy issue was being raised only to defeat the wife's claim, the case also ratifies the fiction that since the 1955 Act Hindu, Sikh, Jain or Buddhist marriages celebrated in India could only be monogamous.[9]

English law also criminalises polygamy under section 57 of the Offences Against the Person Act 1861. In *R v Sagoo* ([1975] QB 885), a Sikh man from Kenya, who was married prior to the adoption of the Indian-inspired legislation there in 1960, then married another woman in England. His conviction for bigamy was upheld on the basis that, while his first marriage had been potentially polygamous, this marriage had been converted to a monogamous marriage as a domicile of choice had been acquired in England. Marrying another time in England, it was held, therefore laid him open to a charge of bigamy. Both these cases illustrate ways in which the Indian and Kenyan official laws were 'received' or reinterpreted by English courts so as to reveal anti-polygamy messages, with the intended effect of intensifying pressures to

---

9   See, to similar effect, Pearl (1986: 39) and Hamilton (1995: 66). For earlier Hindu cases in British courts, see Parashar (1982: 192–93).

drive polygamy underground.[10] On the other hand, the failure to perceive socio-legal realities among ethnic minorities may well reflect wishful thinking about English (and Scottish) law's claims of also having 'abolished' polygamy, along lines of what Menski (2000a) has called 'legocentric hubris'.

This assimilationist attitude crucially informed the statutory reforms contained in the Matrimonial Proceedings (Polygamous Marriages) Act 1972 (later incorporated in the Matrimonial Causes Act 1973 (MCA 1973)) even though this legislation signalled acceptance of the principle that parties to (potentially or actually) polygamous marriages could obtain relief under English matrimonial law. The Report of the Law Commission (1971: 14) put forward one of the key considerations that informed the statutory reforms in the following way:

> Finally, it is rightly argued that immigrants to England are not in a privileged position and are expected to conform to English standards of behaviour. However, it seems to us that parties to polygamous marriages are more likely to conform to English standards if English law imposes on them, so far as is practicable, the same family rights and obligations as are imposed on other married people. The denial of all relief cannot achieve any change in the standards of behaviour of people who have made their home in England. On the contrary, denial of relief not only permits parties to escape from their obligations, lawfully entered into under another legal system, but tends to perpetuate the polygamous situation because the marriage cannot be ended.

The Law Commission was seeking, laudably it may be said, to provide relief in situations where parties were possibly likely to escape responsibilities incurred by entering into plural marriages. However, this was combined with the assimilationist starting point that English legal norms ought ultimately to prevail over any others, and with the underlying aim of assisting in the termination of polygamous unions.

The reforms also added hurdles in a move possibly designed to frustrate further judicial innovation. What became section 11(b) of the MCA 1973 provided that a party to a subsisting marriage cannot validly contract a second or subsequent marriage and that second or subsequent marriage would be void *ab initio*. As far as the 'domestic' law was

---

10 Two earlier prosecutions against *imams* for not following English rules on solemnisation, *R v Mohamed (Ali)* [1964] 2 QB 350 (actually a case from 1943) and *R v Bham* [1966] 1 QB 159, also involve polygamy in the background, and conclude by effectively derecognising *nikah* ceremonies as a condition of avoiding criminal penalties. Another case with similar implications, *R v Rahman* [1949] 2 All ER 165, is a bigamy conviction where the husband already had a first wife in India. This case was formally overruled in *Bham*. All three cases involved English women marrying South Asian men.

concerned, therefore, plural marriages celebrated in England and Wales would not be recognised while, as seen, it was already the case that attempting to enter into such a marriage could lead to criminal charges. Section 11(d) of the MCA 1973 then added to the list of grounds by which a marriage, celebrated overseas after 31 July 1971, could be treated as void:

> (d) in the case of a polygamous marriage entered into outside England and Wales, that either party was at the time of the marriage domiciled in England and Wales.

This sub-section, Poulter (1986: 55–56) points out, was specifically presented as an apparent 'codification' of a pre-existing rule of private international law, despite (or possibly because of) some controversy as to the pre-existing position at common law, and despite the fact that the Law Commission's recommendations in its 1971 Report did not specifically advocate action in this area. Carroll (1984: 67) records Professor Morris's recollection that the sub-section was introduced in response to parliamentary opposition based on the erroneous supposition that the Bill legalised polygamous marriages. Poulter (1986: 56) critically argued that the sub-section was inserted without heed to the likely consequences for immigrant men and their wives:

> ... the 'codification' of this supposed rule into statute law seems to have occurred without sufficient regard being paid to the likely consequences. This is because the provision did not merely prevent a white Englishman who is domiciled here from circumventing the ban on contracting polygamous marriages in this country by purporting to do so abroad. It was framed so widely that it appeared to apply equally to immigrants who had come to Britain from countries where capacity to marry is governed by a personal or religious law which permits polygamy. All the indications are that quite a large number of Muslim immigrants, for example, particularly from the Indian subcontinent, have not been marrying in England but have returned to their countries of origin and there entered into potentially polygamous marriages arranged by their families in accordance with the local and religious law. The return of men to find wives in the Indian subcontinent is partly explained by the comparative shortage of single Asian women living in this country. The apparent effect of the new statutory provision in the case of any such person who had acquired a domicile of choice in England was to render his or her marriage totally void.

Clearly, domicile became the key determinant here as non-English domiciliaries were considered as remaining free to conduct their affairs according to their personal or religious laws with the proviso that key facts such as marriage solemnisation took place outside the UK. Even here problems were being stored up as domicile, and how it is acquired or lost, was hardly an uncontentious issue as we see later (especially in section 5.2.3).

The potential consequences of the developing social scenario, under an English conflicts law that was working itself into a corner, were brought to a head in the well known case of *Hussain v Hussain* ([1982] 1 All ER 369). This case concerned a matrimonial dispute and involved a couple who were in a *de facto* monogamous marriage. They had married in Pakistan in 1979, and the wife later applied to the court for a decree of judicial separation on grounds of the husband's 'unreasonable behaviour'. The wily husband relied on MCA 1973, section 11(d) to deny that he was married at all, the marriage being potentially polygamous, an interpretation then in accord with the views of most commentators (Carroll 1984: 66–67, Poulter 1986: 56). The Court of Appeal, however, wisely disallowed him to rely on this specious reasoning, as he clearly appeared to have been married. The court found that he could not possibly have been potentially polygamously married because, being an English domiciliary, his capacity to marry was governed by English law which only allowed monogamous marriages. He was therefore validly, although monogamously, married. The court was also mindful of Britain's 'increasingly plural society' and, had its decision gone the other way, Poulter observes that it would have had 'widespread and profound repercussions on the Muslim community here' (Poulter 1986: 58). However, the reasoning adopted by the Court of Appeal caused several academics and the Law Commission to comment on its potentially adverse or unclear implications.

The complaints focused on three key issues. First, it was argued that the decision applied only to marriages solemnised after 31 July 1971 and did not clarify the status of those solemnised earlier (Pearl 1986: 46). Secondly, the status of persons who conducted their affairs prior to the *Hussain* decision in the belief that under the MCA 1973 their marriages were void remained unclear (Pearl 1986: 47). Thirdly, where the woman was an English domiciliary, marriages celebrated in a jurisdiction allowing polygamy would still be considered potentially polygamous and therefore invalid under section 11(d) (Carroll 1984: 68–71, Poulter 1986: 58, Pearl 1986: 47). The Law Commission (1985) subsequently advocated recognising actually monogamous marriages of English domiciled women married abroad under laws allowing polygamy, thus removing what now seems like obvious discrimination, although its legal position had been weak at least since the reforms of the early 1970s, if not earlier. Meanwhile, the validity under English law of the marriage of any such woman remained potentially subject to being questioned, and could have had immigration-related consequences that have already been seen under the hated primary purpose rule, and which are thus not difficult to imagine occurring in practice. In that parallel scenario, characterised as a manifestation of heavy-handed 'state masculinism' (Menski 1999), judges acceded to the idea that Asian women in Britain effectively could not choose to marry a partner abroad (*Sumeina Masood* [1992] Imm AR 69, Sachdeva 1993: 155–58). Reported immigration cases raising validity issues on the basis of *potential* polygamy do not seem to have emerged, however, and it seems that parties were normally informed about the invalidity of their marriage under English law but yet granted entry clearance as discussed further below (section 5.2.2).

Poulter pointed out that the underlying problem requiring a more radical solution here was the way in which the concept of domicile operated, and noted that the Law Commission in its post-*Hussain* Working Paper of 1982 had considered the option of allowing Muslim husbands to marry a second wife in Bangladesh or Pakistan, for example, and to give full recognition to such marriages even where the man was considered an English domiciliary (Poulter 1986: 60–61). This option was, however, rejected pending a general rethink about the law of domicile, and it was not revisited in the Commission's 1985 Report. Instead, the recommendations limited themselves to advocating recognition of actually monogamous marriages of English domiciled women married abroad under laws allowing polygamy. It seems that Poulter was rather generous in his interpretation of the Law Commission's Working Paper which specifically ruled out recognition for actually polygamous marriages on the grounds that it would not meet with 'general approval' and because of the difference in treatment among English domiciliaries that this would lead to (Law Commission 1982: 84). Any settlement, if it were to follow the Law Commission's thinking, would reinforce the message that English law would not countenance actually polygamous marriages for English domiciliaries, still thereby treating many ethnic minority men and women, once deemed to have acquired domicile in England, as if their personal laws are subject to absolute control by English law. (A similar position was presumed to prevail in Scotland despite the absence of an equivalent to MCA 1973, section 11(d) (Law Commission 1982: 107).) The recommendations of the Law Commission have now been incorporated into statute by section 5 of the Private International Law (Miscellaneous Provisions) Act 1995 (and section 7 for Scotland), which limits itself to holding valid *de facto* monogamous marriages celebrated in jurisdictions allowing polygamy. While clearly attempting to solve the problem of the potential non-recognition of a huge number of marriages contracted abroad, this legislation also ends up preserving the fiction that English domiciled men and women cannot but enter into monogamous marriages. This mirrors the assimilationist position of English 'domestic' law which is more recently justified on human rights and discrimination grounds (Poulter 1990b).

For ethnic minorities, however, one of the key issues here, which is symptomatic of a wider problem caused by English law (and, it seems, European private international law more generally (see Foblets 1999, Ferrari 2000: 6–8)), is that there is a continuing failure to distinguish between personal law and the relevant jurisdictional law.[11] When English domicile is established, therefore, a person is simply not regarded as capable of contracting into an actually polygamous marriage. The underlying message is that English law seeks to control a person's personal law absolutely in such situations. Given then that the concept of domicile has been seen as the dominant determinant of capacity and that this concept itself is unwieldy and uncertain, this leaves room for all sorts of assimilationist assumptions or exclusionary agendas to be played out by discretionary manoeuvres in actual cases. Marginalising the essentially hybrid legal reality of migrants in such situations will frequently have an immigration bearing.[12] Even in the *Hussain* type scenario, given the couple's actually monogamous marriage, the attribution of English domicile to a Muslim man could still be read as a means of controlling his future freedom of action by barring him from contracting further valid marriages abroad altogether, thus obviating in advance the prospect of future settlement applications by a second wife and her children. The prospect of an English domiciled woman proposing to sponsor a husband who also happens to have a second wife with a potential claim to entry would presumably be totally unimaginable!

5.2.2 Trends in family reunion and the immigration control process

By the mid-1980s, immigration cases could be counted as one of the areas of litigation where questions relating to polygamous marriages were

---

11 Establishing just what is the 'personal law' here may not be a simple exercise, nor does it appear that it would meet with the concerns of all women, see Bano (2000).

12 One line of cases concerns the imputation of polygamy where a prior divorce has not been recognised for failure to comply with the expectations of the official law. *Rukshana Begum Choudhury* (9665) 20 January 1993 (unreported) concerned a refusal to recognise a divorce given to a wife in Bangladesh on the basis that the husband had acquired a domicile in England by that time, and for that reason his subsequent marriage was also not recognised. The Immigration Appeal Tribunal reversed this finding, however, and held that he had never lost his domicile in Bangladesh. In *Mohammed A. Hamid* (14314), December 1996 (unreported) the Immigration Appeal Tribunal heard the appeal of a wife initially refused leave to enter on the basis that her marriage to her Yemeni husband was polygamous. The tribunal held, however, that neither the husband's prior *talaq* to his long-standing first wife, pronounced before an *imam* in Liverpool, nor the subsequent marriage at the Liverpool Islamic Cultural Centre, an unregistered building, were legally effective. See further, Pearl and Menski (1998: 382–98) on the problem of recognition of Muslim divorces in Britain; and Jones and Welhengama (2000: 118–32) and Mayss (2000) on ethnic minority divorces more generally.

featuring prominently, matrimonial and social security cases representing the other key areas (Pearl 1986: 40). The gradual build up of reported and unreported cases in this area can be linked to the changing migration pattern, particularly among South Asian groups in Britain, on the one hand, and the tighter controls that were being applied against their migration to the UK, on the other. Whereas in earlier decades the immigration of men who are referred to by Poulter (section 5.2.1 above) dominated the scene, the 1970s onwards saw the consolidation of families in Britain. It appears that even *among* the South Asian groups the patterns have varied and, to a certain extent, generalisations can be made about this. Ballard (1996a), writing of the Pakistani experience, states that during the 1970s there was a marked shift towards comprehensive family reunion. He (*ibid*: 126) continues:

> While their British citizenship meant that male settlers' rights to reunite families could not be gainsaid, all sorts of administrative obstacles which hindered their ability to exercise those rights began to be introduced, and by the late 1970s lengthy queues had developed at each of the many stages in the process of gaining leave to enter. Yet although this was an effective way of reducing headline figures in the short term, it did not prevent the eventual arrival of persistent applicants, especially when they took their cases to the courts. Thus while the process of family reunion took much longer to complete among the Pakistanis than it had among the Indians ... by 1991 the overwhelming majority of families had been reunited.[13]

Still slower to take off and to peak was the process among Bangladeshis as Ballard (1994b: 20) and Juss (1997: 47–48) have mentioned. Gardner and Shukur (1994: 150) show that in the earlier period Bangladeshi migrant men were 'international commuters' who divided their time between working in the UK and their families in Bangladesh. However:

> By the early 1970s this pattern began to change. New legislation had made movement back and forth between the two countries increasingly difficult, and many migrants had begun to fear that unless they claimed British nationality and brought their dependents to join them, their rights of free movement might evaporate altogether. The whole character of migration swiftly altered: new arrivals were now most likely to be the wives and children of earlier settlers entering officially as dependents. (*ibid*)

This movement then appears to have peaked in the 1980s (Eade *et al* 1996: 151), although it was continuing well into the 1990s (Ballard 1994b: 20). It

---

13 Ballard, apart from identifying the problems encountered in seeking to reunite families among Pakistanis here, draws attention to the facts that this process was delayed as compared with groups from India. For reasons as to why this was the case, see Ballard (1990).

also appears, therefore, that there was a mutually reinforcing effect as between the perception of tighter immigration regulations and the desire to reunite the family rapidly in order avoid stricter controls. This would not, however, rule out the influence of other factors, particularly, the 'growing confidence that it was possible to recreate a fully moral social universe in Britain' (Ballard 1994b: 16), or the desire of women to obtain control over their menfolk (Gardner 1995: 48, Shaw 2000: 53–58).

When we turn to the process of immigration control we find that marriage relationships have often been doubted in South Asian family reunion cases for various reasons (Sachdeva 1993, Juss 1997), but the validity of marriages on the basis of polygamy only seems to be raised in Pakistani and Bangladeshi Muslim cases. One can only speculate at this stage as to the comparative absence of polygamy cases involving applicants from other Asian and African regions or traditions, although it may well be that the comparatively delayed family reunification processes among Pakistanis and Bangladeshis and the immigration controls consequently applied to this movement may provide one explanation. However, we cannot at this stage rule out the role of perceptions about official laws in the countries of origin (see sections 5.1 and 5.2.1 above) in determining South Asian Muslims as more obvious targets of control.

It was widely known that entry clearance officers (ECOs) were expected to conduct routine inquiries about the validity of marriages when dealing with spouse applications. To illustrate the type of consideration involved in such an inquiry Pearl (1986: 40–41) uses the example of a Bangladeshi man who returns to Bangladesh and marries a second wife there, who subsequently gives birth to a son in Bangladesh and then applies for entry clearance to come to the UK. A three-stage test needed to be performed in this illustration:

(1) What is the appropriate 'choice of law' rule which is used to determine the validity of the marriage? In other words, should the officer apply English law, or should he apply the Bangladesh law? Is there an English-law rule which enables him to make this choice of legal system?

(2) The traditional 'choice of law' rule is that the capacity to contract a marriage which is *actually* or *potentially* polygamous depends on the antenuptual domicile of both parties. If this rule is applied, and, as we shall see there are some authorities which suggest that other tests should apply, then two further questions are raised. First, what test is used to determine the parties' domiciles at the time of the marriage? Secondly, assuming it is held that the man is domiciled in England, what is the English law on capacity to contract *actually* or *potentially* polygamous marriages?

(3) Even if the [second] marriage ... is void in English law, does the child have a right of abode as the legitimate son of his father, independent of his mother's claim?

The rules leave considerable discretion in the hands of ECOs who were certainly not obliged automatically to accept the validity of either potentially or actually polygamous marriages. Although the test outlined by Pearl appears complicated, it does not seem that ECOs found it impossible to apply to find that second wives did not qualify for entry clearance on the basis that the second marriage was void under English conflicts law. In order that ECOs could ascertain how the marriage in question ought to be treated, a domicile questionnaire appears to have been in use since at least the mid-1970s. The Commission for Racial Equality (CRE) pointed out, in evidence to the Law Commission (1982: 47–48), that domicile, 'an abstract concept of legal art', was not generally understood and that individuals were not aware that the domicile questionnaire was used for the purpose of ascertaining the husband's domicile at the time of the marriage. It found this objectionable because the document neither explained its purpose nor indicated that it might be desirable for the person required to complete it to obtain prior advice.[14]

In practice, wives of men who were considered as domiciled in Britain were admitted if the marriage was actually monogamous. However, parties to actually monogamous unions were still warned by ECOs that their marriages may not be recognised in the UK if in polygamous form where the husband's domicile was in doubt (Law Commission 1982: 52). As the CRE pointed out in its evidence to the Law Commission, there was inevitably an adverse effect on parties when they were told by Home Office officials that their marriage was void and that, for their protection, they should go through a further ceremony of marriage in the UK (*ibid*: 47–48). Here again we can see indirect pressures to convert potentially polygamous marriages to monogamous form. On the other hand, by allowing entry in practice, ECOs and the Home Office avoided openly raising the issue of the potential invalidity of such marriages, and we have seen that this only came to a head in *Hussain* when a recalcitrant husband sought to obtain an advantage by claiming that under English law his marriage was never valid.

As for the status of children, as raised by Pearl in his third question (above), the Legitimacy Act 1976 provided that a child of a marriage considered void would still be deemed legitimate if at the time of

---

14   For more recent developments on the use of questionnaires to ascertain domicile, see Macdonald and Webber (2001: 423–24).

intercourse resulting in birth both or either of the parties reasonably believed that the marriage was valid (Pearl 1986: 48). It appears, therefore, that refusals were generally made in cases where a wife was party to an actually polygamous marriage and it was concluded that the husband had acquired an English domicile prior to the marriage at issue, even though the children of the marriage may well be considered legitimate and therefore entitled to citizenship or entry clearance. As we shall see (in sections 5.3.2 and 6.3.2) the status of such children seeking entry was also to be downgraded in time.

5.2.3 The emergence of immigration-related cases and the private international law response

The key reported case that reached the IAT in the early phase of development from the mid-1970s is *Zahra and Another v Visa Officer Islamabad* ([1979–80] Imm AR 48, Pearl 1986: 42–43). Tasleem Zahra and Yasar Arafat, citizens of Pakistan, both applied in November 1975 to the visa officer at the British Embassy in Islamabad for entry clearance to join Mr Talib Hussain Shah for settlement in the UK as his second wife and their son.[15] The marriage took place in October 1974. The visa officer was satisfied that the applicant was the sponsor's second wife. However, because he already had a first wife at the time of the marriage and because the view had been formed that the sponsor was domiciled in England at the time, although the marriage may be valid by Pakistani law, under English law the sponsor had no capacity to contract an actually polygamous marriage. The marriage was thus declared void. On appeal, the adjudicator and the IAT upheld this approach. The IAT leaned in favour of the sponsor's response to the domicile questionnaire that he found the climate in Pakistan 'too bad' and therefore wished to retire in the UK. Applying section 11(d) of the MCA 1973 it was agreed that the marriage was void. Therefore UK immigration law had quite early on adopted the so called 'traditional' or 'dual domicile' (or 'prenuptial' or 'ante-nuptial') test to exclude second wives by simply refusing to recognise the validity of their marriages. Pearl (1986: 43) informs us that this meant specifically excluding from the picture the view taken in the foreign legal system, in this case Pakistan, as to validity of marriage, even though that consideration had specifically been mentioned as a sort of saving provision in section 14(1) of the MCA 1973.

---

15 In this case, it appears that the son could not benefit from the Legitimacy Act 1976 as the application predated the statute.

A similar approach was apparently followed in other immigration cases that reached the IAT.[16]

At this time the Immigration Rules (HC 81 (1973), para 37) carried a provision stating that a:

> ... woman who has been living in permanent association with a man ... may be admitted as if she were his wife, due account being taken of any local custom or tradition tending to establish the permanence of the association.[17]

It was also therefore argued before the IAT in *Zahra* that the applicant ought to be allowed entry clearance under this provision. The IAT, however, followed its own ruling in a case involving a Bangladeshi applicant *Johanara Begum* ((1261), 9 June 1978) that had raised essentially the same point, and held that the Rule in question:

> ... is intended to deal with, so to speak, a monogamous situation. If it were to be otherwise an oriental pasha with a harem of several wives might be entitled to bring them all to this country, even if he were domiciled here, provided that he otherwise satisfied the requirements of this paragraph. This is clearly absurd.

That case, we are informed (at ([1979–80] Imm AR 51), was also followed by the tribunal again in *Visa Officer, Islamabad v Zaitoon Begum* ((1642), 5 November 1979).

The disquiet expressed in *Zahra* about the use of the Rules to admit polygamous wives provoked a change in the subsequent restatement of the Immigration Rules of 1980 (HC 395). After restating the 'permanent association' Rule in the above-mentioned paragraph, the 1980 Rules carried a general proviso that:

> A woman is not, however, to be admitted under this provision unless any previous marriage by either party has permanently broken down. Nor may she be admitted if the man has already been joined by his wife, or another woman admitted under this paragraph, whether or not the relationship subsists.

This new paragraph was obviously inserted as a means of 'codifying' the effect of the decided cases thus reducing room for judicial discretion in future, but it also indicated that the immigration judiciary here were influencing the gradual hardening of attitudes by invoking imagined oriental pashas!

---

16   Pearl (1986: 43) mentions two such cases of applicants from Bangladesh: *Johanara Begum and Others v ECO, Dacca* (1261), 9 June 1978, and *Arifun Nessa and Others v ECO, Dacca* (3392), 1984 (both unreported).

17   Equivalent paragraphs also to be found in other Rules in force at the time.

The *Zahra* decision may have been a turning point in that while, in later cases, the tribunal's approach to retention or loss of domicile seems to have kept shifting somewhat, it remained the benchmark as far as the choice of law rules were concerned (Pearl 1986: 43, 45). In other words, here was a decision giving priority to English conflicts of law, thus establishing the essential parameters of legal relevance and perhaps it is not surprising that ECOs were now concentrating on domicile as a means of denying the validity of marriages, and thus denying entry. Corroborating this, Fransman (1989: 204) recalls that 'the respondent in many immigration appeals has sought to argue that the domicile of origin has been abandoned in favour of a domicile of choice'.

The straitjacketing effect of the dominant conflicts discourse meant that there were occasionally very awkward moments for the tribunal which saw the injustice behind some decisions refusing entry. In one case – *Fazalan Bibi and Others v Visa Officer, Islamabad* ((3080), 1984 (unreported), Pearl 1986: 44) – the tribunal took into account, as one of several factors indicating the sponsor's retention of the domicile of origin, the fact that: 'The sponsor is a Muslim and undoubtedly there are aspects of Western culture which he would find repugnant.'! A right result for the wrong reasons? Perhaps, but it may be noted that the tribunal appeared also fairly impressed with the fact that the sponsor's first wife remained in Pakistan. Pearl (1986: 44–45) and Fransman (1989: 204), however, cite several other determinations in which the tribunal appears to adopt a more balanced approach and leans more often in favour of retention of the domicile of origin, thereby also facilitating the recognition of the validity of second marriages.[18]

With Professor Jackson's appointment as Vice President of the tribunal we find, among the reported decisions, two in which a definite change of approach can be seen since *Zahra*. *Rokeya and Rably Begum v Entry Clearance Officer, Dacca* ([1983] Imm AR 163) was another Bangladeshi case of a second wife and daughter of the male sponsor who typically led an 'international commuter' life between Sylhet in Bangladesh and Britain, having first arrived in Britain in 1962. His first marriage took place in Bangladesh in 1969, he became a citizen of the UK and colonies in 1972, and he married the first applicant in 1975 and his daughter by her was born in 1980. It was decided by the ECO and on appeal by the adjudicator that because the sponsor was domiciled in

---

18 There appears to be a parallel between this line of cases and the early liberal approach of the IAT to appeals against the application of the primary purpose rule, which later became significantly tighter, see Sachdeva (1993: 119–22).

England at the time of the second marriage, that marriage was void. The tribunal took care to set out factors for and against the conclusion that the sponsor had acquired a domicile of choice in England and, unlike in *Zahra*, cited authorities that underlined that the burden of proof on those alleging that the domicile of origin had been lost was a heavy one and stated that 'in the typical immigration case of a family split between England and another country the difficulty of satisfying the criteria is considerably increased'. It held that the sponsor's domicile had not changed at the time of his second marriage and allowed the appeal. Thus, here we have a case in which the basic parameters of the so called 'traditional' or 'dual domicile' test were not challenged by the tribunal but, rather, it sympathetically found a way to hold that the marriage was valid by adopting the view that the loss of the domicile of origin had not been convincingly established.

In the second case, *Entry Clearance Officer, Dhaka v Ranu Begum and Others* ([1986] Imm AR 461), the 'traditional' test was itself challenged by the tribunal. This case also involved a Bangladeshi sponsor's second wife and their children. It was found here that the sponsor had initially married an English woman with whom he had four children but that since about 1953 he had not seen her, although he never went through divorce proceedings to end that marriage. He married the first applicant in 1969 in (what was then) East Pakistan. By the tribunal stage, the sole question was about the validity of the second marriage, although at earlier stages it seemed the main issue had been whether the applicants were related as claimed, a frequent inquiry in Bangladesh cases. The question of the sponsor's domicile therefore became a key point in the appeal. It was actually concluded by the tribunal that although he had acquired a domicile of choice in England at the time of his first marriage, he had subsequently *re-acquired* his Pakistani domicile by 1969, so that his second marriage too was valid under the 'dual domicile' or 'prenuptial domicile' test.

The tribunal did not stop there, however. Since the second marriage in this case predated the dateline of 1 August 1971 drawn by the MCA 1973, the tribunal saw no reason to be restricted by section 11(d). Instead, it drew on the Court of Appeal's decision in the matrimonial case of *Lawrence v Lawrence* ([1985] 2 All ER 733) in which either the 'pre-marital domicile' or the 'intended matrimonial domicile' tests (this latter also expressed as the 'intended matrimonial residence' test or the law with which the marriage has a real and substantial connection) were thought to be useful as a way of recognising the marriage at issue. The relevant *dicta* in *Lawrence* had found support in another of the tribunal's decisions – *Rafika Bibi* ((4603) unreported, Mole 1987: 42–43) – already, although as in that case the tribunal in *Ranu Begum* also found that it was difficult to establish the intention of the sponsor after the marriage with certainty as he had intended to return to the UK for work each time after having visited Pakistan/Bangladesh. However, the tribunal went on to find that:

> In so far as the dicta in *Lawrence v Lawrence* opened the gate to consideration of the law which has the most substantial connection with the marriage, we have no doubt that this was the law of Pakistan. All the factors point to Pakistan being the country most connected with the marriage. Even if we had not been able to find that the sponsor had lost his domicile ... we would still have concluded that the law that has the most substantial connection with the marriage was that of Pakistan. We realise that *Lawrence v Lawrence* was not concerned with the validity of polygamous marriages in English law and was concerned with a case where the intended domicile was English. However, as in *Rafika Bibi* we are thankfully relieved from the task of deciding whether, had the sponsor's domicile been English, the marriage should still be considered valid as the law with which the marriage had the most real and substantial connection was Pakistan.

The marriage was held to be valid according to English law as the findings on the two tests coincided, although as reflected in this statement, the tribunal was certainly aware that it had narrowly escaped the burden of ratifying the idea that an English domiciliary was capable of contracting a polygamous marriage in an overseas jurisdiction (albeit only for marriages celebrated prior to 1 August 1971).

The impression that the official position, as far the older marriages were concerned at any rate, was slowly moving to considering the overseas law is reinforced by some remarks made by Webster J in the unsuccessful application for judicial review in *R v Immigration Appeal Tribunal ex p Rafika Bibi* ([1989] Imm AR 1). In that case, although the tribunal had been impressed by *dicta* favouring the 'real and substantial connection' test in the *Lawrence* judgment, it could not decide either that the sponsor's second marriage actually had a real and substantial connection in Bangladesh or that he had retained his domicile there. It had therefore upheld the finding that the second marriage was void, while allowing the appeals of four children of this union. The second wife then somehow arrived at Heathrow some months later claiming entry. When this was refused a judicial review application challenging both the tribunal decision and the immigration officer's refusal was made. Webster J was not persuaded that the tribunal's approach had been unreasonable or perverse. He also refused to entertain the argument that the tribunal ought to have made a decision that Bangladesh law was the most appropriate as: 'the marriage was a Muslim marriage, celebrated in a Muslim community in Bangladesh, that at its date both the sponsor's wives were resident in Bangladesh, and that the only land or property owned by the sponsor was in Bangladesh.' However, in the course of the judgment, Webster J made the following observation:

> Whatever the doubts or dispute there may be as to which of the two rival tests should be applied, I will assume that the real and substantial connection test should be applied if it results in upholding the validity of the marriage which would be invalid tested against dual prenuptial domicile.

This observation also seemed to favour the application of alternative tests, as had the tribunal, with the aim of upholding the marriage if possible.[19]

At the very least, therefore, these newer cases indicate a more relaxed approach. *Rokeya and Rably Begum* shows that the tribunal was willing to find that the domicile of origin had been retained to uphold a second marriage, and in *Ranu Begum*, that it had actually *been recovered*, with the same result. It is possible that the implications of the finding in *Ranu Begum*, that the 'dual domicile' test was likely to be ceased from having a monopoly over the validity of earlier polygamous marriages, may have also worried law makers. That this approach found the support of the High Court could have caused such worries to rise. However, by the time the High Court gave its decision in *Rafika Bibi* on 11 February 1988, the wheels of legislation were already moving to introduce a statutory 'ban' on the entry of second wives, pushing domicile and choice of law questions firmly to the background.[20]

5.3 The ban on second wives: the intervention of statutory control

By late 1980s, UK immigration law was already heavily involved in controlling the settlement of South Asians by legitimating the denial of entry to family members (Juss 1997), while the fully fledged 'primary purpose rule' that served effectively and mainly to exclude a large number of husbands of South Asian women resident in the UK, was also

---

19   The approach was followed in *Sofura Bibi* (8601), 24 February 1992 (unreported), in another case involving a marriage entered into prior to 1 August 1971.

20   Another reason for refusal continued to cause problems, however. This was the contradiction that was often apparent in sponsors declaring that they saw the UK as their future home for the purpose of supporting their spouse's settlement application, and the same information then being used by ECOs to argue that the sponsor's domicile of origin had therefore been lost, leading to a declaration of invalidity of the marital relationship. Refusals based on this line of reasoning were, however, successfully challenged before the tribunal in *Rukshana Begum Chowdhury* (9965), 20 January 1993, and before Sedley J in *R v Immigration Appeal Tribunal ex p Miah* (CO/2100/92), 14 June 1994 (both unreported). See, further, Jackson (1999: 58) and Macdonald and Webber (2001: 423–24).

in full operation by this time (Sachdeva 1993). By the Immigration Act of 1988 and accompanying Immigration Rules UK law then effectively imposed an outright ban on the admission of a wife where another wife had already been admitted. This legislation marked a new departure in the attempt within British law to control polygamy through immigration restrictions. In the following sections I therefore examine the background to and details of the legislation, and also analyse the reaction of the courts in cases challenging decisions made pursuant to this legislation.

5.3.1 The Immigration Act 1988 and accompanying restrictions

The sequence of events leading to the passage of the 1988 Act, as well as several of its provisions are also of interest in this context and are discussed in more detail in Chapter 6. The key provision of the 1988 Act applying to polygamously married wives is found in section 2, although that only relates to their exercising a right of abode or obtaining a certificate of entitlement. Accompanying changes to the Immigration Rules extended the reach of the prohibition to preclude such wives obtaining entry clearance, leave to enter or variation of leave to remain.[21]

Section 2 of the 1988 Act applies to a wife, A, who acquired a right of abode by virtue of a marriage to a man who also had a right of abode as provided for in the Immigration Act 1971. Such a wife is prevented from exercising her right of abode, or from acquiring a certificate of entitlement if there is another woman, B, living, who is the wife or widow of the husband and who is or has, since her marriage to the husband, been in the UK or has been granted either a certificate of entitlement or an entry clearance. The Act therefore envisages that A be prevented from exercising a right of abode acquired as a result of the 1971 Act's patriality provisions if B has previously been or remains in the UK, regardless of whether the husband remains alive. A may only exercise this right where B has been in the UK as a visitor, an illegal entrant or has been granted temporary admission. An exception is also provided if A was present in the UK before 1 August 1988 or if A had been in the UK at any time since her marriage before B became a wife.

The Rule changes prevent wife A from obtaining entry clearance, leave to enter or remain or a variation of leave to remain as a wife of a man who is married to B, if B is or has at any time since her marriage to the husband been in the UK or if she has been granted a certificate of

---

21 These came into force on 1 August 1988 as amendments to the then prevailing statement HC 169, paras 1B–1D; see Moss (1988). They were later incorporated in HC 251 (1990), paras 3–5 and are currently to be found in HC 394 (1994), paras 278–80 with some amendment.

entitlement. Similar exceptions apply in this case, so that entry clearance, leave to enter or variation of leave may still be granted if A has been in the UK before 1 August 1988 having already come for settlement as the wife of the husband or if she has, since her marriage to the husband, been in the UK at any time when there was no wife B. Apart from that, again, A may only obtain entry clearance, leave to enter or variation of leave if B has been in the UK as a visitor, an illegal entrant or has been granted temporary admission. The Rules do not, however, envisage a total ban and wife A could theoretically obtain entry as a visitor, as the prohibition applies to entry or stay as a wife only. It is to be noted that both under the Act and the Rules B and A may not be first and second wives respectively, but rather it is the presence under a certain immigration category of either wife in the UK that precludes the other from enjoying her right of abode or obtaining entry clearance, leave to enter or variation of leave.

Unlike the other changes introduced by the 1988 Act, the polygamy provisions were certainly not seen by legislators as making a great impact on the presence of South Asians in the UK in terms of their numbers. Home Secretary Douglas Hurd (HC Debs, Vol 122, col 785) speaking of what became section 2, stated:

> I do not wish to exaggerate the point. The number of polygamous wives coming here is quite small: we estimate that perhaps 25 or so polygamous households are set up here every year. However, polygamy is not an acceptable social custom in this country. I have no doubt that it would cause serious damage to community relations if it became generally understood that men settled here could continue to bring in a number of wives each. I very much hope that, on reflection, the Opposition will not make an issue of the change. The numbers involved are quite small, but the principle is not acceptable. The sooner we make that clear in the law of the land, the less likely it will be that damage to community relations will result.

Responding to the provisions of the Bill, Roy Hattersely MP (HC Debs, Vol 122, col 189) stated that the Bill was 'less concerned with legislation than with propaganda' and others saw the measure as more politically motivated than about the numbers involved.[22] Still others saw it as justifiable given its gender equality undertones. For example, Anne Widdecombe MP (HC Debs, Vol 122, col 826) observed:

> We have heard of about the 25 cases of polygamy – not a great deal many … But, speaking as a woman, I find polygamy and arranged marriages wholly at odds with what the European Court of Human Rights has said about the equality of women.

---

22   Stuart Randall MP, HC Debs, Vol 122, col 846.

Thus, it seems that unlike some other parts of the immigration control agenda at this time, this was hardly an issue directly relevant to the 'numbers game' as it had come to be known. Rather, it appears more to do with the continuance of 'alien' customs and cultures regarded as unacceptable in Britain. As we have seen, there is a long history of uneasiness about polygamy in Britain and although the initial defences against it were built upon the doctrinal presuppositions of Christianity, these have now metamorphosed into the unacceptability of the custom on grounds of 'community relations' (a term often used as a substitute for 'race relations') or the norms of gender equality and human rights (Poulter 1990b, Poulter 1995, Hamilton 1995: 71–73). Of course, it may also be argued that by focusing on the pluralisation of cultural norms in Britain, wider immigration control agendas could be pursued or justified, as indeed seems to be true of the 1988 Act (see Chapter 6 for details).

5.3.2 The one-wife policy in the courts

The 1988 legislation meant that for actually polygamous couples the prospect of securing full family reunion rights was now overridden by statute, although as seen earlier (at section 5.2.3), the position under private international law had still allowed some room for manoeuvre at the official legal levels. This does not, however, mean that validity of marriages as such is not a concern of the immigration authorities since Jackson (1999: 57) points out that 'polygamy is the issue of validity most commonly faced in the context of immigration', while Macdonald and Webber (2001: 418) state that polygamous marriages, together with *talaq* divorces, were the areas where there were 'particular problems likely to be encountered in immigration cases'. On the other hand, the case law that came after the 1988 legislation is much less concerned with the validity of marriages under private international law than was the case before then, but rather tends to be focused on the limits to the exercise of administrative discretion that now governs the admission of polygamously married wives.

A valiant attempt to declare the Immigration Rules on polygamously married wives *ultra vires* by means of a judicial review challenge in *R v Immigration Appeal Tribunal ex p Hasna Begum* ([1995] Imm AR 249) did not succeed.[23] The case actually involved a woman in a long-standing marriage as a second wife in Bangladesh who had never had accommodation of her own and from the High Court's judgment it looks

---

23 For a similar, and ultimately unsuccessful challenge to the legality of the 'primary purpose rule', see *Rajput v IAT* [1989] Imm AR 350, CA and the discussion by Sachdeva (1993: 147–50).

as if her mother and brother had no longer wanted to maintain her nor to allow her to remain in the same house as them, the brother's wife and their seven children. In the Court of Appeal the circumstances were made slightly clearer in that the brother's evidence indicated that his sister ought to live with her husband, with whom she had never lived, a situation which was of some concern to her mother. It is this background that appears to have motivated the application in the first place, although this is hardly discussed in the judgments. Effectively, here was a challenge to the Rules that sought to get the UK courts to enforce the duties of a husband consistently with South Asian norms. On this reading the husband could be seen as relying on the official legal position to evade his responsibilities. However, in the High Court Tucker J, while sympathetic, did not find the Rules to be *ultra vires*. Neither did Aldous LJ, who gave the leading speech for the Court of Appeal, accept the argument that while the Immigration Act 1971 allowed the making of Immigration Rules that imposed restrictions on the entry of spouses, it did not allow an outright prohibition on the entry of either monogamously or polygamously married spouses.

Attempting to circumvent the official ban on second wives could lead to the jeopardisation of immigration status as found out by the applicant in *R v Secretary of State for the Home Department ex p Zeenat Bibi* ([1994] Imm AR 326, QBD). The case concerns a young second wife of a sponsor who had been in the UK since 1967, registered as a 'British citizen' (probably rather as a 'citizen of the UK and colonies') in 1974, and had gone to Pakistan to marry and return with his wife in 1975. The couple appear to have been childless, as was revealed only in the Court of Appeal's judgment (*Zeenat Bibi v Secretary of State for the Home Department* [1994] Imm AR 550), and it may be that that was the reason (although we are not informed) that the couple returned to Pakistan in 1989 where the husband married the applicant. The applicant arrived in the UK in 1991, but as a visitor, having informed the authorities that she was already engaged to a man in Saudi Arabia. She later revealed that she had been informed by someone who was 'educated' that if she disclosed her true marital status, she would not have a chance of obtaining admission to the UK. After arrival she soon became pregnant and had two children by the time of the hearings. Upon her first pregnancy she applied for variation of leave as a spouse and upon being interviewed with her husband she was declared an illegal entrant, and later informed of the refusal of her application to remain in the UK.

Not much argument seems to have ensued about the validity of the marriage when the application for leave for judicial review was heard, nor when it was renewed in the Court of Appeal. The Secretary of State's letter described the second marriage as 'invalid and polygamous'. Pill J, in the lower court, assumed that the second marriage was not valid because the sponsor had an English domicile, while Russell LJ in the Court of Appeal, assuming validity, pointed out that the Immigration Rules would have frustrated any application as a spouse. Although the Home Secretary's refusal letter proposed to remove the applicant and her two children, neither court was moved to hold that removal was unreasonable in light of the fact that the children, as British citizens, had a right of abode in the UK. This is a particularly disappointing case with the judges blindly following the statutory rules without regard to the human factors involved, but also a logical consequence of the 1988 Act where a party to a marriage seeks at first not to disclose her true status, indicative as we shall see of a wider phenomenon of polygamy moving 'underground', rather than ceasing altogether. Women in this situation find themselves in an extremely weak legal position, subject to harassment and removal by state officials who are free to make hurtful allegations implying *zina* (illicit or unlawful sexual intercourse outside marriage), and potentially by the other parties to the marriage, although that does not appear to have been the situation in this case.

Another reported immigration case, *R v Secretary of State for the Home Department ex p Laily Begum* ([1996] Imm AR 582), involved a widow from Bangladesh who bore four children before her husband died. She was his second wife. She was refused a certificate of entitlement in 1992 as a direct consequence of the 1988 Act, although her four children were issued with British passports. She then sent them to the UK upon which they were sent into local authority care. Some two and half years later she managed to arrive in the UK and claimed asylum when she was refused leave to enter on false American visas. She was allowed to live with her children who were in foster care, although she was refused exceptional leave to remain on the basis that she and the children could continue life in Bangladesh. One of her sons was 18 at the time of the hearing, although she had with her two daughters aged 14 and 16 and another son aged 12. Two of the four children were said to have suffered from severe emotional problems. Among the arguments raised in the application for leave to apply for judicial review was that the Secretary of State had not treated as paramount the interests of the children as would be the case under the Children Act 1989. Dyson J felt, however, that the Secretary of State was not bound by the Children Act and that what weight he placed on the children's interests was for him to decide. This case again shows judicial acceptance of the policy that, even where children have British citizenship, a mother may still be removed or deported from the UK, a flagrant disregard for family life. Nobody seems to have thought it relevant to argue that the mother in this case was initially separated from her children because of the retroactive removal of her right of abode. This case also highlights the different standards of child protection thought appropriate as between the family court jurisdiction and the immigration context.

Much of the case law that emerged, even before the 1988 legislation, involved not only polygamously married wives, but also their children in the background. It therefore must have looked very obvious that UK law was actively engaged in separating families by granting entry to children of mothers who themselves were being refused. In the 1994 restatement of the Immigration Rules (HC 395) a new paragraph (296) was inserted that allowed (even mandated) refusal to children whose mothers would be liable to be refused for being polygamously married. Menski (1994: 118) recalls how this provision was inserted despite arguments against it, partly based on human rights grounds, by representative organisations, and finds it to be a reflection of the 'entirely negative approach to polygamous marriages and children from such marriages'. Whether this provision was inserted in response to the increasing visibility of child-related case law is uncertain, but it would certainly have allowed refusals to be issued in a low-key manner against some children, particularly those who were too young to benefit from the citizenship provisions discussed above (and see Chapter 6).

The position of children of polygamous marriages, previously thought to be entitled to British citizenship, is also now under question by the recent judgment of the Court of Appeal in *Azad v ECO, Dhaka* ([2001] INLR 109, [2001] Imm AR 318). Whereas the conventional wisdom had hitherto been that the Legitimacy Act 1976 operates to allow children to acquire citizen status through the father, even where a marriage may not be considered valid under English law (Pearl 1986: 48), this position now seems to have changed through judicial *fiat*. The Legitimacy Act 1976 merely requires a reasonable belief in one or both of the parties to the marriage as to its validity. Jacob J, giving the only reasoned speech for the Court held, however, that that reasonable belief must be one as to validity under English law, notwithstanding the fact that the marriage in question had taken place in Bangladesh and that the marriage was considered lawful under Bangladeshi law. As discussed in Chapter 6 and elsewhere (Shah 2002b) this case represents an extremely worrying step by the judiciary that seems to be participating in the building of a highly negative private international law position led primarily by immigration control concerns.

As we saw earlier (section 5.3.1) restrictions on polygamy have been increasingly justified on human rights grounds. However, the fact that UK law restricts the immigration of spouses who regard themselves as legitimately married and therefore entitled to reside together in the same country could itself just as well be argued to be a violation of human rights. In the unpublished decision of *Bibi v UK* (Appl 19628/92, 29 June 1992) the European Commission found restrictions on polygamy to be consistent with the provisions of the European Convention on Human Rights (ECHR). As Karen Reid (1998: 277) tells us:

> The Commission found that excluding surplus wives was a legitimate aim under the second paragraph of Article 8 for the preservation of a Christian-based monogamous culture dominant in that society (as pursuing the protection of morals and of rights and freedoms of others). It also recalled its findings in an unpublished Dutch case that a Contracting State cannot be required to give full recognition to polygamous marriages in conflict with their own legal order, referring to bigamy laws.

It therefore appears that the UK government may have attempted to justify restrictions on polygamy in Strasbourg on the basis of the dominance of monogamy as underpinned by Christian norms. I do not, however, have information about what was meant by the 'protection of morals and of rights and freedoms of others' in this context. It nevertheless seems, on the basis of the above case law, that the European human rights fora may not be prepared to countenance complaints against restrictions on polygamously married spouses, whether in the immigration or in any other field. This case law of the Commission obviously assumes importance at the domestic level subsequent to the Human Rights Act 1998.

One may speculate on this basis what the European Court of Justice may make of an application to include a polygamously married wife as a 'spouse' for the purposes of European Community law, for example, under Directive 2004/38/EC (which amends and/or replaces previous family reunification instruments in connection with the free movement provisions). Certainly, Directive 2003/86/EC on family reunification, from which the UK has opted out, contains in Article 4(4) the very restrictive policy already in place in the UK, disallowing the admission of a second spouse, where one spouse is already present, as well as allowing Member State discretion to exclude children of that marriage.[24] Paragraph 11 of the preamble to the Directive reads as follows:

> The right to family reunification should be exercised in proper compliance with the values and principles recognised by the Member States, in

---

24 Ireland and Denmark also have opt outs. One wonders how much this legislation is actually UK inspired, even though the UK has not ultimately participated. The Directive is applicable to third country national family members of resident third country nationals, as long as the latter are not refugees whose family relationships post-date their entry or are not on another sort of humanitarian status. Other legislation is in the pipeline for these groups of persons, which similarly maintains a no admission policy towards polygamous spouses and children of such unions.

particular with respect to the rights of women and of children; such compliance justifies the possible taking of restrictive measures against applications for family reunification of polygamous households.

As with the UK position, other Member States are here taking the position that it may be necessary to exclude wives and children in polygamous marriages to secure the rights of (those?) women and children. It must be a flawed and jaundiced commitment to gender equality which demands the separation of husbands from their wives and fathers and mothers from their children.

5.4 Polygamy as illustrative of the problem of ethnic minority laws

It is apparent that, particularly since the 1988 legislation, UK law draws a particularly hard line against the admission of polygamously married wives, although under the 'domestic' matrimonial law recognition had already been refused, with the possibility of criminal prosecution in existence for even longer before that. It is also notable that legislation against polygamy in this way, if not necessarily directed at Muslims, has been closely associated with controlling the immigration of South Asian Muslims as the case law also appears to indicate. The statutory ban on second wives coincided with the beginnings of political agitation against the Muslim presence in Britain in education and with the peaking of Bangladeshi family reunification, but was very soon overshadowed by the *Satanic Verses* affair.[25]

However, it can be questioned whether the purported ban on polygamy either by prohibiting the contraction of more than one marriage in Britain or by preventing the admission of second wives achieves its actual abolition, assuming of course that this is itself desirable in all situations. There is now considerable evidence to the effect that Muslims living in Britain have generally been able to adapt *shari'a* to the British scene by taking cognisance of multiple legal levels according to what Menski has termed '*angrezi shariat*' – British-Muslim law (Pearl and Menski 1998: 74–77). On the other hand, some Muslims have consciously preferred to keep, or have had to keep, certain legal acts

25 Lewis (1994: 2–7), in his Bradford-focused study, highlights education and the burning of the *Satanic Verses* as the two most prominent issues publicly connected with Muslims in the Britain of the 1980s. Both had their impacts on the legal sphere in different ways. The Education Reform Act 1988 sought to reinforce the notion that worship and religious education in English schools ought to reflect Christian traditions: see Bradney (1989). The *Satanic Verses* affair, meanwhile, led to a debate on the scope of English blasphemy law and, in a wider sense, reinforced to Muslims in Britain messages about their ambivalent status under English law: see Jones and Welhengama (2000: 179–212).

'within the community' so to speak, a situation which the official legal position colludes in perpetuating by the pretence that only English law (or Scottish law[26]) is being followed.[27] How far this is the case for other ethnic minorities remains under-explored, although Menski diagnosed a similar tendency among South Asians more generally over 10 years ago (Menski 1993: 255). Certainly, the evidence concerning polygamy in the reported case law, particularly in the non-immigration sphere, is hardly restricted to Muslims.

At any rate, for Muslims in Britain, Yilmaz (2002a: 348–49) presents specific evidence about the practice of polygamy in that one marriage is contracted under *shari'a* while another marriage may take place under both the official law as well as *shari'a*. The same result may be achieved by declaring only one marriage for immigration purposes, although another marriage may well take place in the UK under *shari'a* only, while the image that the marriage is a monogamous one is retained officially. The polygamy example shows therefore that ethnic minorities have not remained passive recipients of official dictates. Rather, there is evidence of their reliance on their own cultural resources to secure acceptable outcomes for themselves, and they are often able to negotiate between different legal levels in order to do so, thereby calling into question the claims about the dominance of the official legal system.

On the other hand, the evidence cited shows, consistently with that in other jurisdictions, that official bans on social practices such as polygamy are ill-advised and drive the phenomenon underground. The risks of abuse here are many, as is the potential vulnerability of women and children, who may simply be abandoned without a divorce recognised under the personal law of the parties, and without recourse to official legal fora for remedy. If anything, the official law exacerbates the weaker legal position of women and children, often dividing families across continents by disrespecting their choices, as seen particularly in the operation of the post-1988 immigration regime. In the case of *Bibi v Chief*

---

26 It appears that the long-standing ambiguity about the position of persons deemed to have acquired Scottish domicile prior to a second marriage has been resolved by the IAT in favour of following the English approach, that is, to treat the second marriage as void – see *Abida Naseem* (11415), 12 October 1994 (unreported). The case is arguably superseded now by the Private International Law (Miscellaneous Provisions) Act 1995, section 7, to similar effect however (see section 5.2.1).

27 The growing literature about alternative dispute resolution offered by *shari'a* councils of various types in Britain testifies to the widening chasm between Muslims and the official legal system. See Badawi (1995), Carroll (1997), Pearl and Menski (1998: 77–80, 393–98), and Shah-Kazemi (2001). According to recent reports, such tribunals among Muslims, and also Jews and Catholics, have been in operation in Ontario and are officially legitimated under the province's Arbitration Act of 1991.

Adjudication Officer ([1998] 1 FLR 375) the Court of Appeal upheld a refusal to allow a widow of a polygamously married husband to claim a widowed mother's allowance.[28] This case again highlights, in a non-immigration scenario, the wide gap in protection for wives under the official law, and shows that when polygamy issues do come up in official fora the courts are unable to offer relevant solutions.

A similar situation can be seen in the recent case of *A-M v A-M* ([2001] 2 FLR 6) involving a polygamously married Arab couple, also referred to in section 2.3 above. It seems that official legal recognition was only thought to be necessary after legal advice, rightly, indicated that the Muslim *nikah* performed in London would not confer official validity and that other legal problems were therefore likely to arise. Recognition was then sought to be secured by 'forum shopping' in different Arab states. Predictably, the case is over-focused on recognition issues, with Hughes J underlining the importance of following English law rules on solemnisation. One wonders how long English law will be able to continue turning a blind eye to ethnic minority legal facts in this way by insisting on the (sometimes impossible) expectation of compliance with formal requirements as complex issues will inevitably now often arise especially in disputes over property rights.[29]

In light of the clearly unsatisfactory official position in the area of polygamy it may legitimately be asked how the law should develop from here. The issues clearly go beyond the immigration sphere where there is an obvious problem for the reunification of families divided between continents. The solution in the immigration scenario would be to remove the unjustifiable obstacles imposed by the Immigration Act 1988 and under the Immigration Rules. However, there would still remain the aggressive English law position against recognising polygamous marriages for any other purposes. An apparent solution here might lie in reforming English private international law so that marriages contracted validly according to the law in a jurisdiction abroad might be given effect for all relevant purposes in the UK. Nevertheless, even such a reform

---

28 Other similar cases are *R v Department of Health ex p Misra* [1996] 1 FLR 128, QBD concerning entitlement to a pension scheme and widow's benefit where there were two Hindu widows, and *Al Mansorri v Social Security Commissioners*, 12 July 1995, CA (unreported), concerning widows' benefit where the second wife was also deceased.

29 *Gandhi v Patel* [2002] FLR 603 is a recent Hindu case where an inheritance dispute led a widow to resort to court, only to discover that her polygamous Hindu marriage contracted in England was a 'non-marriage', as distinct from a 'void' marriage, thus altogether disentitling her from challenging the will of her deceased husband. While the judgment casts severe doubt on the *fides* of the woman in question this did not, in my view, justify the treatment of the marriage in dismissive terms.

would fail to capture the full extent of the problems arising in this area. The long-term establishment of Asian and African ethnic minorities, and therefore the establishment of Asian and African legal cultures in Europe, leads to questions as to whether private international law offers a realistic prism through which the legal status of such people can be assessed (Foblets 1999, Ferrari 2000). Private international law is too encumbered by notions such as domicile (or nationality or residence) that try to fix parties to a territorially determined jurisdictional law. It is even argued that this way of treating people entrenches their 'foreignness' through legal structures (Ferrari 2000). On the other hand, it is far from being the case that Western legal systems are prepared to move towards the Asian and African model of personal laws. Nevertheless, it cannot be ignored that the UK and other Western societies are pluralising in unprecedented ways and legal systems will have to remain responsive to such developments. Assimilationist strategies, as seen in this case study of polygamy under English law, lead to such phenomena going underground or result in vulnerable persons, generally women and children, being doubly disenfranchised by official law. It therefore remains essential for a justice-focused legal system to remain sensitive to the context and ethnicity of the persons that come before it.[30] In that case, phenomena such as plural marriage, in the sense of polygamous marriage, ought to be accepted as constituting one form of family arrangement within a polyethnic society that may give rise to problems that require resolution by official fora.[31]

---

30 For suggestions centring on the need for state responsiveness to legal pluralism, see Menski (1993) and Yilmaz (2001).
31 As this text was being finalised, the Asylum and Immigration (Treatment of Claimants, etc) Act 2004 came onto the statute book. Section 8(2) allows immigration officers to arrest persons convicted of various criminal offences. Incredibly, one of the offences listed is that of bigamy. This latest legislative signal hardly represents a respect for a diversity of family forms.

Chapter 6
Bangladeshi Legal Pluralism and English Law

Bengal and its surrounding areas were among the chief regions under British rule in South Asia to have provided the traffic of people between the colony and its metropole, as Rozina Visram (2002) shows in her fascinating history of the presence of Asians in Britain for the last 400 years, involving many legal battles over the centuries. Katy Gardner (1995: 34–47) explains in some detail why Sylhetis came to dominate in their representation in the UK, despite initial recruitment by the British all over Bengal. Lewis (1994: 16) points to the fact that 'There were Sylheti restaurant workers as early as 1873 in London', perhaps the start of the huge network of primarily Bangladeshi-owned 'Indian' restaurants that we see all over Britain today in their 'thousands' (Gardner 1995: 48).

In this chapter we examine some of the evidence of reconstruction in Britain of a diasporic group, the Bangladeshis, and the legal issues that arise as a consequence of such processes. Today, Bangladeshis constitute, particularly in London, one of the most densely concentrated of the ethnic minority communities as the 2001 Census results confirm. While their overall UK population has risen to over 280,000, they concentrate overwhelmingly in the London boroughs of Tower Hamlets and Newham. Although the history of Bangladeshis in Britain goes back considerably, in this chapter I concentrate only on some of the relatively recent developments, particularly those which took place with the onset of large-scale family reunification around the time of the creation of Bangladesh out of East Pakistan. I start with a conceptualisation, in legal-pluralist and agency-oriented terms, of the legal implications of the Bangladeshi presence in Britain, and then go on to examine how immigration restrictions, particularly tightened in the 1980s, were aimed at preventing the settlement of Bangladeshis. I then examine some concrete legal problems in reported court decisions, each centring on the status of marriage and children in different ways, with a view to evaluating the extent to which English law takes on board the facts of Bangladeshi legal pluralism in Britain, or the extent to which it generates conflict as a result of its unwillingness to do so.

6.1   The interplay of legal systems, or Bangladeshi legal pluralism

Much of the explanation as to why the Bangladeshi presence in Britain has hardly made a dent in British legal consciousness lies with the nature of, and presuppositions that operate within that system. What are these factors then? First, one can point to the predominant fiction that the state's law is at the centre of things and is able to control and police all aspects of social life within any of the communities that make up contemporary Britain. This ideology is consistent with what John Griffiths (1986) and Marc Galanter (1981, in Jones and Welhengama 2000: 93–94) call 'legal centralism'. It is the belief that all normative orders can be displaced by the state's legal system which then becomes the sole governing factor in legal terms. Whatever is not recognised or stipulated by state law is considered legally irrelevant and therefore not a concern for lawyers or legal academics. Such assumptions are common to Western legal systems that are predicated on the superiority of state-sanctioned law. The 'official' (Chiba 1986: 5–6) British state law thus presents itself very much as the 'dominant' (Hooker 1975) legal system.

Secondly, the problems presented by legal centralism are compounded by its combination with ethnocentrism within the legal system and among its ideologues. Thus, not only is the state law considered the only relevant regulatory factor, but also it is not seen as necessary for the state to respond with equidistance to all the communities that make up its population. There are clear cultural biases that inform law making and that are also strongly inclined to displace the influence of non-Christian, non-Western normative systems. Santos (2002: 250–51) would probably regard this equation between the 'nation' and the 'state', which permeates into the legal field, as an 'ethno-cratic' situation, whereby the repression (Glenn 2000: 50–53) of other legal orders is in place at all levels, despite a rhetorical recognition by government officers that Britain today is a multicultural society. The fact of a plural social base is not deemed to require the pluralisation of the official legal system. Rather, there remains the expectation that various 'others' must assimilate to the norms of the majority as a condition of legal protection. Thus, the state law presents a system of 'ethnic penalties' (Modood and Berthoud 1997: 144–45), such that the more 'ethnic' one is seen to be, the more the likelihood of marginalisation or penalisation.[1]

Bangladeshis have evidently not just followed English law upon arrival in Britain, and much less do they follow English law in

---

1   This is not to accept the view that only some, usually racialised, ethnic minorities are 'ethnic'. Theoretically, each of us has one or more 'ethnic' identities. In areas of Bangladeshi concentration in London, the ethnic minorities may well be members of all other groups!

Bangladesh, as proponents of the common law's triumph over non-Western legal cultures would have it. Indeed, we know far too little about the legal system of Bangladesh. However, its basic set up seems to resemble other South Asian legal systems, with which it also shares a common history in several ways (Monsoor 1999: 59–120). A key point for us is that the state is actually a relatively distant phenomenon in psychological terms. It is modelled on the Asian (and African) paradigm of a 'soft state' which, while formally superior, is not interested in dictating the terms of everyday life and law for most people (Menski 2000a: 11). We might best describe this scenario as one of assisted self-control, in that the primary regulating factor is the society and its sub-units, but not the state which allows a larger zone of self-regulation to the units of society. This model, with ancient roots in South Asia (Stein 1980: 264–84, Menski 2000a: 149–72, and discussed further in Chapter 3), runs on assumptions that are quite different to the Western state system with its legal-centralist ideology.

Another key distinguishing feature is the place of personal laws in South Asian legal systems. Thus, we find that it is officially recognised that different religious or tribal communities will follow their personal law systems in matters of family, property and religion – accordingly the state gets involved in administering Muslim law, Hindu law, and so on. This is a pre-colonial fact, recognised by the colonial Indian state in its own peculiar way, and it continues to inform the basic *modus operandi* of legal systems all over South Asia today. However, in Bangladesh, as in Pakistan, this system has come under tension with the twin drives for 'Islamisation' and uniformisation (Menski and Rahman 1988, Menski 1997b: 18–23), leading to further forms of ethno-cratic development, and to the flight of non-Muslim refugees from Bangladesh.[2] It would still appear, however, that in contrast to the Western model, South Asian legal systems allow a wide scope for the operation of personal law systems, as well as facilitating their official recognition. These differences in understanding about the place of the state in the context of its social framework have a crucial role to play in conceptualising the transplantation of Bangladeshi legal culture in Britain, and they are arguably key determinants in its cognitive interaction with English law.

With migration to Britain one can expect that legal patterns that are followed at the personal level are continued unless we make the very unsound assumption that all one's cultural baggage gets lost on the

---

2   This situation has not prevented Bangladesh being listed in June 2003 as a 'safe' country for the purposes of asylum decision-making in the UK under the Nationality, Immigration and Asylum Act 2002; see Stevens (2004: 207–08).

sea voyage or flight to Britain! We therefore find that there is a transplantation of Bangladeshi, predominantly Sylheti legal culture to the *bideshi* setting. With the earlier stages of male dominated migration from Bengal/East Pakistan, some *bideshi* habits may have been adopted and there is some evidence in the reported cases that some of these men had formed relationships with local women.[3] However, with the arrival of families in more recent decades we have seen the hardening of societal strictures in all sorts of ways (Ballard 1994b: 14–18). We will therefore see quite different stages of legal reconstruction and interaction on the road to the establishment of *desh bidesh* (Gardner 1993), to make Roger Ballard's (1994a) formulation, *desh pardesh* more Bengali-specific.

At this stage, it is worth emphasising that theorising and fieldwork about the ethnic minority presence in the UK have moved on, despite official dogmas about the respective place of state and society as well as inherent cultural biases. Thus, we already have some material that argues for the recreation of South Asian legal cultures in diasporic contexts (chiefly, Menski 1993). For Bangladeshis the material on Muslim law, or '*angrezi shariat*' (Pearl and Menski 1998, Menski 2001b) is most relevant, given the overwhelming concentration of Muslims among this group. The concept of *angrezi shariat*, an Urdu term meaning British Muslim law (*ingreji shoriyot* in Bangla/Sylheti), is understood as the Muslim legal cultures recreated within the British setting.

I do not see this as only indicating the introduction of the textual or doctrinal *shari'a*; it should rather be seen as the more or less conscious process of developing a *living law* in the diaspora.[4] Thus, it is that Ballard argues for greater attention to be paid, not to the concepts of the doctrinal *shari'a*, but to everyday notions of *rivaz* (*rewaj* in Bangla/Sylheti) on which maintenance of honour is crucially predicated. This should incorporate the elements of 'Hindu' custom and the female-centred ritual order, apparently very strong in the Bangladeshi setting (Gardner 1995, Monsoor 1999: 48–51), although tending nowadays to be dismissed as mere 'cultural' artefacts by young Muslim students in Britain in their avowedly increasing commitment to Islam (Gardner and Shukur 1994: 161–63, Lewis 1994: 8, Ballard 2001a). It could also incorporate adaptations to English legal requirements such as the registration of marriages. A thoroughly hybrid process is therefore presented and it is evident that all Muslim communities have been engaged in this process

---

3   See cases cited at Chapter 5.2.1 This is backed up for Pakistanis more generally by Shaw (1988: 46–49) and Shaw (2000: 55–58), and for Bangladeshis by Gardner (1995: 48).
4   The term living law is borrowed from the work of Eugen Ehrlich; see Menski (2000a: 114–19).

to some degree, the Sylhetis no less.[5] Because this process is a dynamic one (Yilmaz 1999), it means that actual fieldwork knowledge is required to appreciate how the cultures have adapted to their new settings.

What is the status of this emergent Muslim law then? While there were demands in the 1970s from Muslim spokesmen that the state recognise *shari'a* officially, these demands have not been met (Poulter 1990b). Muslims have also been campaigning for recognition under the anti-discrimination and blasphemy laws, but these more limited demands have also been pushed away by a state that has been making confident strides towards secularism for decades now. This form of secularism is not the Indian form of equidistance to all faiths but, drawing on liberal answers to intra-European religious conflicts, demands the 'privatisation' of religion, although the long-standing officially established position of the Church of England gives this problem a particular English flavour (Bradney 1993, Hamilton 1995). Some concessions, particularly at local level (Nielsen 1988, 1992, Shah 1994) on issues such as education, mosque building and slaughter regulations are granted, however, and this probably remains the most viable strategy for obtaining recognition at present (Yilmaz 2000). According to the classification that we met earlier, therefore, Muslim law, whether in doctrinal form, or – much more relevant – in the sense of a living legal system, has been pushed firmly into the 'unofficial' sphere. It is uncertain whether this general position will change in the near future, although there is no doubt that there exist serious, and no doubt culturally-loaded, reservations in the West about the compatibility of Muslim laws with human rights norms (Poulter 1990b, 1998).

Apart from the diasporic reconstruction at the level of kinship and religious structures, the Muslim response meanwhile seems to have turned to what Hart (1961) might call the creation of 'secondary' rule systems in the form of dispute resolution fora as a parallel non-state court system that demonstratively illustrates that the English legal system offers inadequate protective mechanisms (Badawi 1995, Carroll 1997, Pearl and Menski 1998: 77–80, 393–98, Shah-Kazemi 2001, Yilmaz 2001). From an internal Muslim perspective, these patterns might look like the re-emergence of a familiar dialectic in Islamic jurisprudence between self-controlled order at family and wider community level, and the input of jurists as exponents of Islamic jurisprudence, although they seem to be an innovation specifically in response to the diasporic condition.

---

5   The availability of the internet means that the process of ascertaining *shari'a* rules on any particular issue becomes even more diffuse; see Yilmaz (2003).

6.2 Immigration restrictions: preventing the establishment of *desh bidesh*

Before going on to examine some of the recent, almost contemporaneously decided cases, it is useful to examine the immigration law response to the prospect of Bangladeshi settlement in Britain. The immigration system is, after all, where much of the legal encounter between Bangladeshis and the English law has been taking place in the last two decades. The reasons are obvious to anthropologists and ethnographers who have noticed that the establishment of *desh bidesh*, and thus the regrouping of families in Britain, took place at a later stage for Sylhetis than it did for the other South Asian groups from India or Pakistan. There was thus a shift from the men's 'international commuter' lifestyle to the arrival of wives and children from the 1970s, peaking in the 1980s, but continuing through the 1990s (Ballard 1994: 20, Gardner and Shukur 1994: 150, Gardner 1995: 114–21, Eade, Vamplew and Peach 1996: 151, Juss 1997: 47–48). If the decision to reunite families was at least in part motivated by a strategy to avoid waiting for a time when controls would get even stricter, as Gardner and Shukur (1994: 150) indicate, the immigration law system had, by the mid-1980s, fine-tuned its restrictive machinery against South Asian settlement such that Bangladeshis found themselves experiencing some of its worst aspects.

Indeed, from the mid-1980s we find that restrictions were tightened further, specifically in response to Bangladeshi regrouping in Britain. Thus, in August 1985, the Immigration Rules that spouses and fiancées were required to meet before obtaining entry clearance were changed so that those applying to enter had also to satisfy the authorities that there would be no recourse to public funds (Sachdeva 1993: 93–100). This coincided with the gradually worsening economic position of Bangladeshi men because of deindustrialisation in sectors where they were over-represented (Lewis 1994: 22, Gardner 1995: 48). Many men could still claim exemption from the application of these 'public funds' requirements, however, as they had been working in Britain since before the Immigration Act of 1971.[6] A clause (section 1(5)) had been inserted into this Act guaranteeing Commonwealth men who had settled in Britain prior to 1973 that their conditions for family reunion would be no worse. As Sachdeva writes, section 1(5) was 'originally enacted to give confidence to Commonwealth citizens settled here that increasingly restrictive immigration policies were not aimed at driving them away or

---

6   The 1971 Act came into force on 1 January 1973, and so this date was normally applied to assess eligibility.

preventing their families joining them in the UK' (Sachdeva 1993: 40). The full impact of the Rule changes was therefore not evident immediately.

A visa requirement imposed in the autumn of 1986 for visitors from Bangladesh, Pakistan, India, Ghana and Nigeria effectively came to control strictly travel to Britain (Joint Council for the Welfare of Immigrants 1987, Drabu and Bowen 1989), and it had its impact even on those dependants with a claim to British citizenship. The most serious attack on Bangladeshi families came about in the Immigration Act of 1988, however, and Gardner (1995: 49–50) has rightly observed its crucial importance:

> British Bengali men who did not bring their wives and children to the UK in the 1970s may now find themselves embroiled in complicated and expensive legal wrangling, which may take years to resolve, especially since the Immigration Act 1988 now means that their dependants are no longer guaranteed entry. Countless trips may have to be made to the British High Commission in Dhaka by family members in Bangladesh. Sometimes by the time a case is processed, the conditions of entry are no longer valid. Many rural Sylhetis, like ordinary people in the UK, have only a vague idea of the immigration laws, and none at all of their rights. The documentary evidence which is acceptable in British courts simply does not exist in rural Bangladesh, for few people know their exact age, let alone have a birth certificate to prove it. The skill of a family's lawyer may well tip the scales in deciding who gets their entry and who does not, and it is the poorer and less well-connected who inevitably lose out.

The 1988 Act did away with the above-mentioned guarantee in the 1971 Act, thereby allowing the subjection of Bangladeshis to the stringent and ever more demanding requirements of the Immigration Rules on family reunion. It is therefore no coincidence that a huge number of refusals have been made under the public funds criteria since then. This is attested to by the fact that public funds cases constitute a significant proportion of the litigation dealt with by the IAT (Gillespie 1992, McKee 1995, Hussein and Seddon 1996, Wray and Quayum 1999).[7]

The 1988 Act also attempted to neutralise another trump card in Bangladeshi hands. Many South Asian men, Bangladeshis (formerly East Pakistanis) being the most important group here, who came to work in the UK in the earlier periods of post-war migration, acquired a right of abode under the 'patriality' provisions of the Immigration Act 1971.

---

7   For a contemporaneous account showing much case study evidence from the mid-1980s about the process of controlling family reunion, which at the time affected Bangladeshis to a significant degree, see Sondhi (1987). The following summary shows, however, that the state's capacity of control was increased subsequent to Sondhi's account.

While South Asian men could not generally establish such a right through ancestral connections or birth in the UK, many were able to do so after five years' residence in the UK, or by registering in the UK as citizens of the UK and colonies (CUKCs) as Gardner and Shukur (1994: 150) have indicated. Importantly, under the patriality provisions such men could also pass a right of abode on to their wives, including second wives and children, who therefore enjoyed an unfettered right to enter the UK. Further, the children of patrial men who had registered themselves as CUKCs became entitled to claim the status of British citizens by descent upon the coming into force of the British Nationality Act 1981.[8] They could therefore travel to the UK without the need for certificates of entitlement, even on Bangladesh passports, and without being subject to immigration control (see in detail Fransman 1986, 1989: 210–31). The key events that culminated in the 1988 Act being passed again reinforce the impression that the main targets of control were family members from Bangladesh. Fransman (1989: 215) recounts the cumulative effect of the 1986 and 1988 legal changes:

> The Bangladesh British citizens by descent began to arrive in 1985 and during 1986 the numbers increased substantially. However, as of 16 October 1986, the UK government made Bangladeshis visa nationals. As a matter of law, those claiming British citizenship by descent did not require visas but the airlines, fearful of financial penalties, simply refused to carry any Bangladesh passport holder without a visa. The result was that in all but a few isolated cases the flow of claimants from Bangladesh was halted.

> The government, however, was not satisfied with a mere *de facto* prevention of direct arrivals of claimants of British citizenship by descent. The introduction of visas may have placed a hurdle in the path of claimants wishing to travel direct to the UK but did not affect their legal right to do so. Accordingly, after the 1987 election the government announced its intention to amend the law and so to extinguish the statutory entitlement.

Thus, the 1988 Act (in section 3(1)) imposed a requirement on all claimants to the right of abode or British citizenship to establish that status by obtaining a certificate of entitlement or a British passport when seeking to enter the UK. This provision obviated the risk of those previously eligible for entry simply arriving at a British port, and rather attempted to ensure that controls were applied at diplomatic posts abroad where any adverse publicity could be avoided.

The 1988 Act also had specific implications for those in polygamous marriages. Some of the earlier immigration case law seems to indicate, at

---

8   The 1981 Act came into force on 1 January 1983, and the legal effects of key events such as births depend on whether they occurred on either side of that date.

best, an ambivalent official attitude to the recognition of polygamous marriages, and a refusal to allow family reunion could often result, even though the persons involved had always considered themselves married under their personal law. The 1988 Act and accompanying Immigration Rules changes then introduced a prohibition on the entry of a polygamously married wife where another wife had already been admitted to Britain. This can also be read as a direct attack on Bangladeshi families as the practice of polygamy seems to be have been most prevalent with this group as compared with other South Asians. As we saw in Chapter 5, although this change may not have been significant in terms of overall numbers, it was also indicative of the fact that the UK legal system was prepared to tolerate the separation of families, and of mothers from their children, ironically as a way of signalling its civilisational superiority. As discussed further below, such posturing has also led to the downgrading of the rights of Bangladeshi children, who are now deemed illegitimate by English law. A more general point that can be made about the immigration restrictions is that, not only are they aimed at curbing the settlement of Bangladeshis in Britain, but the way in which particular legal conflicts are handled shows much evidence of ethno-cratic assumptions in full play within English law. This then has its own function in signalling to Bangladeshis that assimilation to the dominant norm system is expected.

6.3   Bangladeshis in English law: case studies in legal ethno-cracy

If we take the two elements identified earlier – of legal-centralism and ethno-cracy – together we find that there is ample scope for the dismissal, marginalisation or distortion of Bangladeshi legal culture within English legal fora. On the other hand, we can also find at least some evidence that English judges cannot escape from having to grapple with evidence of Bangladeshi legal reconstruction in Britain, despite the official mono-culturalist policy. The three reported cases show how these patterns work themselves out in concrete situations. All three cases are linked to the extent that they all deal with the issue of marriage, albeit in different contexts; all three are also, directly or indirectly, concerned with the status of children from the marriages. One concerns recognition of a long-standing marriage contracted in Bangladesh in the absence of evidence of registration or indisputable documentary evidence. The second is concerned with the consequences of a polygamous marriage for the status of children. The third, which is discussed in a separate section considering the challenging issues it raises, concerns the dreaded mixed marriage and the question of renaming and circumcising the child once the couple has split up.

6.3.1   Sanctity of marriage or over-reliance on kagzi evidence?

In our first case, *R (Shamsun Nahar) v Social Security Commissioners* (21 December 2001, QBD (Admin Ct), [2001] EWHC Admin 1049), the underlying question was whether the applicant was entitled to a widow's pension as the surviving wife of a Bangladeshi man. There was some evidence that she had already fought a long legal battle with the immigration authorities to obtain a certificate of entitlement to the right of abode on the basis of her marriage. Her initial appeal against refusal of a certificate was allowed but then, on further appeal by the entry clearance officer (ECO), the matter was remitted by the Immigration Appeal Tribunal (IAT) to another adjudicator who also allowed the appeal. The IAT refused leave to appeal further, and the applicant finally arrived in the UK with her son. Throughout the immigration proceedings, the validity of the marriage, which had taken place 'in accordance with Muslim tradition and practice' in (what was then) East Pakistan in 1952, was accepted. Also, a document described as a 'marriage deed' had been accepted as valid.[9]

The applicant's claim for a widow's pension had already been made while she was in Bangladesh and, having been interviewed at the British High Commission in Dhaka, her claim was refused by an adjudication officer. It was in the social security proceedings that the whole question of whether she was married at all was then raised. The 'marriage deed' was produced before the Social Security Appeal Tribunal on appeal. The document was referred to a 'document examination officer' within the Department of Social Security. He was of the opinion that it was highly unlikely that the marriage deed was actually issued in 1952. Munby J's judgment then sets out what followed:

> On 27 February 1998 the Social Security Appeal Tribunal refused the claimant's appeal, having found on the balance of probabilities that it had not been established that a valid marriage had been contracted between the [claimant] and Abdul Kadir [her deceased husband]. The Tribunal's full reasons were issued on 1 June 1998. Referring to the expert's opinion the Tribunal described the marriage deed as suspect. The Tribunal mentioned that the claimant's solicitor had referred to the decision of the [immigration] adjudicator of 22 July 1997 and went on to record the presenting officer's riposte that that decision had been based on the supposed validity of the marriage certificate. The Tribunal concluded on the balance of probabilities that the marriage deed was a forgery.

---

9   Having said this, Sondhi (1987: 28–41) and Juss (1997: 89–108) show evidence from several Bangladeshi cases where documents verifying family relationships were not accepted as valid.

The challenge before Munby J then concentrated on the extent to which the social security appeal proceedings ought to have followed the findings as to validity in the immigration proceedings. It was held that there was no such obligation on them, and the judgment is essentially a review of authorities on this and related points. In fact, the judge held that even when a party has satisfied one government department of the existence of a certain relationship, other departments may lawfully reopen the issue of validity.

The problem that needs to be highlighted here, however, is that it was unhelpful for the social security proceedings to have focused on the genuineness or otherwise of the 'marriage deed', on which the whole effort of establishing validity of the marriage seemed to have depended. As seen, doubts as to the genuineness of the 'deed' seem to get progressively greater through the social security proceedings. What ought to have been revealed at some stage in those proceedings was that marriage laws in South Asia are not premised on registration systems; although such systems do exist they are not mandatory and informal and customary marriages are invariably recognised. It is common practice for people to obtain secondary documentation in order to show that the relevant relationship exists when such a need arises. While such documents can never be absolute proof that the relationship claimed exists, neither should it have been assumed that if the documents were not drafted at the time of the relationship's coming into being (for example at the time of a marriage ceremony), that a *forgery* had been committed, or that the marriage in question is necessarily invalid.

Munby J did recognise in the judgment that:

> The claimant thus finds herself in an unenviable and invidious position and, I do not doubt, one which seriously affects her standing in and treatment by her community. As [her counsel] points out, the effect of the Commissioners' decision is to brand her son M as illegitimate.

Despite this acknowledgment, no significant effort seem to have been made to satisfy any doubts about the relationships through appropriate means. If validity of the marriage was at issue, then there are other rules that could have been used. This must be assumed to be more than an isolated case as Pearl and Menski (1998: 171) have commented:

> In quite a few cases, absence of witnesses or more generally lack of documentation of a Muslim marriage entered into in South Asia has been an issue for the determination before the British courts and tribunals. While the South Asian courts ... lean in favour of recognising such marriages as valid, European judges appear to need constant reminders of the existence of a strong presumption in favour of marriage in Muslim law.

Crucially, it does not appear that this was picked up by the lawyers arguing the case and they managed to divert the issue by getting the judge to decide on one of the finer points of English administrative law. In so doing, they missed the essential issue, as did Munby J himself, despite having recognised that a finding of invalidity would have undesirable consequences for the applicant and her son. Not only would the decision leave her worse off in financial terms, but English law would also be making allegations of *zina* (*jina* in Bangla/Sylheti) against her, while leaving the status of her son in question.

We saw in section 2.4 that Menski has criticised the fact that the South Asian elements in a particular case would end up being quite distorted once lawyers got hold of the matter, and this is precisely what happened here. It seems that the lawyers here have gone off on a complete tangent, arguing legalistic points at the expense of the woman in question, while totally ignoring relevant points about Muslim or Bangladeshi law. Incredibly, although the present writer had commented on the High Court's decision in this case as summarised here (Shah 2002a), the Court of Appeal upheld that decision ([2002] EWCA Civ 859), three senior judges apparently unable to see the, by this stage, ridiculous position the legal proceedings had reached. The sub-heading to this section and its reference to '*kagzi*' meaning 'of paper' is thus a hint at the obsession of British decision-makers with paper evidence and paper trails, repeatedly ignoring crucial, legal relevance of the ritual sphere.[10]

6.3.2 Questioning the legitimacy of children

As discussed in Chapter 5, the English (and Scottish) law attitude to the recognition of polygamous marriage has long been ambiguous, if not altogether hostile. This hostility has not been sustainable over the longer term because courts were inevitably placed in a position of having to decide on the consequences of such marriages, especially when matrimonial relief was sought. In the early post-war decades, the judicial response was pragmatic, but still ethnocentric – convert the marriage to a monogamous one mentally and then provide relief. In the early 1970s, however, legislation was specifically passed to allow courts to provide relief in polygamous marriages that had broken down. At the same time, in a thoroughly assimilationist move, it was stipulated that no marriage

---

10 See also my complaint in section 1.4 about recent cases on marriage solemnisation where entirely inadequate approaches seem to be being adopted, with the one proviso that the presumption of marriage makes its necessity felt in English law again.

celebrated in England and Wales could be polygamous, and the marriages of English domiciled men were void if contracted in polygamous form (Matrimonial Causes Act 1973 (MCA 1973), section 11). English law was thus attempting to assert control over non-European men here. Read literally, the provisions of this legislation would have meant that those South Asian men who had married under Muslim or Hindu law that allowed polygamy were not validly married, even if the marriages were actually monogamous.

The Court of Appeal (in *Hussain v Hussain* [1982] 1 All ER 369) stepped in to remedy partly this anomaly by holding that, since no English domiciled men were capable in law of entering into polygamous marriages, all such marriages were valid. However, the effect of the legislation and this case was still that those women married to men who were already married could have their marriages treated as invalid under English law if their husbands were considered as domiciled in England. Thus, many actually polygamous marriages were treated as such when second or third wives made their applications to enter Britain. Even though the reforms of the early 1970s were predicated on extending the protection of the matrimonial relief laws to polygamously married women, the cumulative effect of subsequent developments has been to penalise those women by derecognising their marital unions altogether. We have also seen in Chapters 5 and section 6.2 how the immigration law positions of such wives declined further.

However, children of such marriages were still considered legitimate under the Legitimacy Act 1976 and thus able to inherit British citizen status from their fathers, just as described above (Pearl 1986: 48–49). Or so it was thought! The decision of the Court of Appeal in *Azad v ECO, Dhaka* (10 May 2001, [2000] WL 1918688 (CA), [2001] INLR 109, [2001] Imm AR 318) puts the whole thing in doubt. The applicant child, born in Bangladesh in 1984, was a son by a third wife. An application was made for a certificate of entitlement to the right of abode in the UK on his behalf. It was also recognised that this would be a test case for all other children by the father's second and third wives. By the Court of Appeal stage, some matters had already been conceded, specifically that the marriage between the applicant's father and mother was considered void under English law, even though valid under Bangladesh law, as the father was already domiciled 'in the UK'. The father, it was conceded, knew that to be so, and so it was the mother's belief as to validity on which the case would turn. This is because section 1 of the Legitimacy Act 1976 (as amended) provides in the relevant part as follows:

> 1–(1) The child of a void marriage, whenever born, shall ... be treated as the legitimate child of his parents if at the time of the insemination resulting in the birth or, where there was no such insemination, the child's conception

(or at the time of the celebration of the marriage if later) both or either of the parties reasonably believed that the marriage was valid.

...

(3) It is hereby declared for the avoidance of doubt that subsection (1) above applies notwithstanding that the belief that the marriage was valid was due to a mistake as to law.

As the court saw it, the main question was whether the mother's belief was one as to validity under English law or under the *lex loci celebrationis*, that is, Bangladesh law. In an extremely briefly reasoned speech Jacob J, with whom Laws and Kennedy LJJ fully agreed, held that the question ought to be whether she had a reasonable belief in the validity of the marriage under English law. Jacob J also felt that, as there was no evidence as to the mother's state of mind, no finding could be made as to her belief. He dismissed the test in an earlier IAT case (*Begum*, 16 March 1990) in which Professor Jackson had suggested that the tribunal would be prepared 'to approach the matter on the basis that it would suffice if one parent had no reason to believe that the marriage would be invalid in English law'. Given that there was no material from the third wife as to her belief about the position under English law, the tribunal's decision in the present case was upheld.

This is an extremely worrying judgment. For observers who are used to decisions on South Asian laws being largely driven by immigration concerns, it probably does not come as much of a surprise. However, it means that decision-makers are now able to refuse citizenship to, or for that matter the enjoyment of other rights by and the imposition of obligations upon, children of polygamously married parents on the basis of an absence of proven belief about validity under English law that was held by a spouse, even though that marriage was considered legal in the place where it was performed and, crucially, under the *personal laws* of the parties concerned. Further, the decision on citizenship rests on an initial finding of illegitimacy that would have thoroughly offensive overtones, not only to Bangladeshis (as recognised by Munby J in *Shansun Nahar* discussed at section 6.3.1 above), but also to a significant number of communities now settled in Britain. Not only may it already be considered offensive enough that English law does not respect polygamous arrangements allowed under the laws of large sections of the world's population, but it may not go unnoticed that English law is so easily prepared to declare children of such unions illegitimate.

That such law can be created by judicial *fiat* in an extremely short judgment and with a reasoned speech made by only one judge, is a further sign that immigration concerns are now creating a private international law that seems to have lost all perspective. Where is this trend now likely to stop? If one is prepared to extrapolate on the basis of this judgment, are we also to treat as illegitimate children of second marriages that take place after a first marriage has been dissolved by an extra-judicial divorce? Even though recognised under other legal systems, it is certainly the case that such divorces are routinely being derecognised by UK decision-makers who are supported in this by case law from the highest courts (Pearl and Menski 1998: 382–98, Jones and Welhengama 2000: 118–32, Mayss 2000). As seen in the *Shamsun Nahar* case (section 6.3.1 above), there are even cases where English law has trouble recognising first marriages where no official element of registration is involved. The fact that most legal systems in the world are happy to continue recognising such marriages does not seem to make a difference in English law, however. Rather, in the face of increasing social and ethnic pluralism, English law seems again to retreat further into an ethno-cratic posture.

6.4   Towards a Londoni-Bangla law? [11]

The third, and in some respects ground-breaking case, is *Re S (Change of names: cultural factors)* (15 May 2001, [2001] 2 FLR 1005) decided in the Family Division of the High Court. Although Wilson J's judgment really deserves an article by itself, this section is restricted to remarking on what I see as its most significant aspects. The case involves a Bangladeshi Muslim girl who had arrived in the UK in 1990 from Bangladesh, was now 22 years old and a British citizen. She had eloped with her child's father, a Sikh by 'religion and culture' and now 28 years old, and an Indian national who had obtained indefinite leave to remain in the UK by virtue of the marriage. They had married when she was 17 and he 22, and she thereby became ostracised by her parents and brother, having only minimal contact with her family through her younger sister. In time, the marriage broke down, and the father applied for a contact order from the court. The mother made a cross-application to resist that and also to have the child's three Sikh names changed so that he would be accepted by her natal family, with whom she had now become reconciled, and by the larger Bangladeshi community.

In the event, Wilson J refused to grant permission for the child's names to be changed by deed poll, stating that the child should continue to be aware of the Sikh part of his identity and that, should he wish to have his names changed officially, then he could do so when he came of

---

11   The term 'Londoni', indicating those with families settled in Britain, is related by Katy Gardner (1995) from her fieldwork evidence in Sylhet.

age. The judge did, however, allow the mother to continue to use a Muslim name for him, including registration with the school and medical and dental practices. The judge decided that the child should be brought up as a Muslim, since it was impractical for him to be brought up as a Sikh at the same time, although he observed that this did not preclude him being encouraged to respect the Sikh faith. He therefore accepted that the child could be circumcised. He finally ordered that contact by the father should be maintained at a contact centre twice a year.

While these overall conclusions by the judge could obviously be discussed further, what makes the case stand out specially is the lengths that Wilson J goes to use the cultural backdrop, particularly as concerns the mother, to arrive at the end result. Indeed, he starts off by remarking that:

> It is difficult for a white judge to understand, let alone to articulate, the depth of the shock which the mother's family suffered and of the shame which she brought upon it, as well as upon herself, by running away with and marrying a Sikh man.

This is a rare example of a *white judge* admitting in effect that his cultural distance prevents him from deciding the issues in the case alone. In fact, he goes on to credit the assistance of the lawyers in the case both of who seemed, judging by their names, to be South Asian Muslims, if not Bangladeshis, as well as the benefit of reports by experts on 'Indian [*sic*] law, culture and religion', who had been employed by either side. The use of the adjective 'Indian' may reveal something about the persistence of old colonial paradigms, which also feature elsewhere in the judgment. In fact, the reports were by one expert on South Asian Muslim law and an expert in Islamic and Middle Eastern studies. It is quite possible that they, together with the lawyers, swayed the judge in taking notice of the very specific ethnic background of the parties concerned. In fact, hardly any evidence about Sikh traditions is introduced in the case.

The quoted passage is also but one illustration of the judge's treatment of the mother's position and conduct through the proceedings as being intimately linked to her status in her family and in her wider community. In other words, the judgment shows some awareness throughout that whatever decision was made had to be seen, not from an individualistic perspective, but must take into account the mother's and her child's future chances of successfully maintaining their social position in their wider context, even though this had been obviously affected somewhat by the mother's history. Wilson J thus refers to her having transgressed the taboo against having sexual relations outside marriage, and that too with a non-Muslim man, that her portrayal of the father's behaviour towards her was at least partly motivated to assist in her own reconciliation with her family and that she could still aim for remarriage within her community.

In several places in the judgment there are references to the fact of this community context. The judge thus also refers to the 'East London Muslim community', 'the Muslim community' and 'the East London Bangladeshi community'. The very localised nature of the mother and her child's social context also seems to be recognised by specific references to the East London setting. Is this actual judicial recognition of the fact that different localities are now influenced by particular ethnic minority legal cultures? Is it possible to argue that this is also *official* recognition of the fact of legal reconstruction, of a 'translocal' (Ballard 2001b), legal *desh bidesh*? Certainly, Menski (1988: 11, 1993: 262, Pearl and Menski 1998: 59–61) has observed that patterns of local concentration have their particular significance for legal reconstruction. It is thus certainly possible to argue that judges cannot escape the relevance of local knowledge and developments and that this judgment shows a proactive taking-on-board of such phenomena. If we are saying that 'law' is anyway much more about lived cultures, rather than just positivist dictats 'from above', then the idea should not be so hard to grasp. It is thus certainly possible to argue that we are seeing a movement from the 'unofficial' to the 'official' levels here.

On the other hand, the precise manner in which this is done also carries its own dangers. Wilson J begins his judgment by referring to religious conflicts from South Asia and their transplantation to the British scene as 'ugly clashes between Hindus and Muslims in Bradford'. While he may have perceived this as a relevant backdrop to his evaluation of the factual scenario, one may ask about the extent to which his decision really need have rested on such conflicts. Indeed, the judge seems to view things as very much moving from the 'political' to the personal level, when he notes: 'how long-standing conflicts in the subcontinent become cruelly translated into personal lives.' It can be argued that this specifically British way of viewing South Asian pluralism (or the limits thereto) has the unfortunate effect of exaggerating what Ballard (1996b) has described, in the Punjabi context, as the '*quamic*' or communal elements of religiosity that emerged specifically as a reaction to British colonial policy in India. Elevation of these, effectively male-centered, *qaumic* elements has the side-effect of suppressing many more common elements of religiosity and world view among South Asians. Highlighting political conflict among these groups enables the white judge to then place himself above all this and thus appear as a neutral arbiter, and further to reconstruct these in the British context. If this judgment also carries the hallmark of ethnocentrism, then it does so in a much more subtle way, and this is a possible line of action in the future of the reluctantly-pluralising English legal system. Whether this will be in interest of the groups concerned, and whether it will successfully contribute to building sustainable pluralism, remains open to question. We saw in section 3.3 that the collection of Census figures in 2001 along lines of religion was initially directed at gaining a measure of religious groupings amongst South Asians, but one must ask whether this tends to the ossification of politicised, *quamic* categorisations, again at the probable expense of pluralism inherent within and between South Asian (and indeed all) religions traditions.

Whether the *Re S* decision, or at least its more positive features, ends up as a mere flash in the pan, or as a limited concession in line with the more general tendency of approaching ethnic minority laws within the English legal system, or whether it will have a lasting significance, is difficult to estimate at this stage. Given the firm resistance to seeing the pluralisation of the official legal system, observers may not want to be too sanguine about its relevance. Were it not for the combination of circumstances in this case, including its factual situation, the strategy pursued by the lawyers, including the calling of expert evidence, the fact that no white litigant was involved, some sympathy from the judge and the absence of an overriding statutory rule that the judge considered binding, this case could easily have looked quite different. However, one can also wonder how far avoidance strategies are a real option for judges any more, given the rapid pluralisation of the British social order. If a case such as *Re S* shows clearly that the recognition of the interlinkage between law, culture and religion (as indeed Wilson J notes) in the South Asian context, and the need for this to be taken into account in the British courts, then could it not be argued that this should not be done just in an isolated case, but as a more general policy approach? Indeed, in the next chapter we interrogate the question of the 'reception' of South Asian law in the official legal sphere further. For Bangladeshis, meanwhile, life under English law, with its in-built superiority complex, continues to remain difficult.

Chapter 7
Expert Opinions on South Asian Laws in Immigration Cases

In the 1990 issue of *Immigration and Nationality Law and Practice* Professor Werner Menski, an expert on South Asian laws at London's School of Oriental and African Studies, wrote an article outlining the need for immigration advisers to be informed about South Asian legal systems (Menski 1990). In so doing, he highlighted the relative lack of knowledge about these systems among practitioners and ways in which this could be overcome, by consulting existing writing and through education programmes. In his detailed study of the immigration control process, Satvinder Juss (1993: 132–35) makes some critical observations about the lack of knowledge amongst immigration adjudicators of South Asian customs, cultures, religions and ways of life. More than 10 years on we might find that such observations about the lack of knowledge of South Asian laws would not be significantly different today, and may indeed be even worse. In the same period we have seen the continued expansion of immigration, and the rapid establishment of asylum, as areas of legal practice, a fact that makes the knowledge-gap even more yawning. We have seen in Chapter 2 the importance of education in ethnic minority laws, with South Asian laws being an important component of such teaching given the UK's immigration history. An equally important corollary of this, especially in immigration laws, must be reflection on legal systems *in* South Asia. Not only does this background constitute a crucial component of the 'legal baggage' that people bring with them, or simply navigate through, in their 'translocal' lifestyles, but such knowledge has a vital bearing on the kind of questions that come up frequently in the immigration law context. This chapter draws upon my personal experience of the writing of expert reports and reflects on the value that one might place upon them as a means of informational input to the legal process in the immigration context, as well as in the wider sense of disseminating knowledge of South Asian laws.

7.1   Interaction with legal advisers

How does one identify whether an expert report is required in any particular case? Werner Menski highlighted the fact that, at the time of his writing, a number of existing books by both UK-based and South Asian writers could be consulted, but warned that they might be too technical, not contain the sort of information required, or they could simply mislead the reader. More texts usefully filling existing gaps in the literature have appeared since that time, particularly on the family law dimension (see Pearl and Menski 1998, Monsoor 1999, Menski 2001a, 2003). While these may not be conclusive or may not furnish the reader with the precise points that are required, they might certainly provide the practitioner with a better starting point from which to address the expert.

Experienced lawyers will often have developed an instinct about the need for better information about a disputed point of fact or law and will tend to take the initiative to contact an expert. The ILPA *Directory of Experts* (1997, now in a new internet edition) is a useful database of information about country experts in a wide number of fields. There is now also a pool of expertise, organised under the auspices of the Centre for Applied South Asian Studies (www.casas.org.uk), which seeks to provide an interface between academia and the practice world, and in areas that are not restricted to law. With the growth of South Asian communities in Britain, this sort of knowledge base is likely to assume a far greater importance than is currently realised.

Jim Gillespie (2001) recently wrote about the role of experts in the asylum context, highlighting the need to provide clear instructions as to what is needed from an expert. However, some legal advisers will often be unsure about what they really require or what sort of expert should be consulted on a particular matter. In my experience, key points might surface only after discussion with legal advisers, and this might indicate the importance of making contact as early as possible. Often an expert might be able to clarify whether a particular line of argument may or may not be worth running, even before a report is commissioned. Ideally, one would almost always prefer to be in contact with the client him or herself so as to pick out things that the legal adviser might not have thought to be of importance.

The fact that I also specialise in immigration and refugee law is, I find, a particular advantage. This is particularly so because of the level of communication that can be struck almost immediately since the legal adviser does not have to explain complicated bits of immigration law before introducing the main issue. On the other hand, one also often finds that advisers are not always trained in public or private international law, or on the finer points of international refugee law; nor may adjudicators or judges be on firm ground in such areas. One can therefore also have some useful input at that level. I am sometimes concerned that there is a tendency to rely on experts for the most basic information, although this is partly understandable given the time pressures on practitioners. It does, however, indicate that much public money may be wasted, and unnecessary anxiety caused to clients, where basic issues could easily be thrashed out earlier on in the decision-making process. Sadly, official legal procedures seem to rank point scoring above these more basic concerns.

One example shows, however, that badly thought out lines of argument are not always due to the problem of time. Take the case of an adviser whose client was born in Indian Kashmir, and trained as a militia in Pakistan. He was due to be removed to Pakistan. The adviser was adamant on running the argument that as her client was born in Indian Kashmir, he was therefore a Kashmiri national (as indeed the client insisted), and that that could be used to resist removal to Pakistan. She had not even considered that, as he was born in what is Indian territory, legally he might be an Indian national and removed to India even if removal to Pakistan was successfully contested! This indicates a lack of knowledge about basic principles of international law relating to the acquisition of nationality and its consequences, and this may be put down to the narrowness of training rather than time pressure.

7.2   'Legal' or 'non-legal' information?

I have often had to say that I cannot prepare reports on political situations on any particular country. I would not advise, for example, on the accessibility of Indian territory to Taliban-linked militia groups in the assessment of possible risk to a client. Neither would I say that I advise only on strictly 'legal' situations. In the South Asian context, the line between 'law' and 'society' is never as clearly demarcated, as one tends to assume is the case for Western legal systems. However, this is the stage at which our preconceived notions about South Asian law – that it is but an offshoot of the common law system, or that statutory laws necessarily provide accurate guidance on law 'on the ground', as it were – interfere with a proper assessment of any legal issue or principle. Many experts and High Commission/Embassy personnel and overseas lawyers generally unfortunately restrict themselves to such assessments due to the positivistic biases of their training. However, disregarding what one might call the 'socio-legal' dimension crucial to an understanding of South Asian legal issues, that can lead to giving unduly narrow, even inaccurate and false impressions.

I find it nearly always necessary to take into account and to draw attention to how the socio-cultural issues interact with the 'legal' issues at stake. Thus, in one case, I thought it crucial to explain by reference to Gujarati socio-cultural norms why a young, orphaned woman who had been raped, and was now applying for entry clearance on compassionate grounds, could not be expected to have recourse to the official criminal law system given attitudes to the public airing of such matters, as well as the potential for further victimisation had she done so. I also had to anticipate the possibility that the Home Office might point out that she could have resorted to her brothers' 'protection' and therefore drew a sort of psychological profile of her brothers from the information given, and thereby argued that her brothers were not capable of or willing to protect their sister's interests. Similarly, in a Tamil case, it had to be explained why a son would be thought to be the more appropriate carer for elderly parents than married daughters who were residing in Sri Lanka. In inter-family adoptions it may be necessary to highlight the importance of male heirs who would be expected to perform essential sacraments upon a parent's death. The examples are many and varied.

Thus, while the border between the 'legal' and 'non-legal' is often not an easy one to draw, it will be important to bring out the wider issues in such cases, particularly as a way of explaining how socio-cultural presuppositions inform the behaviour of the parties involved and therefore inevitably impact on the 'legal'. This might come dangerously close to assessing the credibility of clients and, in recent cases, the benches have warned that experts ought not to give their opinion as to credibility. Thus, in *R v IAT ex p Ez-Eldin* [2001] Imm AR 98, Blofeld J noted:

> I doubt if an expert's opinion of an applicant's credibility is, in itself, admissible. Credibility is essentially a matter solely for the court or Tribunal that hears the case.

One must therefore remain careful not to pronounce too strongly about such matters, while pointing to relevant factors as objectively as possible. In practice, this may not be so easy or smooth. As in *Ez-Eldin*, the expert might have relied on certain facts as given by the client which are subsequently found not to be credible, thereby compromising part or whole of the expert opinion. However, at the same time, one cannot ignore the fact that even assessments of credibility, which in my opinion are too readily formed, can be illuminated by cross-cultural knowledge. Admittedly, these are not necessarily 'legal' issues *per se* and can involve matters such as demeanour, the way in which questions are answered, and so on. In any case, the somewhat strict line sought to be drawn in cases such as *Ez Eldin* is not always possible to sustain, and really reflects the desire for objectivity to which the benches always seem to aspire but can never really reach.

7.3 Overcoming dominant legal approaches

A more general barrier is created by legal processes in the UK, which tend to import certain cultural presuppositions that distort South Asian legal principles, thus preventing their correct application in factual situations. At the worst end of the scale, actors within the legal system tend to hold somewhat negative attitudes towards Asian and African laws, regularly delegitimising legal acts following South Asian patterns. A Professor of Comparative Law recently pointed out to me that there has generally been a difference in the way that the Home Office and the Foreign Office (and formerly the Colonial Office) have tended to treat matters of Asian and African laws. During the colonial period, recognition was given to such laws abroad, while the Home Office tended to take the view that English law should prevail. It seems that negative, Eurocentric attitudes, nowadays being driven by immigration control concerns, are becoming more entrenched the further we move away from the colonial period.

These are problems that affect the whole legal system – from the training of practitioners and case preparation, right through to judicial decision. One key explanation here is the imposition of dominant Western positivist approaches to South Asian legal matters, and therefore the expectation that South Asian legal patterns should mirror the Western model. If they do not, and they almost always do not, then the accusation all too easily levelled is that these systems are failing to protect the people concerned sufficiently or are breaching human rights principles. It is ironic that officials level such accusations while their decisions might have the effect of denying legal agency and the enjoyment of human rights to the persons concerned! Spijkerboer (2000) has instructively argued that such differences between North and South are distorting assessments of the situation of refugee women.

The adviser or the expert therefore has the added burden of confronting such prejudiced and legally sanctioned forms of discrimination at the risk of being accused of 'dodginess' him or herself (Menski 2002a)! We saw in section 6.3.1 evidence of the continuity of approach that Pearl and Menski (1998: 171) had identified – that judges need constant reminders about the lack of necessity of documentation and witnesses in Muslim marriages from South Asia. However, official intransigence has been taken a step further in the immigration sphere. Immigration laws are creating their own sphere of *non-recognition*, particularly as regards South Asian laws, and in defiance of conflicts of law principles. No area is immune from attack here; marriages (Sachdeva 1993, Menski 2001a: 10–12, Macdonald and Webber 2001: 418–24, 426–31, and Chapter 5), divorces (Pearl and Menski 1998: 382–96, Mayss 2000, Macdonald and Webber 2001: 424–26) and adoptions (Mortimore 1994, Macdonald and Webber 2001: 455, McKee 2002: 35–36) are just some of the prominent examples. I recently wrote a report concerning an inter-family Sikh adoption in India where the Home Office lawyers were alleging that the system of adoptions as recognised under the Hindu Adoptions and Maintenance Act 1956 was violative of human rights! Considering the in-built discrimination against such adoptions in the Immigration Rules, this was adding a further barrier to objective assessment of the issues.[1]

Once reports are submitted, the important question is how they are received. It is understandable, as Jim Gillespie (2001) pointed out, that courts and tribunals have become concerned about experts who tend to be partial, often pushing their own political agendas in asylum cases. Yet there is another dimension that needs to be discussed more openly. There is a palpable perception among the experts on South Asian issues that decision-makers are increasingly dismissive of expert reports, thereby calling into question the willingness of courts and tribunals to overcome the sorts of entrenched attitudes highlighted above.

One cannot help getting the feeling that in the immigration system, decision-makers are driven by control considerations at the expense of just treatment of cases. Thus, a marriage registrar in Scotland refused to accept my report to the effect that an extra-judicial divorce had been effected, thus undermining an Indian woman's claim to remain in the UK with her intended second husband. The contention of divorce was rejected, not on grounds of any faults in the legal arguments, but because I had used words such as 'seems to have been'. Thus, an attempt not to usurp the function of officials by carefully avoiding the making of categorical findings was turned around as a device to reject the validity of a legal act on the flimsiest of grounds. In a recent case involving a Hindu man from Bangladesh, a report by Werner Menski was dismissed summarily despite the provision of details of the systematic failure of the Bangladeshi authorities to protect Hindu property owners (Appeal No HX/25277/2002). Although this area needs to be researched in more detail, it does seem that the long-observed 'culture of disbelief' continues to prevail among official authorities.

7.4   Of academic value?

While expert reports are written primarily to have an impact within legal proceedings, they may serve other, rather more inchoate, but nonetheless important ends. As an academic, it is valuable for me to have the opportunity to write reports as a way of engaging in a dialectical

---

1   It so turned out that the Court of Appeal reversed this contention by holding that for the immigration law not to recognise the system of adoptions was itself violative of human rights; see *Singh v Entry Clearance Officer New Delhi* [2004] EWCA Civ 1075, *The Times*, 15 September 2004.

relationship between the theory we learn and teach and the 'real world' of actual cases. In this way, we as academics also learn about what sorts of problems are being thrown up at the practice end, and how existing knowledge can be adapted to respond to them. I have found such reports very useful in teaching students about the ways in which what they are learning can be used constructively, and as illustrations that South Asian law remains of vital importance in practice despite the impressions that 'mainstream' legal education and literature provide. This does not mean that there is necessarily agreement about the approaches that I adopt when writing reports and some students have also been critical of my own and other experts' reports. This is a very healthy state of affairs in which the important thing is not agreement but the debate itself.

It remains an unfortunate fact that, beyond their use value in the case at hand, reports that are written after expending considerable research efforts generally do not see the light of day, and are frequently not even mentioned in determinations or judgments, a case of further silent treatment.[2] In my view, good reports can constitute an important information resource and one is aware of several ideas to publish such reports as alternative law reports. That would be an important development in this field, which will contribute to the development of South Asian law in immigration sphere and beyond. This is, however, far from claiming any particular *authority* for statements of law contained in these reports. As was mentioned in sections 1.4 and 6.4, we cannot be certain whether this is a transitional phase in the development of awareness of South Asian laws, and Asian and African laws generally. From this point the British legal system could move either in the direction of further suppression of South Asian legal systems, or move toward a more open acknowledgment of legal pluralism. Given the continuing growth in the Afro-Asian population in Britain, with its many translocal connections throughout the world, it does not seem that the British legal system can maintain a standstill position.

---

2   Note the similar treatment of the expert report in Zoora Shah's appeal discussed in section 4.3, based on personal experience, this is far from being a unique situation in the criminal law sphere either.

Chapter 8
Who do we think we are? British Nationality in the European Context

We saw in Chapter 3 how the history of UK citizenship and nationality law has been fluctuating over the decades. It took on an expansive form when Britain gained an empire abroad but has, in more recent times, been contracting, particularly as a means of controlling immigration. In this chapter we examine a portion of this recent history as it connects to Britain's involvement in the European integration process. Peo Hansen (2004) has recently argued that the construction of a European identity involves denial of Europe's connection with large numbers of people in the 'non-European' parts of the world. This case study on nationality law can thus be seen in this wider context and, in particular, the decision of European Court of Justice (ECJ) in the *Manjit Kaur* case can be viewed as the latest in long series of events tending to exclude Asian British nationals. 'The East, which has been insinuating itself into England from the earliest times' (Shah, I 1999: 77) is thus continuously repressed in the effort of integration in Europe.

The exercise of the Community law freedoms relating to workers, services, establishment as well as residence rights relating to students, independent and retired persons is premised upon a person holding the nationality of a Member State of the European Community.[1] This precondition has, since the Treaty on European Union, been transposed to the effective exercise of citizenship of the Union. It has normally been presupposed that one should look to the nationality or citizenship law of a particular Member State to decide the question whether a person may exercise Community freedoms or, in the new scenario, citizenship of the

---

1 That holding nationality of a Member State was a precondition to the exercise of Community freedoms was not necessarily the impression given by the Treaty of Rome of 1957, which spoke, in Article 48 (now Article 39) of 'workers of the Member States'. Secondary Community legislation subsequently enacted of course does refer to nationality.

Union (Nascimbene 1996: 4).[2] However, this principle by itself did not solve the problem of deciding who would be a UK national for EU purposes. This is because UK nationality had for several decades been split into several sub-citizenships and also because holders of only some of these statuses were declared by the UK government as eligible to exercise rights of EU citizenship. There were five different statuses under the last comprehensive statute on UK nationality law, the British Nationality Act 1981: British citizens, British Dependent Territories citizens (BDTCs), British Overseas citizens (BOCs), British subjects and British protected persons (BPPs). Another status, that of British Nationals (Overseas) (BN(O)), was added by the Hong Kong Act 1985 and the Hong Kong (British Nationality) Order 1986.[3] BDTCs are now renamed British Overseas Territories citizens (BOTCs), and are also granted British citizenship under the British Overseas Territories Act 2002.

It was only with a recent decision of the ECJ in Case C–192/99 *R v Secretary of State for the Home Department ex p Manjit Kaur*, given on 20 February 2001, that nearly three decades of uncertainty about the status under European law of British nationals who have been denied the possibility of exercising a right of abode in the UK for an even longer period was ended. This chapter first provides a summary of the key changes in UK immigration and nationality law that led to the removal of the rights of abode for certain classes of UK nationals. It then examines the circumstances which led to their exclusion from the definition of UK nationals for Community law purposes, and also recounts their further marginalisation under UK and Community law. That the Nationality, Immigration and Asylum Act 2002 sought to reconcile the long-standing deprivation of rights of entry to some classes of British passport holder (Shah, R 2003b), as in Manjit Kaur's case, does not detract from the need to study British nationality in its European context. For many of those affected by British nationality law in its European context, it may not be so important that Britain corrected its 'thirty year wrong', but that it took 30 years for that to be done.

---

2   The concept of EU citizenship should not strictly be projected backwards prior to the coming into force, on 1 November 1993, of the Treaty on European Union, since it was that agreement that introduced the concept of citizenship into EU law. A sharp distinction as between the concepts of nationality and citizenship is not maintained in this chapter, although either concept can have a specific meaning or usage depending on the context, and states also differ in their practice.

3   The 1986 Order also anticipates the creation of more British Overseas citizens in case of potential statelessness as a result of the transfer of Hong Kong to the People's Republic of China; see Shah, P (1995).

8.1 Immigration and nationality law prior to the UK's membership of the Community

Under the British Nationality Act 1948, an expansive definition of British nationality encompassed, broadly speaking, people living in the UK and those under colonial domination (who together became citizens of the UK and Colonies (CUKCs)) as well as people who lived in what became independent countries in the British Commonwealth. Both CUKCs and citizens of independent Commonwealth countries qualified as 'British subjects', and were simultaneously known as 'Commonwealth citizens', with the freedom to reside in the UK. The British Nationality Act 1948 was chiefly concerned to provide a mechanism by which a population of a country who were previously primarily classed as CUKCs could have their status changed to reflect their new position as citizens of a newly independent country.[4] At the same time, their right to reside in the UK remained legally intact. Another group of British nationals known as 'British protected persons' (BPPs) took that status by virtue of a connection with a protectorate or protected state such as former princely states in India or the kingdoms in Uganda and, as far as is known, they were not treated differently from British subjects for immigration purposes until more recently.

As is now widely known (see section 3.2), many people, *inter alia* from the Caribbean, South Asia, Hong Kong, West Africa, Aden and Somalia took advantage of work opportunities in the UK after the Second World War, leading to the largest level of Afro-Asian immigration the UK had ever seen. This movement was accompanied by the 'return' of an innumerable number of 'white' migrants upon decolonisation. Their 'invisibility' in immigration terms underlines the racist aspects of immigration control for much of the post-war period. It was not long before immigration controls were contemplated in top government circles, and 'race riots' in the late 1950s gave the final fillip to politicians to introduce controls on entry.[5] Thus, while in nationality law terms,

---

4   Conferment of citizenship of an independent Commonwealth country was, of course, a matter for the domestic law of the state concerned, but the 1948 Act provided a means by which its effect could be recognised for the purposes of UK nationality law. The Act was also concerned to keep British status, in the form of British subjects without citizenship, for those who would fall outwith the provisions of the laws in such Commonwealth countries.

5   There are two key studies which are based on declassified government documents covering the period from the end of the Second World War to the 1960s. They show that attempts were made before the introduction of statutory control to limit the number of entrants to the UK by administrative means such as the issue of documentation – see Paul (1997) and Spencer (1997).

most of these people were still treated as British subjects, the Commonwealth Immigrants Act 1962 predicated control on the place of issue of a person's passport. If a British subject was issued with a passport by the UK government, then he or she remained free from control. The 1962 Act also brought in powers to control BPPs without regard to whether the persons concerned had obtained the nationality of any other state. Although this formula was seemingly neutral in its impact, as it brought most British subjects and BPPs outside the UK under control, it was known that discretion could easily be exercised to allow white Dominion citizens to enter the UK with minimal fuss (Dummett and Nicol 1990: 183).

Under the 1962 Act, passports issued by the UK government did not include those issued to people in an existing British colony, and so they also came under control, as a planeload of Mauritians found out in 1967 (*R v Secretary of State for the Home Department ex p Bhurosah* [1968] 1 QB 266, [1967] 3 All ER 831). However, a passport issued in a British High Commission did not bring the person concerned under control. Thus it was that many Asians from the Indian sub-continent living in East African states, and who retained British nationality on the basis of British assurances made at the time of independence in the early 1960s, also remained free from control. Manjit Kaur, the applicant in the key case on British nationality in the European context decided by the ECJ, was one such person, having been born in Kenya in 1949. Many such people, especially from Kenya, began to arrive in the UK from the mid-1960s as a result of Africanisation programmes in East African countries that discriminated against South Asians settled there. The UK government acted swiftly and curtailed the freedom to move for this group by the Commonwealth Immigrants Act 1968. The 1962 Act was thus amended to require possession of CUKC status by virtue of the holder having been born, adopted, registered or naturalised as such in the UK, or having a parent or grandparent in that position, in order to remain free from immigration control.[6] Manjit Kaur would have lost her freedom to live in the UK at this time, although she presumably, like many of her fellow British passport holders, did not hold the nationality of any other state. It has already been noted that the 1962 Act had also silently introduced powers to control British protected persons, and many Asians settled in East Africa could thereby already be brought under control, although this did not become apparent in practice until around the time of the passing

---

6   The most detailed study on the 1968 Act is Steel (1969). Lester (2002) provides
    information from recently declassified documents about cabinet discussions prior
    to the Act's passage.

of the 1968 Act. It is therefore more appropriate, as far as practical effects were concerned, to speak of British passport holders rather than distinguishing between CUKCs and BPPs, although it is true that there has been a subsequent divergence in the juridical status of the two groups to the effect that BPPs have been deemed not to have *ever* enjoyed a right of abode in the UK.[7]

Since the passing of the Commonwealth Immigrants Act 1968, legal entry to the UK for British passport holders from East Africa was to be secured by applying for a voucher issued under a quota system at a British High Commission. The criteria for the issue of vouchers remained vague and discretionary. They discriminated against women applicants who found it very difficult to qualify as 'heads of household', and waiting times could extend for years on end.[8] For present purposes, it is important to note that this system allowed the UK government to delay indefinitely the issue of vouchers and thereby restrict the entry of persons seemingly entitled to them. It also meant that there was no obligation on the UK to grant entry and residence to persons arriving without vouchers, a position in which Manjit Kaur found herself.

8.2 The Immigration Act 1971 and the first UK Declaration on Nationality

The subsequently key Immigration Act of 1971 was being debated at the same time as the UK's entry as a member of the EEC was being negotiated. Indeed, both the European Communities Act 1972,

---

7 The position contended for in the text is borne out by Home Secretary, Robert Carr's, statement at the time of the Uganda Asians crisis when he stated: 'I feel sure that when we gave the opportunity to these people who had been either citizens of the UK and colonies [or] British protected persons to apply for our passports, we must have intended – speaking for myself, I did intend – that one of the rights they acquired, but not the only right, would be the right to come to this country if they were expelled and had nowhere else to go', House of Commons Official Report, 5th series, Vol 843, cols 261–63, 18 October 1972. Steel (1969) does not appear to distinguish between the position of CUKCs and BPPs, again indicating that the practical difference was not important at this time. It is also known that BPPs were included as eligible for consideration under the quota voucher scheme. On the later reinterpretation of BPPs' legal position, see *R v Immigration Officer ex p Thakrar* [1974] QB 684, QBD and CA, and Shah, P (2000b: 92–94) for further discussion.

8 On the voucher scheme generally see Moore and Wallace (1975: 30–51), Shah, R (1992), Shah, R (1999). In the latter article Shah, R (1999: 9) comments: 'Since the scheme operates entirely at the will of the government and has remained unchallenged and unscrutinised by the courts the problems thrown up by its working have remained equally unaddressed and unresolved.' The judiciary accepted the discretionary and sex discrimination aspects of the voucher scheme – see, for example, *Amin v Entry Clearance Officer Bombay* [1980] 2 All ER 864, CA and HL. On this and other cases on the operation of the voucher scheme, see Shah, P (2000b: 80–84, 89–92).

implementing Community law domestically, and the Immigration Act 1971 came into force at the same time on 1 January 1973. The link between public racism and the control of immigration was already established by the Commonwealth Immigrants Acts of 1962 and 1968, and at the time that the UK negotiated for entry into the EEC the rhetoric of Enoch Powell must have been fresh in the minds of policy makers in Britain. The 1971 Act was itself passed amidst governmental claims that 'primary immigration' to the UK would be stopped.[9] While providing a framework of control necessitated due to successive statutes that introduced complex provisions, the Act itself added to the complexity by its formula of patriality.[10] A 'patrial', and thus someone who enjoyed a right of abode in the UK, was (broadly) defined as:

(1) A CUKC who had that citizenship as a result of birth, adoption, naturalisation or registration in the UK or any of the islands.

(2) A CUKC who at the time of his or her birth or adoption had either one parent or grandparent who had acquired CUKC status at the time of that birth or adoption by the means described at 1 above.

(3) A CUKC who had at any time completed five years' ordinary residence in the UK or islands, and was considered as 'settled' as defined in the Act.[11]

(4) A Commonwealth citizen (British subject) one of whose natural or adoptive parents was, at the time of birth or adoption, a CUKC by reason of birth in the UK or islands.

(5) A Commonwealth citizen, being a woman, who was married to a patrial.

These apparently new categories, in fact, broadly ensured the continuation of much of the position achieved as a result of Commonwealth Immigrants Acts of 1962 and 1968. There were some new

---

9 Dummett and Nicol (1990: 223–27) recount some of the extreme right wing voices that were influencing debates on immigration at the time. Enoch Powell had opposed the 1971 Act on the basis that a restrictive redefinition of British nationality should have been undertaken at the same time. That was, indeed, eventually done under the British Nationality Act 1981.

10 On the background and implications of the Immigration Act 1971, see Dummett and Nicol (1990: 216–27), Evans (1983: 68–72) and Sachdeva (1993: 27–39). For legal details see Macdonald and Blake (1991: 103–06) and Fransman (1989: 115–21), who focus on the notion of 'patriality'.

11 Becoming 'settled' seems to acquire much importance in immigration law from this time. It basically means ordinary residence without being subject under the immigration laws to any restriction on the period of stay, as originally provided in the Immigration Act 1971, s 33(1). Being granted settled status is ultimately an exercise of discretion by the immigration authorities, and is by no means automatic or available as of right. See, further, Macdonald and Blake (1995: 98–106) or Macdonald and Webber (2001: 126–32).

beneficiaries, however, particularly those in category 4. Leading practitioners in immigration law, Macdonald and Blake (1991: 104), comment on the patriality formula thus:

> Obviously the majority of persons who qualified as patrials, because of their ancestral connections with the UK, came from the 'old' Commonwealth countries and from families of British colonial administrators. Few, if any, of non-European origin qualified.[12]

Commonwealth citizens who were living in the UK could, nevertheless, become patrials by applying for registration as CUKCs after five years' residence and becoming 'settled'. It is important to mention this as it relates to the then current debate about who would qualify for free movement rights under Community law.[13] Meanwhile, someone in Manjit Kaur's position could acquire patriality under category 3 above, but this would be conditional on being admitted to the UK, completing the five-year residence requirement and becoming 'settled', all of which depended on exercises of discretion by the UK immigration authorities.

How did this complicated reformulation of immigration and nationality law feed into the contemporaneous EEC negotiations? It would still somehow have to be decided who of the potentially expansive category of people who could still call themselves British subjects under the 1948 Act would have the right to qualify for free movement under the Community Treaties. (BPPs had, it seems, been written off altogether by this time.) And what influences would determine this question? It is quite possible that recently declassified documents may provide some clues to these questions. Certainly, available evidence of discussions at the time reveals that the anti-immigration concerns prevalent in Britain were also influencing decisions about EEC membership.

---

12 A person coming under category 4 would more likely acquire patriality if his or her mother was born in the UK or islands, since a person with a father born there would be a CUKC by descent under the British Nationality Act 1948 and would qualify as a patrial under category 2 anyway.

13 The position of this group can be seen to be gradually worsening under immigration and nationality law over time. Under the 1948 Act, a Commonwealth citizen could register as a CUKC after only a year's residence. Under the 1962 Act such persons could register as CUKCs only after completing five years' residence as of right. Under the 1971 Act, registration as a CUKC became discretionary except for (a) those who were accepted for settlement prior to the 1971 Act coming into force and had completed five years' residence in the UK or (b) patrial citizens of independent Commonwealth countries who had been ordinarily resident in the UK for five years or had been in Crown or other approved employment. Discretionary registration involved ordinary residence in the UK (or a colony) for five years and being 'settled' or in relevant employment and satisfying the Secretary of State (or a Governor) about character, language ability and future residence or employment intentions. See Fransman (1989: 92–96) and Macdonald and Blake (1991: 97) for details.

Hugh Tinker, in a preface to an excellent study by Böhning (1972: vii–viii) on the migration implications of the UK's membership of the EEC, observed that unlike some of the founding Member States which tended to treat nationals of Italy, Turkey or North African states as 'guest-workers':

> Britain, with all its failings, has regarded people from overseas seeking work in our island as immigrants (we have thousands of temporary European workers in our midst, but for most purposes we ignore them). Because these immigrants have been characterised as a 'problem', and a great deal of political mileage has been made out of this problem, our European neighbours – soon to be our supranational partners – believe that there is a disease in Britain which may infect them when we come in. Fantasies are not wholly confined to the British Isles, and the vision of a horde of Sikhs and Pakistanis disembarking at Calais and the Hook of Holland, waving their British passports, has already been created in many European minds.

Böhning (1972: 131–32) himself, in his extremely informative book, also notes the prevailing mood in the context of examining the prospects for allowing free movement rights to those Commonwealth citizens who, while not registered as CUKCs, had already established themselves in Britain:

> … the Commonwealth citizens of independent Commonwealth countries referred to are predominantly coloured, and it would certainly not please the anti-immigration lobby in this country to have economic, social, and legal rights extended to the Black British which would put them on a par with white British, nor would it please the racialist element in Community countries to see Black British grasping the opportunity to work on the Continent.

Böhning (1972: 132–33) also observed that Eurocrats and continental politicians were baffled by the complexity of the immigration and nationality laws of the UK, and by the then current Immigration Bill. He argued that while the Commission in Brussels could have accepted the inclusion within any definition of British nationals those who enjoyed civil rights (although not necessarily enjoying a right of abode) in the UK, and therefore possibly covering resident Commonwealth citizens, that option appears to have been rejected in favour of a narrower one by late 1971. As for UK passport holders such as Manjit Kaur, mainly now remaining in East Africa, it was claimed that they would be eligible for free movement in the EEC after five years' residence.[14] As discussed above, while this may have been the case under the ensuing Immigration

---

14 Böhning cites a statement by Geoffrey Rippon, Chancellor of the Duchy of Lancaster, to that effect. Also quoted in part by Dummett and Nicol (1990: 227).

Act of 1971, this condition could only be fulfilled once legal entry with a discretionary quota voucher as well as 'settled' status was secured.

Meanwhile, the definition of British nationals for the purpose of exercising free movement rights in the EEC was not set out in the Immigration Act 1971, the European Communities Act 1972, nor in the Treaty of Accession between the UK and the then Member States. Instead, the definition was made the subject of a Declaration by the UK government, appended to the Final Act of the Treaty of Accession, which read as follows:

> As to the UK of Great Britain and Northern Ireland, the terms 'nationals', 'nationals of Member States' or 'nationals of Member States and overseas countries and territories', wherever used in the Treaty establishing the European Economic Community ... or in any of the Community acts deriving from those Treaties, are to be understood to refer to:
>
> (a) persons who are citizens of the UK and Colonies or British subjects not possessing that citizenship or the citizenship of any other Commonwealth country or territory, who, in either case, have the right of abode in the UK, and are therefore exempt from UK immigration control;
>
> (b) persons who are citizens of the UK and Colonies by birth or by registration or naturalisation in Gibraltar, or whose father was so born, registered or naturalised.

This was the most restrictive option of those that had been under consideration in the UK's negotiations as far as is known, and the obviously racist connotation of the policy behind the Declaration was not lost on Böhning (1972: 154) who remarked that, *inter alia*, coloured citizens of the UK and Colonies legally settled in the UK but not for the requisite five years remained without the freedom of movement, while white citizens of the UK and Colonies who never settled in the UK obtained the right: 'The insidious distinctions are wholly consistent with an immigration policy which rightly bears the trade mark racialist.'

Other expressions by writers also reveal the uneasy tension between the territoriality principle and ethnicity. Hartley (1978: 73, 85) disagreed with Böhning, emphasising the view that territoriality being a prevailing principle, it had to be conceded that for French or German nationals to be allowed to work in Gibraltar but not in Hong Kong, Gibraltarians also ought be allowed to work in France or Germany, and workers from Hong Kong not. Edens and Patijn (1972) also emphasise the territoriality considerations involved in not extending free movement rights to nationals residing in overseas or associated territories.[15] Arguments

---

15 But see the reply and rebuttal by Böhning (1973).

justifying different treatment on the principle of territoriality do not however address the issue of the status of British nationals without any other nationality, such as Manjit Kaur and many others, who were excluded from the Declaration, and does not square with the special position of the Channel Islanders and Manxmen who, despite not being covered under the territorial scope of the Treaties, came to be treated as eligible for free movement rights upon mere five years' residence in the UK, while their right to take up residence in the UK remained unimpeded (Evans 1983: 238–39). Nor does it square with the position of Falkland Islanders, who retrospectively obtained British citizenship for the purposes of the later British Nationality Act 1981 (Fransman 1989: 190–93). On Gibraltar, Evans (1983: 204–05) observes:

> The technical explanation for the inclusion of Gibraltarians is that it aligned the territorial scope of Community law with its international personal scope: the political explanation is probably that it extended the right of free movement to only a small number of people, of European origin, whose presence in the Member States was unlikely to cause any of the social or economic problems that were feared might be occasioned by large numbers of blacks and Asians who could not easily be 'intergrated' into the host society.

There were many others, like Manjit Kaur, who although not having another nationality, remained outside the scope of the declaration altogether.[16]

Another document also appended to the Final Act, the 'Joint Declaration on the Free Movement of Workers' by the old and the new Member States and the President of the Council of the European Communities, read:

> The enlargement of the Community could give rise to certain difficulties for the social situation in one or more Member States as regards the application of the provisions relating to the free movement of workers. The Member States declare that they reserve the right, should difficulties of that nature arise, to bring the matter before the institutions of the Community in order to obtain a solution to this problem in accordance with the provisions of the

---

16 British subjects without citizenship (BSWCs) referred to in (a) were another category of persons who, because they might be left out of the citizenship law of an independent Commonwealth country, were recognised under the British Nationality Act 1948. As indicated in the Declaration, only those BSWCs with a right of abode in the UK qualified thereunder. Any such person would have to have qualified under partiality categories 4 or 5 of the Immigration Act 1971 as indicated above.

Treaties establishing the European Communities and the provisions adopted in application thereof.

While this document does not appear to have been raised in the *Manjit Kaur* proceedings it nevertheless conveys, albeit indirectly, the thinking of the time, and shows that the idea of a restrictive and discriminatory immigration policy for Europe is not a new one. It is quite probable and unsurprising that British immigration and nationality law was not understood well until late in the day by continental counterparts, and so nor was the scope of the Declaration on nationality.[17] Nevertheless, there is a suspicion that the Joint Declaration was designed to exclude even those non-white Commonwealth citizens who acquired CUKC status and consequently qualified for full free movement rights, as well as later generations of people already settled in the UK. Of this document Böhning (1972: 155) writes:

> The charge of racialism must also be levelled at the Joint Declaration. It is known that the Dutch Government purported that Black Britons "would take advantage of" the free movement provisions and go to the Netherlands in great numbers, and these contentions were believed to be shared by the Germans ... This political pressure was finally formalised in this incredibly vague Joint Declaration which, although not visibly applicable to Black Britons, is in reality only directed against them – for no other reason than their colour and regardless of the fact that the majority of Black UK nationals will have been born and educated in the UK and will have worked and voted there.[18]

More specifically, in arguing against the legality of this measure, Böhning (1972: 157) writes:

> The original provisions obviously did not meet the Dutch-German objections to an assumed influx of coloured citizens of the UK. The Joint Declaration gives the Netherlands and Germany and every other country the assurance that measures could be taken, at least until challenged in Court, which are not authorised by the present free movement regime. One cannot help feeling, however, that this deliberately vague document hides a more specific agreement reached during the entry negotiations and read

---

17 Edens and Patijn seem to admit as much in their rebuttal postscript to Böhning's rejoinder, (1973) Vol 10 *Common Market Law Review*, p 85.

18 Evans (1983: 206) also suspects that the Joint Declaration is explained by the possibility 'that a substantial number of black or Asian United Kingdom nationals might exercise their rights under Community immigration law'.

into the minutes of a meeting, which is kept secret for fear of contradicting too openly the existing system.[19]

It remains to be seen whether the reluctant release of documents by the EU institutions or the release of UK government records may yield something more concrete about the thinking at the time. However, it is already clear from existing evidence that there was nervousness among Britain's future partners in the Community about the possibility of non-white people migrating there as a result of UK membership and that the UK obliged with a restrictive, essentially racist definition of persons it considered qualifying for free movement. Whether a policy motivated by such concerns should receive the imprimatur of the European Court and European law is obviously an important question.

8.3 The British Nationality Act 1981 and the second UK Declaration on Nationality

A decade after the Immigration Act 1971 and the UK's membership of the EEC, British nationality law was altered by the British Nationality Act 1981, which came into force on 1 January 1983. With this Act, the UK government sought to reconcile the split that had occurred over the previous two decades as between nationality and immigration status. A person who held British nationality status did not obviously hold a right of abode in the UK, a position that would appear to contradict even the ECJ's declaration in *Van Duyn v Home Office* (Case 41/74, [1974] ECR 1337, at para 22), the first major litigation involving the UK government before that Court, that 'it is a principle of international law, which the EEC Treaty cannot be assumed to disregard in the relations between Member States, that a state is precluded from refusing to its own nationals the right of entry and residence'. However, it is perhaps not

---

19 Hartley (1978: 75), on the other hand, does not make much of the legal relevance of the Joint Declaration, describing it as 'purely political', but he also perceives the felt need for other Member States to be on guard despite the British Declaration on nationality: 'It should be pointed out that the other Member States, at whose instigation the British declaration was no doubt made, seem to have felt that it was not sufficiently restrictive. Therefore, the Member States made a Joint Declaration on the Free Movement of Workers at the time of the signing of the Treaty of Accession.' Edens and Patijn (1972: 326–27) also reproduce the Joint Declaration and state that it had been 'formulated as an escape clause for the present and future member States [because] during the negotiations the view has always been taken by the negotiating parties that the EEC provisions concerning the free movement of workers apply in principle to Commonwealth citizens, who have the right of abode in the United Kingdom'.

surprising that the purported coincidence of British citizenship and immigration law under the 1981 Act has been described as 'a bit of an optical illusion' (Macdonald and Blake 1991: 2).

A further and more credible aim behind the 1981 Act was to declare to people still claiming British nationality, but who had lost the right of abode some years ago, that they should not entertain the prospect of immigration to the UK any longer.[20] In the event, those CUKCs with a right of abode, or patrial CUKCs, obtained the new status of British citizens, while existing colonial citizens became BDTCs.[21] British nationals associated with a former colony, like Manjit Kaur, became BOCs. Of the three categories, only British citizens have a right of abode, while persons in the other two categories did not gain it. It was known at the time that holders of BOC status included South Asians from East Africa, people of Indian or Chinese origin in Malaysia, people of Syrian descent in West Africa, of Cypriot descent in South Africa, and of UK descent in Argentina (Dummett and Nicol 1990: 243). However, it was difficult to know with any precision how many BOCs there were worldwide. At the time of the passing of the 1981 Act it had been officially claimed that there were over 200,000 BOCs without any other citizenship, although this appears to be an exaggeration, as does the official estimate of over two million BOCs with another citizenship, mostly in Malaysia. Some 25,000–30,000 of the East African Asians had already arrived in the UK upon expulsion from Uganda by the Idi Amin regime in late 1972, although many others had gone to India and Pakistan to wait for entry vouchers to be admitted to the UK, while yet others opted for residence in the Indian sub-continent or in other countries (Dummett and Nicol 1990: 243).[22] Many in this latter group would have retained BOC or BPP status. The official exaggeration of numbers was probably designed to ensure little opposition in not granting full immigration rights to East African Asians as the main group who remained without another citizenship: '… if this group, of which the UK passport holders from East Africa form only a part, were to have

---

20 See the comments of government officers as noted by Blake (1982: 182–83) and Dummett and Nicol (1990: 249).

21 The largest number of these at the time was in Hong Kong. On the impact of this and other legislation for the people of Hong Kong, see Menski (1995).

22 Dummett and Nicol (1990: 243) also state that the Indian queue was stated by the UK government to be at 39,000, although in 1981 there were some 12,500 people, including dependants, in this queue. Many of the applicant 'heads of households' of this group can be assumed to have been reclassified as BOCs by the 1981 Act. Some estimates suggest that the number of BOCs without another nationality could be as low as 100,000; see Gillespie (2000: 147).

British citizenship, the potential immigration commitment would be so large as to be quite unacceptable.'[23] It was stated that, instead, this group should remain in the special voucher queue and that, since it was deemed desirable that the country of birth be regarded as responsible for remedying the situation, BOC status should be made non-transmissible.[24]

For BOCs and BDTCs, acquisition of a right of abode was now made conditional on acquiring British citizen status, which was to be done through registration as such after five years' residence and being 'settled' by that time. This was a change of position since the Immigration Act 1971 because, under that Act, for people who were then CUKCs, a right of abode could be acquired after five years' residence and having 'settled' status, without any further formality (category 3, section 8.2 above). As discussed below, this change fed into a new definition of UK nationals for Community purposes, consequently making the exercise of Community freedoms that much more difficult. It is not the case, therefore, as the ECJ appears to suggest later on in the *Kaur* judgment, that the 1981 Act did not alter the legal position of this group at all.

The enactment of the 1981 Act, with its new categories of citizenship, naturally necessitated a reclarification of the UK's view as to which of its nationals now qualified for Community free movement rights. This was not done in the 1981 Act itself, despite a European Parliament resolution to the effect that a clear definition of UK nationals for Community purposes should be included in it (Evans 1983: 239). In 1982, the UK government lodged with the Italian government, as the 'guardian of the Treaties', a new Declaration on the definition of UK nationals as follows:

> In view of the entry into force of the British Nationality Act 1981, the Government of the UK of Great Britain and Northern Ireland makes the following Declaration, which will replace, as from 1 January 1983, that made at the time of signature of the Treaty of Accession by the UK to the European Communities:
>
> As to the UK of Great Britain and Northern Ireland, the terms 'nationals', 'nationals of Member States' or 'nationals of Member States and overseas countries and territories', wherever used in the Treaty establishing the

---

23   British Nationality Law: Outline of the Proposed Legislation, Cmnd 7987 (July 1980), para 26.
24   *Ibid*, paras 27 and 103. For a critique of this position see Blake (1982: 191). It is interesting to note that in Kenya, nationality law revision has retroactively *deprived* Asians among others of citizenship obtained at the time of independence in 1963; see Shah, R (1992).

European Economic Community ... or in any of the Community acts deriving from those Treaties, are to be understood to refer to:
(a) British citizens;
(b) Persons who are British subjects by virtue of Part IV of the British Nationality Act 1981 and who have the right of abode in the UK and are therefore exempt from UK immigration control;
(c) British Dependent Territories citizens who acquire their citizenship from a connection with Gibraltar.[25]

This Declaration does not in itself change much of substance, except in so far as it adopts the underlying effect of the British Nationality Act 1981 which, as already outlined, makes British citizenship harder to acquire than was the acquisition of patriality under the Immigration Act 1971. It is important to note, therefore, that the new Declaration did not ratify a simple change of wording but, rather, an actual alteration in status for the people concerned, something that seems to have been ignored in the Advocate General's opinion and Court judgment in the *Manjit Kaur* case. As Evans (1983: 205–06) observed, the racial overtones that Böhning and others had seen as dominant in the early 1970s continued to prevail:

> If the definition of those exempt from UK immigration control or of those entitled to British citizenship, can be said to be racially motivated or biased, then the definition of UK nationals for the purposes of Community law is vulnerable to the same charge.

Since the 1982 Declaration there was no further movement in the UK's position as to nationality for Community purposes, even when new nationality statuses, particularly with respect to the transfer of power in Hong Kong, were created. Provision for the acquisition of a new nationality status in anticipation of the lapse of BDTC status for many Hong Kong people was made by the Hong Kong (British Nationality) Order 1986. This Order provided for the new status of BN(O) to be acquired by application in Hong Kong, and for the acquisition of BOC status upon potential statelessness on the transfer of power in 1997. The acquisition of these statuses did not change the holders' position under UK immigration law, however, even for Hong Kong's mainly South Asian ethnic minorities who would not automatically acquire Chinese nationality. This is perhaps not surprising as it reflects the maintenance of the pre-existing position that no further immigration commitments from ex-colonial territories should be accepted. It is notable that Portugal

---

25   The British subjects referred to in (b) are substantially the same category of persons recognised previously as British subjects without citizenship under the 1948 Act. They should not to be confused with 'Commonwealth citizens', a category equated to 'British subjects' under the British Nationality Act 1948.

opted for precisely the opposite route when transfer of Macau (unlike Hong Kong, an economically depressed area) was being negotiated, without much objection from the other Community Member States, it seems.[26] Interestingly, a case involving a BN(O) by the name of *Hung* was also reportedly referred to the ECJ by the High Court at about the same time, and was pending hearing on the same issue of principle as *Manjit Kaur*, although it was later dropped.[27]

By the mid-1980s, despite initially favourable indications, the European Convention on Human Rights organs had decided that they were not interested in protecting *de facto* stateless British nationals (see Shah, P 2000b: 95–97). At the time of the negotiations for the Treaty on European Union there was clearly some discussion about the nationality issue again which may have been the result of any number of factors. It was around the time that the *Surinder Singh* case (Case C–370/90 *Singh* [1992] ECR I–4265, [1992] 3 All ER 798) was being litigated in the European Court of Justice. There is also evidence of several cases of BOCs, particularly involving Asian women from East Africa or India, who were being refused leave to enter or remain in Britain, and it appears that British courts maintained their support of the perceptibly tighter Home Office policies at this time.[28] It is quite possible, therefore, that some further litigation against the UK government on the nationality question was being planned, threatened or anticipated in Luxembourg as the final international avenue of redress. Notably, the Member State governments annexed to the Final Act of the Treaty on European Union 1992, Declaration No 2 on the nationality of a Member State, as follows:

> The Conference declares that, wherever in the Treaty establishing the European Community reference is made to nationals of the Member States, the question whether an individual possesses the nationality of a Member State shall be settled solely by reference to the national law of the Member State concerned. Member States may declare, for information, who are to be

---

26 For details on the 1986 Order and the position of Hong Kong's ethnic minorities, see Menski (1995). Finally, the British Nationality (Hong Kong) Act 1997 provided for the acquisition of British citizenship and therefore the right of abode in the UK for *de facto* stateless people. For evidence of continuing problems in establishing eligibility under the 1997 Act, see Gillespie (2000: 148).

27 This information is reported by Gillespie (2000: 146). A possible difference in the two cases could have been that in *Hung* the applicant was not *de facto* stateless, presumably having a claim to the nationality of the People's Republic of China.

28 See, for example, *R v Secretary of State for the Home Department ex p Patel* [1993] Imm AR 257, QBD and [1993] Imm AR 392, CA; *R v Immigration Appeal Tribunal ex p Nargis Sunsara* [1995] Imm AR 15. See Shah, P (2000), pp 97–98 for further discussion.

considered their nationals for Community purposes by way of a declaration lodged with the Presidency and may amend any such declaration when necessary.

Given the survey of events relating to the question of UK nationality it would be reasonable to assume that this Declaration, while adopted multilaterally, was instigated or at least supported by the UK government.[29] The Declaration could be read as a notice to judges and others that they should not usurp the 'reserved domain' of states in the sphere of nationality. Whether this was in anticipation of, or in reaction to, the possibility of litigation in Europe is an open question but it certainly coincides with the UK's visibly harsher policies particularly against Asian women British passport holders such as Manjit Kaur.

8.4   The *Manjit Kaur* case

Manjit Kaur was born in Kenya in 1949, thereby becoming a CUKC under the British Nationality Act 1948. Following the entry into force of the 1981 Act, she became a BOC automatically by operation of that Act. We are not told either in the Advocate General's opinion or in the ECJ's judgment that, initially, Ms Kaur had applied for an entry clearance to come to settle in the UK in 1987, and having been refused, she had applied for entry as a visitor and was again refused. She also lost her appeals against this refusal.[30] She somehow entered the UK in 1990 and, as we are told in the Advocate General's opinion, following several temporary periods of residence in the UK, and while once again in the UK, she reapplied for leave to remain on 4 September 1996. On 20 March 1997 she applied to the High Court for judicial review of the decision of 22 January 1997 by the Home Secretary refusing her leave to remain. In an argument clearly designed to link her situation to Community law, she stated that she wished to remain and obtain gainful employment in the UK and periodically to travel to other Member States in order to make purchases of goods and services and, if necessary, to work there.

---

29   It is possible that this Declaration was also of some interest to the Federal Republic of Germany in its post-unification phase, as it is another Member State that has sought to define the scope of its nationality for Community purposes by means of a prior Declaration. For background, see Hartley (1978: 80–82), and for recent immigration of 'ethnic Germans' to the Federal Republic, see Marshall (2000: 33–34). The Declaration may also have reflected Member State unease about the precise scope of the concept of European citizenship at the same time being introduced by the Treaty on European Union.

30   The case history is most fully set out in the reference by Lightman J in *R v Secretary of State for the Home Department ex p Kaur (Manjit)*, 11 December 1998, CO/985/97.

The High Court referred to the ECJ the question as to the effect of the 1972, 1982 and 1992 Declarations, particularly in a situation where the nationality law of a particular state identifies only some of its nationals as having the right to enter and remain in that state. It asked what the relevance would be in this context of Article 3(2) of the Fourth Protocol to the European Convention on Human Rights (ECHR) which provides that no one shall be deprived of the right to enter the territory of the state of which he is a national. It also asked what the extent of Article 8a(1) of the EC Treaty (now Article 18) is, in particular, whether it entitles a person to enter and reside in a Member State that granted nationality even where the law in that Member State does not confer such a right, and whether it also covers matters that are wholly internal to a Member State.[31] Not only would this reference have opened up the issue of UK nationality for Community law purposes, but it could have provided the ECJ with an opportunity to shed new light on the scope of the relatively recent provisions on citizenship of the Union, as well as the reach of human rights norms in the Community context.

Advocate General Léger's opinion, issued on 9 November 2000, envisaged two possible ways to tackle the issue, neither of which would confer a result favourable to Ms Kaur. The first option would be to construe her as eligible to be recognised as a UK national for Community law purposes, in which case she would still not be able to establish a factor linking her to Community law as she could not show a cross-border element in her situation. On the other hand, she could simply be seen as not coming within the terms of the 1972 and 1982 Declarations on UK nationality and would therefore be ineligible to exercise Community law rights at all. The Advocate General did, however, address the question, in a footnote, as to whether Ms Kaur could avail herself of the protection of Article 3 of the Fourth Protocol to the ECHR. It will be noted that the UK is not itself a party to the Fourth Protocol; it has merely signed but not ratified it. As far as Community law is concerned, however, this fact in itself does not prevent reliance on it.[32] He states:

> Admittedly, the Court ruled in *Singh* ... that, as provided by Article 3 of the Fourth Protocol to the European Convention for the Protection of Human

---

31 Article 8a(1) (now Article 18) reads: 'Every citizen of the Union shall have the right to move and reside freely within the territory of the Member States, subject to the limitations and conditions laid down in this Treaty and by the measures adopted to give it effect.'

32 The ECJ has maintained that it draws from 'guidelines supplied by international treaties for the protection of human rights on which Member States have collaborated or of which they are signatories'. See Case 4/73 *Nold v Commission* [1974] ECR 491, [1974] 2 CMLR 338.

Rights and Fundamental Freedoms, a state may not expel one of its own nationals or deny him or her entry to its territory (paragraph 22). Should the Court consider that rule to be applicable, both generally and in this particular case, this would have the effect of limiting Member States' rights in the matter. It ought, however, to be borne in mind that while fundamental rights do form an integral part of the general principles of law with which the Court must ensure compliance, this is subject to the condition that the area to which the case before it relates falls within the scope of Community law (see, for example, Case C–260/89 *ERT* [1991] ECR I–2925, paragraphs 41 and 42). I submit precisely that the notion of 'citizenship of the Union' does not cover relations which a Member State may have with its nationals in regard to rights of entry and residence within its territory if there is no issue concerning their freedom to move from one Member State to another.

In effect, this statement also requires a Community linking factor before a claim founded on Article 3(2) can be made. Is it possible, therefore, that in a future case a person who can show such a factor, but who falls outwith the UK Declaration on nationality, may still claim the protection of the Fourth Protocol via Community law? This option appears to have been ruled out by the ECJ.

The Court, instead of asking whether there was a Community linking factor despite Manjit Kaur not having moved, or whether the reach of Article 8a(1) might confer hitherto unknown rights to persons in her position, took the route of deciding on the legal effect of the 1972 and 1982 Declarations, and therefore effectively asked whether Manjit Kaur had Union citizenship at all. The judgment notes that in *Micheletti v Delegacion del Gobierno en Cantabria* (Case 369/90, [1992] ECR I–4239) the Court had stated that: 'under international law, it is for each Member State, having due regard to Community law, to lay down the conditions for the acquisition and loss of nationality.' It goes on to state that the UK, 'in light of its imperial and colonial past, defined several categories of British citizens whom it has recognised as having rights which differ according to the nature of the ties connecting them to the UK'. The 1971 Act, according to the Court, 'reserved the right of abode within the territory of the UK to those citizens who had the closest connection to that state'. Meanwhile, the 1972 Declaration was intended to clarify the scope *ratione personae* of the relevant Community provisions, which was a particularly important issue for the other Member States, who were fully aware of its contents, and the conditions of the UK's accession were determined on that basis. It followed, according to the Court, that the Declaration must be taken into account for determining the scope of the Accession Treaty *ratione personae*. It states further that the: 'adoption of that declaration did not have the effect of depriving any person who did not satisfy the definition of a national of the UK of rights to which that person might be entitled under Community law. The consequence was rather that such rights never arose in the first place for such a person.' As for the 1982 Declaration, it was apparently common ground that it had been necessitated by the enactment of the British Nationality Act 1981, that it substantially designated the same categories of persons as the 1972 Declaration and that it did not alter Ms Kaur's situation as regards Community law. Further, it had not been challenged by other Member States. It was therefore necessary to refer to the 1982 Declaration, which replaced the 1972 Declaration. Due to this conclusion on the nationality issue, the Court found it unnecessary to consider the other questions set out by the High Court.

The opinion of the Advocate General and the judgment of the Court are both notable for their brevity and lack of willingness to tackle much of the history behind the 1972 and 1982 Declarations. The UK government's submission, as set out in the Court's judgment, is similarly brief and highly selective; it stated before the Court that the Declarations on nationality were made necessary because of the many people who had no close connection with the UK who nevertheless retained its nationality because of its 'imperial and colonial history', and because the law on British nationality was complex and recognised various categories of nationals to which different rights attached. However, as outlined above, above all there were racial factors that had motivated the UK's formulation of its immigration and nationality policy, which directly fed into its making of the 1972 Declaration. There were also demands at the time by the existing Member States that a narrowly defined class of persons should benefit from free movement rights, one of the main concerns being the possible migration to their territories of non-white British nationals. Indeed, as it turned out, the definition adopted in the 1972 Declaration was considered *too wide* for comfort by other Member States. As a result, they insisted on adding a Joint Declaration to the Final Act to the UK's Treaty of Accession, to guard against the consequences of decisions by those non-white Commonwealth citizens who may eventually qualify for free movement rights.

In all this, the position of UK nationals such as Manjit Kaur who were mainly in East Africa and who did not possess another nationality was particularly weak as they had lost their right to reside in the UK, and were not considered worthy of special consideration in the Community scheme. Indeed, their position under the domestic law was worsening, as indicated by the enactment of the Immigration Act 1971 and the British Nationality Act 1981. It is quite inaccurate for the ECJ to state that the 1982 Declaration did not affect the position of such people as they were now additionally required to register as British citizens under the 1981 Act before they were considered eligible to exercise Community rights. It is disappointing that neither the Advocate General nor the Court has been prepared to consider this history of marginalisation and creation of statelessness over the years. Is it enough for the Court to refer to this history of marginalisation as simply a consequence of the UK's 'imperial and colonial past'? Are these questions only a matter of the past, and did they not affect the present reality for so many persons? The fact that the UK and East Africa have had a considerable history and presently have a series of overlapping links along ethnic and kinship lines seems to be irrelevant here. The territorial principle therefore asserts ascendancy over any other regulatory order based on kinship or ethnicity. More bluntly, it appears that in this case European judges appear unwilling to face the question of legalised racism head on.

The narrow legal effect of the *Manjit Kaur* decision is that British nationals other than those included in the 1982 Declaration cannot benefit from the free movement provisions of the EC Treaty. Only British citizens, BDTCs by virtue of a connection with Gibraltar and British subjects who already have a right of abode in the UK would so qualify. In a wider sense, however, the decision will be remembered as one more in a long list of failures to face up to the historic problem of racism in Europe. While institutions in the EU are making laudable efforts to legislate against discrimination on racial, religious and other grounds, these efforts appear quite hollow if the attitude is to look the other way when faced with concrete situations. It is hardly surprising that the prevailing official attitude continues to maintain that if one is not white one cannot be British nor a national of another Member State of the EU. One UK Asian woman MEP, Neena Gill, has complained of precisely this sort of attitude when stating that she is routinely stopped by immigration officials in Europe, despite having a special pass to denote that she is an MEP: 'While my other colleagues go straight through immigration, I get stopped so that they can check I am an MEP.'[33] Most non-white travellers within Europe will say that this is not an isolated example, and the ECJ's judgment will certainly not help. Indeed, this short history of UK nationality law in the European context shows that the notion of European citizenship, influenced as it is by national law concepts, is being given shape in a way that is ethnically loaded.

Meanwhile, the human rights point based on Article 3(2) of the Fourth Protocol to the ECHR could arguably have been dealt with quite

---

33 Payal Nair, 'Flying high. Britain's first Asian woman MEP'. In: *Asian Voice*, 3 March 2001. See also Suzanne Simmons-Lewis, 'You're no Brit you're Black', in *The Voice*, 30 October 2000 reporting on the case of Rafiu Odetayo who was arrested by German police and spent four weeks in prison after UK consulate staff denied, upon inquiries being made by German police, that there were any black British.

differently. As described above, the Advocate General chose to state in a footnote that this Article was not of assistance as there was no Community linking factor. The Court does not deal with it at all. Could it not have been considered that the existence of a Community linking factor was itself prevented by virtue of the non-application of Article 3(2) by the UK government, as surely it is the thinking that some British nationals should not enjoy the right of abode in the UK which has led to their exclusion from the free movement provisions by the making of the Declarations on nationality? Of course, such an interpretation would not be favoured by other Member States – the German, French and Italian governments and the Commission, as far as we know from the ECJ's judgment, argued against an expansive interpretation by pointing out that it is up to each Member State to determine the categories of persons to be recognised as citizens. Possibly it was not helpful that the UK government is not itself a party to the Fourth Protocol, although this should not have been a necessary obstacle to a proactive interpretation of the reach of Community law by the ECJ, and it is notable that the Advocate General did not mention that as a specific consideration.

Although the question of the UK's ratification of the Fourth Protocol has been canvassed recently in the government's White Paper on Overseas Territories, this does not appear to have been premised upon the extension of full citizenship to BOCs, BPPs or BN(O)s. The British Overseas Territories Act 2002 was passed consequent to the White Paper. This Act effectively grants British citizen status to the now much-reduced group of BDTCs (now BOTCs). This group will now enjoy the benefit of free movement rights under Community law on a non-reciprocal basis. Therefore, although those remaining BDTCs have subsequently become British citizens, the White Paper (as quoted by Gillespie 2000: 147) states:

> We do not intend to offer British citizenship to British Overseas Citizens. Many have access to or have acquired dual nationality. Many have access to the UK through our voucher scheme. Moreover we have particular responsibility to people in areas for which we have sovereign responsibility.

The White Paper thus made no attempt to solve the problem of the *de facto* stateless BOCs, BPPs or British subjects. The statement above rather seems to maintain the preference expressed at the time of the passing of the British Nationality Act 1981 that BOCs ought to be recognised as nationals wherever they live. This was in flat contradiction to the promises given to the Indian and other governments at the time of the Commonwealth Immigrants Act 1968 that the UK would retain responsibility for these people despite that Act. Finally, however, it has been provided that those British nationals – specifically BOCs, BPPs and British subjects – mainly connected with African countries, can register as

British citizens under the Nationality, Immigration and Asylum Act 2002, as long as they have not acquired any other nationality (Shah, R 2003b). These recent statutory changes may be a happy postscript by which to round off Britain's colonial experiment, although the scepticism it has generated through the years, exported to a Europe with its own ambivalences about cultural diversity, remains just one in a long series of legal pluralisms in conflict.

Conclusion |

While this book comes to its final stages of writing we have been watching developments in the case of a young Muslim girl, Shabina Begum, in Luton who challenged her school in court to allow her to wear a *jilbab* to school (*R (on the application of Begum) v Headteacher and Governors of Denbigh High School* [2005] EWCA Civ 199). This case starkly illustrates that we are working within a framework that attempts to cope with legal pluralism in the context of Britain's cultural diversity. While the outcome of the case will have been very important to Shabina Begum herself and to many others in her position, it is useful to focus on the legal postulates that led to the conflict going to court. In the terms of the debate with which we set out, we could see this case as illustrating the conflict between the legal postulates of modernity and uniformity on the one hand, and of individual legal agency on the other. The former are strongly adhered to by the official legal order, while Shabina Begum relied on her own interpretation of the requirements of her faith. It also illustrates the interaction between the modern state's law and unofficial personal or religious law.

In the larger context, and in common with many of the case studies that we have discussed in this book, we can propose that the chief problem for the British legal order is the *recognition of difference*. Difference is the fulcrum upon which much of the conflict between modern, state law and other legal orders tends to turn. Quite how to reconcile the demand of homogeneity and the recognition of difference is a major challenge for modern legal systems, and not just in Britain. It is the increasing unsustainability of the former in the face of rapid legal pluralisation, and the conflict that that continues to generate, which needs to be resolved by embracing the postmodern conditions of the British legal order today. At the epistemological level, the main challenge must therefore be ceasing to assume that all are equal and acknowledging that *all are different*, that all conceive of law in different ways, and therefore demand different things and situation specific solutions. If that problem can be cracked, then resolution of other problems should become more readily apparent. The question is are we serious enough about identifying legal pluralism in conflict and ready to take the steps that are needed?

One place to begin this process is the stage of legal education. It is in legal education and in writing about law where the first steps to change the mindset, the *mentalité*, as Legrand (1996) has it, towards a more open appreciation of difference can be taken. Legrand indicates that it is really away from the national power centres that the comparative law, as difference, can be studied. Melissaris (2004) seems to argue that it is away from the institutionalised legal system, and in the academy, that legal pluralism can be accommodated and legal alternatives investigated. These remarks are in themselves indictments of the capacity of the official legal order to accept difference in its own terms, since both writers seem to say that legal pluralism cannot be accommodated by it. As far as ethnic minority legal studies are concerned, however, we still face huge problems even within the academy as such studies are nobody's favourite and no brownie points will be won for discussing such problems, except for appreciation from students. Yet as one of my students once told me, academics are the 'priests' of the legal system, and we therefore often have to ask ourselves where the balance is to be struck between serving the established order and challenging it.

Our survey of writings by the 'priests' of constitutional law shows a dire need to reorient our focus and stop concentrating on received ideas, but to have some critical distance from them so that our analysis can correspond to the social reality around us. We need to examine the gap between the official order and the unofficial order, and to make our writing more reflective of the surrounding ontological and epistemological conditions around us. If social scientists such as Werbner (2002) can provide lucid studies of participation in the public sphere by Pakistanis in diaspora, then why is it that legal academics are so resistant to analysing the same issues? Chiba (1989: 157) noted that the key to the identity postulate in modern countries is their constitutionalism. In particular, constitutional law must be investigated as the justification of the status quo, or as the provider of mechanisms for change with the transplantation of other forms of law. In our study we saw that Afro-Asian laws, increasingly present in the unofficial sphere, are hardly ever mentioned as relevant to official accounts of constitutional law. As Glenn (2000) and others have argued, we therefore see a repression of other traditions within the 'system' of constitutional law. Thus it appears that we are going around in circles when it comes to assessing the issue of voting patterns of ethnic minority people, and the perceived lack of interest among ethnic minority people for the official political order, unless we begin to discuss Afro-Asian concepts of the relationship between state and society. I have proposed that these other models be considered, but it is far from being a comprehensive analysis and clearly much more work needs to be done in this area. Again, the key seems to be the rediscovery of a 'jurisprudence of difference' which the premoderns knew well, and which Macpherson seems to have refashioned for postmodern conditions.

One of the most difficult fields of official legal power to deconstruct is the criminal law sphere. While forms of legal pluralism are readily apparent in fields such as family law, in criminal law we have a staggering silence, with even the literature on 'race' and crime taking an almost wholly assimilationist position. It appears that the power of the maxim of equality before the law has taken deep roots in the psyche so as to prevent pluralist analysis. Otherwise we have Poulter's writings, typically overselling the capacity of English criminal law to be flexible enough in appropriate situations. Could it not be that even here ethnic minority laws are in full operation and conflict with the official order constantly? The argument here has been that the field of criminal law therefore represents one of the key arenas for the investigation of legal pluralism in conflict, as illustrated by cases of homicide. Excavating this area indeed reveals that Asian legal systems allow for the legal agency of the individual, even to kill under certain circumstances, as against the modern state's power to determine the terms of legitimate violence. These systems also offer a different order of punishments and penances than envisaged by the official system. As it is, however, these are not given any attention in official practice where modernist assumptions dominate, another example of outright repression, which appears to be the emerging fate of ethnic minority laws in Britain.

Throughout our discussion we have argued that family and kinship systems represent the dominant mode of social organisation and self-regulation amongst ethnic minorities. This is the sphere that most often comes into conflict with the official legal order which posits a rival form of social organisation premised on citizenship of the modern nation-state. Our case study of polygamy reveals this starkly. We see the most direct clash, since the official legal system has for long held quite ambivalent or, more often, hostile views about the practice of polygamy. On the other hand, even though it may not be practised so frequently, it is actually endorsed, within limits, by the legal orders of large sections of humanity. We therefore have the stage set for the application of Eurocentric assumptions against the principles of Afro-Asian legal orders, another in a long series of repressions of other legal traditions that this book documents. As with many other aspects of the state's attempt to control, or even eliminate, ethnic minority laws, it is the immigration sphere which turns out to be the site of much conflict. However, the polygamy example also shows that the official sphere is ultimately impotent and can only show its disapproval of the practice. Thus, the larger point here may be that ethnic minority laws tend to resurface in some form even though the state attempts by various means to repress unwanted practices. Instead, it turns out that the official law penalises the very women and children whom it seeks to protect in the name of progressive Christian or modern human rights values.

As an ethnic minority group, Bangladeshis have experienced some of the harshest forms of state regulation. We saw that of the main South Asian groups in Britain, Bangladeshi men were the last to take off on the road to sponsoring family members to reside in Britain. This meant that the legal system was fully armed to control this stream of people and much of the official law on this, as we have seen, is linked to immigration in some way. Increasingly, we also see that Bangladeshi family forms have come under the spotlight and British judges seem to have generally penalised them rather than offering relevant solutions. It is remarkable that the Court of Appeal can so offensively rule that a Bangladeshi child's parents are not validly married and that he is therefore illegitimate, while a Bangladeshi woman can be told by the High Court that she was never married to the man as whose widow she now claims a pension. On the other hand, we have also see evidence in the *Re S* case that judicial notice is taken of the concentration of the ethnic minority population in certain parts of Britain and that changes to the local unofficial legal order can be recognised. It would be interesting to watch whether such a case is followed up by a more systematically receptive approach to ethnic minority laws, although it is doubtful that conditions are favourable for that to happen.

A key issue which is thrown up by the *Re S* case, as with the *Zoora Shah* case before it, is the role of expert reports in official courts and tribunals. While in *Zoora Shah* we find that a wholly hostile attitude seems to have been taken to Roger Ballard's report, in *Re S* the judge was very receptive to the reports by the experts on both sides. We also examined in some more detail the writing of reports in the immigration sphere which forms one site in the official sphere where the role of experts has come to be quite key, and where discussions about comparative law come to the fore. On the one hand, it is a recognition by the official system that it needs to have relevant information, especially about legal systems abroad, if it is to make sound decisions. On the other hand, we also see that immigration officials and tribunals are doing their bit to construct a view of overseas or ethnic minority laws as unacceptable in Britain. This may be explicable by the very obsessive control mindedness in some areas of the immigration system. However, it generates a dynamic which permeates the whole legal order which is anyway not very receptive of Afro-Asian legal orders if they appear to go against the basic assumptions of Western legal systems. Yet I see report writing as a key means by which information about translocal processes can be put into the official level; as a way that we ourselves can obtain training to analyse these processes more deeply and as a useful resource for training students about *doing* legal pluralism in present day Britain.

Finally, we recount one more chapter in the story of British nationality in the post-war period. Not only did we see that nationality law was hijacked for immigration control purposes but that this found a reinvigorated expression in the process of deeper European integration. We see that since Britain joined the European Community/Union, its definition of British nationals was reconfigured further to exclude Asian British passport holders. In our main case study, the *Manjit Kaur* case, we therefore find that Britain's colonial and postcolonial connections with the Afro-Asian world were covered up, much as Lord Denning had seen fit to do in the *Thakrar* case. Thus, nationality law seems to have moved blindly along, ignoring the deep translocal, intercontinental linkages that Britain and its minority communities sustain through their own networks, providing another illustration of the modern nation-state and the European super-state imposing their rules on the self-regulatory orders of such communities.

We are now in a position to reflect on the key issues that were identified in Chapter 1. I discussed in several chapters the problem of what Chiba called the identity postulate of a legal culture. This was considered to be a crucial element of any socio-legal entity, as it provides the means by which transplanted law may be accommodated within the exiting order, possibly resulting in a new amalgam to reflect the changed scenario. In the British case we see that the constitutional system seems, at present, to prevent the open acknowledgment of the presence of the transplanted legal orders of diasporic ethnic minority communities. In many other areas of law too we have seen that the legal orders of ethnic minorities, as unofficial orders, have not been sanctioned or recognised by the official order, which thereby attempts to manage, control, suppress or extinguish them. Far from accepting this situation, ethnic minorities continually recreate their laws by making subjective choices that are satisfying to them from a cultural point of view. The basis for legal pluralism in conflict is thus set.

As Menski (2000a) points out, the acceptance of Afro-Asian legal orders in the world faces considerable hurdles, and this global situation has a severe impact on the view taken of ethnic minority legal orders which are new, hybrid variants of these Afro-Asian legal orders. Basic differences in the legal postulates of these competing orders also create a difficult environment for the acceptance of Afro-Asian laws in the diaspora. The dominant Western mode of social organisation sees law as the monopoly of the modern, territorial, centralising and homogenising nation-state, asserting the position that the state controls society, and with severe ambivalence towards religion as a source of law. The legal postulates of ethnic minorities, on the other hand, tend to stress the (trans-)local, kinship-based, flexible, situation-specific forms of justice, and are often inspired or supported by religious values and practices. In this book I have sought to argue that these basic differences in the assumptions which underlie the different legal orders create another ground for legal pluralism in conflict. It remains difficult to see the co-existence of these different orders in harmony unless adjustments are made to the official system to make it more responsive to the socio-legal orders within its scope.

Bibliography

Alexander, C (2000) *The Asian Gang: Ethnicity, Identity, Masculinity*, Oxford: Berg

Allen, CK (1964) *Law in the Making*, 7th edn, Oxford: Clarendon Press

Allen, C (2003) *Fair Justice: the Bradford Disturbances, the Sentencing and the Impact*, London: Forum Against Islamophobia and Racism

Allott, A (1980) *The Limits of Law*, London: Butterworths

Allott, A (1990) 'Religious pluralism and the law in England and Africa', in Hamnett, I (ed) *Religious Pluralism and Unbelief. Studies Critical and Comparative*, London: Routledge, pp 205–25

Anderson, JND (1951) 'Homicide in Islamic law', in *Bulletin of the School of Oriental and African Studies*, pp 811–28

Anderson, JND (1954) *Islamic Law in Africa*, London: HMSO

Ansari, H (2002) *Muslims in Britain*, London: Minority Rights Group International

Anwar, M (1979) *The Myth of Return: Pakistanis in Britain*, London: Heinemann

Aspinall, P (2000) 'Should a question on "religion" be asked in the 2001 British Census? A public policy case in favour', in (December 2000) Vol 34, No 5 *Social Policy and Administration*, pp 584–600

Badawi, Z (1995) 'Muslim justice in a secular state', in Michael King (ed) *God's Law Versus State Law. The Construction of an Islamic Identity in Western Europe*, London: Grey Seal, pp 73–80

Baldwin, R (1995) *Rules and Government*, Oxford: Clarendon

Ballard, R (1976) 'Ethnicity: theory and experience', in Vol 5, No 3 *New Community*, pp196–202

Ballard, R (1990) 'Migration and kinship: the differential effect of marriage rules on the processes of Punjabi migration to Britain', in Clarke, C, Peach, C and Vertovec, S (eds) *South Asians Overseas. Migration and Ethnicity*, Cambridge: Cambridge University Press, pp 219–49

Ballard, R (1992) 'New clothes for the emperor? The conceptual nakedness of Britain's race relations industry', in Vol 18, No 3 *New Community*, pp 481–92

Ballard, R (ed) (1994a) *Desh Pardesh. The South Asian presence in Britain*, London: Hurst & Co

Ballard, R (1994b) 'Introduction: the emergence of *desh pardesh*', in Ballard, R (ed) *Desh Pardesh. The South Asian presence in Britain*, London: Hurst & Co, pp 1–34

Ballard, R (1996a) 'The Pakistanis: stability and introspection', in Peach, C (ed) *Ethnicity in the 1991 Census. Volume 2: The Ethnic Minority Populations of Great Britain*, London: HMSO, pp 121–49

Ballard, R (1996b) '*Panth kismet dharm te quam*: continuity and change in four dimensions of Punjabi religion', in Singh, P and Thandi, SS (eds) *Globalisation and the Region: Explorations in Punjabi identity*, Coventry: Association for Punjabi Studies, pp 7–38

Ballard, R (1996c) 'Negotiating race and ethnicity: Exploring the implications of the 1991 Census', in Vol 30, No 3 *Patterns of Prejudice*, pp 3–33

Ballard, R (1996d) 'Islam and the construction of Europe', in Shahid, WAR and Koningveld, PS (eds) *Muslims in the Margin*, Kampen Kok Pharos, pp 15–51 also at www.art.man.ac.uk/CASAS/Papers/islam.doc

Ballard, R (unpublished) 'Common law and uncommon sense: the assessment of "reasonable behaviour" in a plural society', at www.casas.org.uk

Ballard, R (2001a) 'Popular Islam in Northern Pakistan and its reconstruction in Britain', Paper presented at the International Workshop on Islamic Mysticism in the West, Buxton, Derbyshire, 22–24 July 2001 (also at www.casas.org.uk)

Ballard, R (2001b) 'The impact of kinship on the economic dynamics of transnational networks: reflections on some South Asian developments', Paper presented at Workshop on Transnational Migration, Princeton University, 29 June – 1 July 2001, also at www.casas.org.uk and at www.transcomm.ox.ac.uk

Ballard, R (2003) 'On the consequences of being ideologically off the wall: Some reflections on the academy's response to ethnic pluralism', Paper presented to the Dynamics of Change in Higher Education, 3–4 April 2003

Bano, S (2000) 'Muslim South Asian women and customary law in Britain', in Vol 4 *Journal of South Pacific Law*

Bassiouni, CM (1982) '*Quesas* crimes', in Bassiouni, MC (ed) *The Islamic Criminal Justice System*, London: Oceana Publications, pp 203–09

Berman, HJ (2003) *Law and Revolution II. The Impact of the Protestant Reformations on the Western Legal Traditions*, Cambridge, Mass: The Belknap Press/Harvard University Press

Bevan, V (1986) *The Development of British Immigration Law*, London: Croom Helm

Biondi, A (1995) 'The reform of Italian nationality law', in Vol 9, No 3 *Immigration and Nationality Law and Practice*, pp 89–91

Blackburn, R and Plant, R (1999) *Constitutional reform: The Labour Government's constitutional reform agenda*. London and New York: Longman

Blake, C (1982) 'Citizenship, law and the state', in 45 *Modern Law Review*, pp 179–97

Boele-Woelki, K (ed) (2003) *Perspectives for the Unification and Harmonisation of Family Law in Europe*, Antwerp: Intersentia

Bognador, V (1997) *Power and the People: A Guide to Constitutional Reform*, London: Victor Gollancz

Böhning, WR (1972) *The Migration of Workers in the United Kingdom and the European Community*, London: Oxford University Press for the Institute of Race Relations

Böhning, WR (1973) 'The scope of the EEC system of free movement of workers: a rejoinder', in Vol 10 *Common Market Law Review*, pp 81–86

Bowling, B and Philips, C (2002) *Racism, Crime and Justice*, Harlow, England: Longman

Bradney, A (1989) 'The Dewsbury Affair and the Education Reform Act 1988', in Vol 1, No 2 *Education and the Law*, pp 51–57

Bradney, A (1993) *Religion, Rights and Laws*, Leicester: Leicester University Press

Brazier, R (1991) *Constitutional Reform: Re-shaping the British Political System*, Oxford: Clarendon

Brown, LC (2000) *Religion and State: Muslim Approaches to Politics*, New York: Columbia University Press

Bryceson, D and Vuorela, U (eds) (2002) *The Transnational family: New European Frontiers and Global Networks*, Oxford and New York: Berg

Bunglawala, Z (2004) 'Muslims in the UK labour market', in [June 2004] Vol 22 *Discrimination Law Association Briefings*, pp 6–8

Burrows, R (2000) *Devolution*, London: Sweet & Maxwell

Carroll, L (1984) 'Definition of a "potentially polygamous" marriage in English law: a dramatic decision from the Court of Appeal (*Hussain v Hussain*)', in Vol IV, Nos 1-2 *Islamic and Comparative Law Quarterly*, pp 61–71

Carroll, L (1997) 'Muslim women and "Islamic divorce" in England', in Vol 17, No 1 *Journal of Muslim Minority Affairs*, pp 97–115

Cashmore, E and McLaughlin, E (eds) (1991) *Out of order: Policing Black People*, London and New York: Routeledge

Castles, S (2004) 'Why migration policies fail', in (March 2004) Vol 27, No 2 *Ethnic and Racial Studies*, pp 205–27

Castles, S, Booth, H and Wallace, T (1993) *Here for Good: Western Europe's Ethnic Minorities*, London: Pluto

Cavadino, M and Dignam, J (2002) *The Penal System: an Introduction*, 3rd edn, London: Sage

Chiba, M (1986) *Asian Indigenous Law in Interaction with Received Law*, London and New York: KPI

Chiba, M (1989) *Legal Pluralism: Toward a General Theory Through Japanese Legal Culture*, Tokyo: Tokai University Press

Chiba, M (1998) 'Other phases of legal pluralism in the contemporary world', in Vol 11, No 3 (September 1998) *Ratio Juris*, pp 228–45

Cohen, A (1974) 'The lesson of ethnicity', in Cohen, A (ed) *Urban Ethnicity*, London: Tavistock, pp ix-xxiv

Cohen, R (2000) 'Review article: The incredible vagueness of being British/English', in Vol 76, No 3 *International Affairs*, pp 575–82

Collinson, S (1993) *Europe and International Migration*, London: Pinter

Conaghan, J (2002) 'Law, harm and redress: a feminist perspective', in Vol 22, No 3 *Legal Studies*, pp 319–39

Cook, D and Hudson, B (1993) *Racism and Criminology*, London: Sage

Cooper, D and Herman, D (1999) 'Jews and other uncertainties: race, faith and English law', in Vol 19, No 3 *Legal Studies*, pp 339–66

Copland, I (2000) 'The political geography of religious conflict: Towards an explanation of the relative infrequency of communal riots in the Indian Princely States', in Vol 7, No 1 *International Journal of Punjab Studies*, pp 1–27

Cotterrell, R (1997) 'The concept of legal culture', in Nelken, D (ed) *Comparing Legal Cultures*, Aldershot: Dartmouth, pp 13–31

Cotterrell, R (2003) *The Politics of Jurisprudence*, London: LexisNexis

Cotterrell, R (2004) 'Law in culture', in (March 2004) Vol 17, No 1 *Ratio Juris*, pp 1–14

Coulson, NJ (1964) *A History of Islamic Law*, Edinburgh: Edinburgh University Press

Day, TP (1982) *The Conception of Punishment in Early Indian Literature*, Waterloo, Ontario: Wilfrid Laurier Press

Derrett, JDM (1963) *Introduction to Modern Hindu Law*, London: Oxford University Press

Derrett, JDM (1968) *Religion, Law and the State in India*, Delhi: Oxford University Press

Derrett, JDM (1976) *Essays in Classical and Modern Hindu law*, Vol 1, Leiden: EJ Brill

Devlin, P (1965) *The Enforcement of Morals*, London: Oxford University Press

Doongaji, D (1986) *Crime and Punishment in Ancient Hindu Society*, Delhi: Ajanta Publications

Drabu, K and Bowen, S (1989) *Mandatory Visas. Visiting the UK from Bangladesh, India, Pakistan, Ghana and Nigeria*, London: Commission for Racial Equality

Dummett, A and Nicol, A (1990) *Subjects, Citizens, Aliens and Others: Nationality and Immigration Law*, London: Weidenfeld and Nicolson

Dyson, KHF (1980) *The State Tradition in Western Europe: A Study of an Idea and Institution*, Oxford: Martin Robertson

Eade, J, Vamplew, T and Peach, C (1996) 'The Bangladeshis: the encapsulated community', in Peach, C (ed) *Ethnicity in the 1991 Census: Volume 2: The Ethnic Minority Populations of Great Britain*, London: HMSO, pp 150–60

Edens, DF and Patijn, S (1972) 'The scope of the EEC system of free movement of workers', in Vol 9 *Common Market Law Review*, pp 322–28

Edwards, S (1998) 'Beyond belief – the case of Zoora Shah', in Vol 148, No 6839, *New Law Journal*, 8 May 1998, pp 667–68

Edwards, S and Welstead, M (1999) 'Death before familial dishonour', in Vol 149, No 6891 *New Law Journal*, 4 June 1999, p 867

Elst, K (2001) *Who is a Hindu? Hindu Revivalist Views of Animism, Buddhism, Sikhism and other Offshoots of Hinduism*, New Delhi: Voice of India

Enright, S (1991) 'Multi-racial juries', in Vol 141, No 6513 *New Law Journal* 19 July 1991, pp 992–96

Evans, J (1983) *Immigration Law*, 2nd edn, London: Sweet & Maxwell

Ferrari, S (2000) 'Introduction', in Ferrari, S and Bradney, A (eds) *Islam and European Legal Systems*, Aldershot: Ashgate, pp 1–9

Ferrari, S and Bradney, A (eds) (2000) *Islam and European Legal Systems*, Aldershot: Ashgate

Foblets, M-C (1999) 'Conflicts of law in cross-cultural family disputes in Europe today. Who will reorient conflicts law?', in Foblets, M-C and Strijbosch, F (eds) *Relations familiales interculturelles/Cross-cultural Family Relations*, Oñati: International Institute for the Sociology of Law, pp 27–45

Foley, M (1999) *The Politics of the British Constitution*, Manchester and New York: Manchester University Press

Fransman, L (1986) 'Family settlement cases: a denial of statutory rights', in Vol 1, No 1 *Immigration and Nationality Law and Practice*, pp 5–15

Fransman, L (1989) *British Nationality Law*, London: Fourmat

Fryer, P (1984) *Staying Power. The History of Black People in Britain*, London: Pluto Press

Ganz, G (2001) *Understanding Public Law*, London: Sweet & Maxwell

Gardner, K (1993) '*Desh-bidesh*: Sylheti images of home and away', in Vol 28, No 1 *Man*, pp 1–15

Gardner, K and Shukur, A (1994) '"I'm Bengali, I'm Asian, and I'm living here". The changing identity of British Bengalis', in Ballard, R (ed) *Desh Pardesh. The South Asian Presence in Britain*, London: Hurst & Co, pp 142–64

Gardner, K (1995) *Global Migrants, Local Lives: Travel and Transformation in Rural Bangladesh*, Oxford: Clarendon

Ghai, Y (2000) *Autonomy and Ethnicity: Negotiating Competing Claims in Multi-ethnic States*, Cambridge: Cambridge University Press

Gidoomal, R, Mahtani, D and Porter, D (2001) *The British and How to Deal with Them: Doing Business with Britain's Ethnic Communities*, London: Middlesex University Press

Gillespie, J (1992) 'Maintenance and accommodation and the immigration rules: recent developments', in Vol 6, No 3 *Immigration and Nationality Law and Practice*, pp 97–100

Gillespie, J (2000) 'The Overseas Territories White Paper and Protocol 4 of the ECHR – the ILPA response', in Vol 14, No 3 *Immigration and Nationality Law and Practice*, pp 142–50

Gillespie, J (2001) 'Expert evidence in asylum cases', in Vol 15, No 1 *Immigration, Asylum and Nationality Law*, pp 88–91

Glenn, HP (2000) *Legal Systems of the World*, Oxford: Oxford University Press

Gordon, P (1988) 'Black people and the criminal law: rhetoric and reality', in Vol 16 *International Journal of the Sociology of Law*, pp 295–313

Goulbourne, H (2002) *Caribbean Transnational Experience*, London: Pluto

Gray, J (2000) *Two Faces of Liberalism*, Cambridge: Polity Press

Griffith, JAG (1991) *The Politics of the Judiciary*, 4th edn, London: Fontana

Griffiths, A (2002) 'Legal pluralism', in Banakar, R and Travers, M (eds) *An Introduction to Law and Social Theory*, Oxford: Hart, pp 289–301

Griffiths, J (1986) 'What is legal pluralism?', in No 24 *Journal of Legal Pluralism and Unofficial Law*, pp 1–56

Hameso, SY (1997) *Ethnicity in Africa: Towards a Positive Approach*, London: TSC

Hamilton, C (1995) *Family, Law and Religion*, London: Sweet & Maxwell

Hansen, P (2004) 'In the name of Europe', in Vol 45, No 3 *Race and Class*, pp 49–62

Harden, I and Lewis, N (1986) *The Noble Lie: The British Constitution and the Rule of Law*, London: Hutchinson

Harlow, C and Rawlings, R (1984) *Law and Administration*. London: Weidenfeld and Nicolson

Hart, HLA (1961) *The Concept of Law*, Oxford: Oxford University Press

Hartley, TC (1978) *EEC Immigration Law*, Amsterdam: North Holland

Hartley, TC and Griffith, JAG (1981) *Government and Law: An Introduction to the Working of the Constitution in Britain*, 2nd edn, London: Weidenfeld and Nicolson

Harvey, J and Bather, L (1977) *The British Constitution*, 4th edn, Basingstoke: Macmillan Education

Hinchcliffe, D (1970) 'Polygamy in traditional and contemporary Islamic law', in Vol 1, No 8 (November 1970) *Islam and the Modern Age*, pp 13–38

Hoge, W (2002) 'Britain's nonwhites feel un-British, report says', in *New York Times*, 4 April 2002

Hoggett, B, Pearl, D, Cooke, E and Bates, P (2002) *The Family, Law and Society: Cases and Materials*, 5th edn, London: Butterworths

Hood, R (1992) *Race and Sentencing: A Study in the Crown Court*, Oxford: Clarendon Press

Hood Phillips, O, Jackson, P and Leopold, P (2001) *Constitutional and Administrative Law*, 8th edn, London: Sweet & Maxwell

Hooker, MB (1975) *Legal Pluralism*, Oxford: Clarendon Press

Hudson, B (1989) 'Discrimination and disparity: The influence of race on sentencing', in Vol 16 No 1 (October 1989) *New Community*, pp 23–34

Huntington, SP (1993) 'The clash of civilisations?', in Vol 72, No 3 *Foreign Affairs*, pp 22–49

Hurnard, ND (1969) *The King's Pardon for Homicide Before AD 1307*, Oxford: Clarendon

Hussain, AM (2001) *British Immigration Policy under the Conservative Government*, Aldershot: Ashgate

Hussein, R and Seddon, D (1996) 'Recourse to public funds and indirect reliance', in Vol 10, No 2 *Immigration and Nationality Law and Practice*, pp 50–53

Hutchinson, AC (1999) 'Beyond black letterism: ethics in law and legal education', in Vol 33, No 3 *The Law Teacher*, pp 301–09

Immigration Law Practitioners' Association (1997) *Directory of Experts on Conditions in Countries of Origin and Transit*, 2nd edn, London: ILPA

Ivor Jennings, W (1966) *The British Constitution*, Cambridge: Cambridge University Press

Iwuji, E (1983) *Marriage Form in Nigeria*, Rome: Tipolitografia

Jackson, D (1999) *Immigration: Law and Practice*, 2nd edn, London: Sweet & Maxwell

Jacobson, J (1997) 'Perceptions of Britishness', in Vol 3, No 2 *Nations and Nationalism*, pp 181–99

Jain, KB (1990–91) 'Polygamy in *Shastric* law – a study in comparison with *Shari'ah* rules', in Vols X & XI *Islamic and Comparative Law Quarterly*, pp 169–86

Joint Council for the Welfare of Immigrants (1987) *Out of Sight. The New Visit Visa System Overseas*, London: JCWI

Jones, E (1998) *The English Nation: The Great Myth*, Phoenix Mill, Stroud, Gloucestershire: Sutton Publishing

Jones, R and Welhengama, G (2000) *Ethnic Minorities in English Law*, Stoke on Trent: Trentham

Joppke, C (1998) *Immigration and the Nation-State: the United States, Germany, and Great Britain*, Oxford: Oxford University Press

Juss, S (1993) *Immigration, Nationality and Citizenship*, London: Mansell

Juss, S (1997) *Discretion and Deviation in the Administration of Immigration Control*, London: Sweet & Maxwell

Kakar, S (1982) *Shamans, Mystics and Doctors. A Psychological Inquiry into India and its Healing Traditions*, Delhi: Oxford University Press

Kanwar, M (1989) *Murder and Homicide in Pakistan*, Lahore: Vanguard

Kanyadago, PM (1991) *Evangelizing Polygamous Families. Canonical and African Approaches*, Eldoret, Kenya: AMECEA Gaba Publications

Kelley, DR (1997) *The Writing of History and the Study of Law*, Aldershot: Variorum/Ashgate

Kenyon, R and Hill, H (2994) 'Race equality schemes reviewed', in Vol 21 (February 2004) *Discrimination Law Association Briefings*, pp 3–7

Kershen, AJ (1997) *London: The Promised Land? The Migrant Experience in a Capital City*, Aldershot: Ashgate

King, M (ed) (1995) *God's Law Versus State Law: The Construction of an Islamic Identity in Western Europe*, London: Grey Seal

Kogen, M (1987) 'Karman: Buddhist concepts', in *The Encyclopedia of Religion*, Vol 8, New York: Macmillan, pp 266–68

Lahiri, S (1999) *Indians in Britain: Anglo-Indian Encounters, Race and Identity*, London: Frank Cass

Law Commission (1971) *Family Law: Report on Polygamous Marriages*, Law Commission Report No 42, London: HMSO

Law Commission (1982) *Polygamous Marriages: Capacity to Contract a Polygamous Marriage and the Concept of a Potentially Polygamous Marriage*, Law Commission Working Paper No 83 and the Scottish Law Commission Consultative Memorandum No 56, London: HMSO

Law Commission (1985) *Private International Law: Polygamous Marriages – Capacity to Contract a Polygamous Marriage and Related Issues*, Law Commission Report No 146, Scottish Law Commission Report No 96, London: HMSO

Legrand, P (1996) 'How to compare now', in Vol 16, No 2 (July 1996) *Legal Studies*, pp 232–42

Legrand, P (1997) 'Against a European Civil Code', in Vol 60, No 1 *Modern Law Review*, pp 44–63

Lester, A and Bindman, G (1972) *Race and Law*, London: Penguin

Lord Lester of Herne Hill, (2002) 'Thirty years on: The East African Asians case revisited', in (Spring 2002) *Public Law* 52–72

Lewis, P (1994) *Islamic Britain: Religion, Politics and Identity Among British Muslims*, London: IB Tauris

Lippman, M, McConville, S and Yerushalmi, M (1988) *Islamic Criminal Law and Procedure*, New York and London: Praerger

Macdonald, IA and Blake, NJ (1991) *Immigration Law and Practice in the United Kingdom*, 3rd edn, London: Butterworths

Macdonald, IA and Blake, NJ (1995) *Immigration Law and Practice in the United Kingdom*, 4th edn, London: Butterworths

Macdonald, IA and Webber, F (eds) (2001) *Immigration Law and Practice in the United Kingdom*, 5th edn, London: Butterworths

Mac an Ghaill, M (2000) 'The Irish in Britain: the invisibility of ethnicity and anti-Irish racism', in Vol 26, No 1 *Journal of Ethnic and Migration Studies*, pp 137–47

McConville, M and Baldwin, J (1982) 'The influence of race on sentencing in England', in Vol 26 No 2 *Criminal Law Review*, pp 147–55

McLeod, WH (1989) *Who is a Sikh?*, Oxford: Oxford University Press

McKee, R (1995) 'A burden on the taxpayer? Some developments in the role of 'public funds' in immigration law', in Vol 9, No 1 *Immigration and Nationality Law and Practice*, pp 29–31

McKee, R (2002) 'Recent developments – an overview', in Vol 16, No 1 *Immigration, Asylum and Nationality Law*, pp 34–38

Mahony, WK (1987) 'Karman: Hindu and Jain concepts', in *The Encyclopedia of Religion*, Vol 8, New York: Macmillan, pp 261–66

Makdisi, J (1990) 'An inquiry into Islamic influences during the formative period of the common law', in Heer, N (ed) *Islamic Law and Jurisprudence*, Seattle and London: University of Washington Press, pp 135–46

Malik, KN (1997) *India and the United Kingdom: Change and Continuity in the 1980s*, New Delhi: Sage

Mansour, AA (1982) '*Hudud* crimes', in Bassiouni, CM (ed) *The Islamic Criminal Justice System*, London: Oceana Publications, pp 195–201

Marshall, B (2000) *The New Germany and Migration in Europe*, Manchester: Manchester University Press

Mason, D (1995) *Race and Ehnicity in Modern Britain*, Oxford: Oxford University Press

Mason, D (2003) *Explaining Ethnic Differences: Changing Patterns of Disadvantage in Britain*, Bristol: The Policy Press

Mayer, A (1987) 'Law and religion in the Middle East', in Vol 35 *American Journal of Comparative Law*, pp 127–84

Mayer, A (1990) '*The shar'ah*: A methodology or a body of substantive rules?', in Heer, N (ed) *Islamic Law and Jurisprudence*, Seattle and London: University of Washington Press, pp 177–98

Mayss, A (2000) 'Recognition of foreign divorces: unwarrantable ethnocentrism', in Murphy, J (ed) *Ethnic Minorities, their Families and the Law*, Oxford, UK and Portland, Oregon: Hart, pp 51–70

Melissaris, E (2004) 'The more the merrier? A new take on legal pluralism', in Vol 13, No 1 *Social and Legal Studies*, pp 57–79

Menski, WF (1987) 'Legal pluralism in the Hindu marriage', in Burghart, R (ed) *Hinduism in Great Britain: The Perpetuation of Religion in an Alien Cultural Milieu*, London and New York: Tavistock, pp 180–200

Menski, WF (1988) 'Uniformity of laws in India and England', in Vol VII, No 11 *Journal of Law and Society* (Peshawar), pp 11–26

Menski, WF (1990) 'South Asian laws in British legal practice: a matter for immigration lawyers?', in (April 1990) *Immigration and Nationality Law and Practice*, pp 63–66

Menski, WF (1993) 'Asian laws in Britain and the question of adaptation to a new legal order: Asian laws in Britain?', in Israel, M and Wagle, NK (eds) *Ethnicity, Identity, Migration: the South Asian Context*, Toronto: Centre for South Asian Studies, University of Toronto, pp 238–68

Menski, WF (1994) 'Family migration and the new Immigration Rules', in Vol 8, No 4 *Immigration and Nationality Law and Practice*, pp 112–24

Menski, WF (ed) (1995) *Coping with 1997: The Reaction of the Hong Kong People to the Transfer of Power*, Stoke on Trent: Trentham

Menski, WF (1997a) 'Race and law', in Ireland, P and Laleng, P (eds) *The Critical Lawyers' Handbook 2*, London and Chicago: Pluto, pp 61–75

Menski, WF (1997b) 'South Asian Muslim law today: an overview', in Vol 9, No 1 *Sharqiyyat*, pp 16–36

Menski, WF (ed) (1998) *South Asians and the Dowry Problem*, Stoke on Trent: Trentham

Menski, WF (1999) 'South Asian women in Britain, family integrity and the primary purpose rule', in Barot, R, Bradley, H and Fenton, S (eds) *Ethnicity, Gender and Social Change*, Basingstoke: Macmillan and New York: St Martin's Press, pp 81–98

Menski, WF (2000a) *Comparative Law in a Global Context. The Legal Systems of Asia and Africa*, London: Platinium

Menski, WF (2000b) 'From imperial domination to Bhaji on the Beach: fifty years of South Asian laws at SOAS', in Edge, I (ed) *Comparative Law in Global Perspective*, Ardsley, New York: Transnational Publishers, pp 121–44

Menski, WF (2001a) *Modern Indian Family Law*, Richmond, Surrey: Curzon

Menski, WF (2001b) 'Muslim law in Britain', in No 62 *Journal of Asian and African Studies* (Japan), pp 127–63

Menski, WF (2002a) 'Chameleons and dodgy lawyers: reflections on Asians in Britain and their legal reconstruction of the universe', in *Britain, India and the Diaspora: Changing Social and Historiographical Perceptions* (Vol XXVIII, No 2 *Indo-British Review*, Millennium issue), pp 89–103

Menski, WF (2002b) 'Immigration and multiculturalism in Britain: New issues in research and policy', in Vol XI [2002] *KIAPS: Bulletin of Asia-Pacific Studies*, Osaka, pp 43–66

Menski, WF (2002c) 'Hinduism', in Levinson, D (ed) *Encyclopaedia of Crime and Punishment*, Thousand Oaks: Sage Publications, Vol 2, pp 827–31

Menski, WF (2003) *Hindu Law. Beyond Tradition and Modernity*, New Delhi: Oxford University Press

Menski, WF and Rahman, T (1988) 'Hindus and the law in Bangladesh', in Vol 8, No 2 *South Asia Research*, pp 111–31

Merry, SE (1988) 'Legal pluralism', in Vol 22, No 5 *Law and Society Review*, pp 869–96

Milsom, SFC (1969) *Historical Foundations of the Common Law*, London: Butterworths

Modood, T (1992) *Not Easy Being British: Colour, Culture and Citizenship*, Stoke on Trent: Trentham

Modood, T (1996) 'If races do not exist, then what does? Racial categorisation and ethnic realities', in Barot, R (ed) *The Racism Problematic: Contemporary Sociological Debates on Race and Ethnicity*, Lewiston: The Edwin Mellen Press, pp 89–105

Modood, T (1998) 'Anti-essentialism, multiculturalism and the 'recognition' of religious groups', in Vol 6, No 4 *The Journal of Political Philosophy*, pp 378–99

Modood, T, Berthoud, R et al (1997) *Ethnic Minorities in Britain*, London: Policy Studies Institute

Mole, N (1987) *Immigration: Family Entry and Settlement*, Bristol: Jordan and Sons

Monsoor, T (1999) *From patriarchy to gender equity. Family law and its impact on women in Bangladesh*. Dhaka: The University Press Ltd.

Moore, SF (1978) *Law as Process*, London: Routledge & Kegan Paul

Moore, R and Wallace, T (1975) *Slamming the Door: The Administration of Immigration Control*, London: Martin Robertson

Morgan, G (1985) 'The analysis of ethnicity: conceptual problems and policy implications', in Vol XII, No 3 (Winter 1985) *New Community*, pp 515–22

Morris, HF (1972) 'Indirect rule and the law of marriage', in Morris, HF and Read, JS *Indirect Rule and the Search for Justice. Essays in East African legal History*, Oxford: Clarendon, pp 213–50

Mortimore, C (1994) *Immigration and Adoption*, Stoke-on-Trent: Trentham Books

Moss, PRH (1988) 'Statement of changes in the Immigration Rules HC 555: a note for practitioners', in Vol 3, No 3 (October 1988) *Immigration and Nationality Law and Practice*, pp 54–56

Nandy, A (2002) 'Telling the story of communal conflicts in South Asia: interim report on a personal search for defining myths', in Vol 25, No 1 (January 2002) *Ethnic and Racial Studies*, pp 1–19

Nargolkar, V (1974) *Crime and Non-violence*, Poona: Sulabha Rashtriya Granthamala Trust

Nascimbene, B (1996) 'Introduction', in Nascimbene, B (ed) *Nationality Laws in the European Union*, Milan: Giuffré Editore, pp 1–19

Nesbitt, E (1997) '"We are all equal": young British Punjabis' and Gujaratis' perceptions of caste', in Vol 4, No 2 *International Journal of Punjab Studies*, pp 202–18

Nicolle, D (1987) *The Normans*, London: Osprey Publishing

Nielsen, J (1988) 'Muslims in Britain and local authority responses', in Gerholm, T and Lithman, Y (eds) *The New Islamic Presence in Western Europe*, London: Mansell, pp 53–77

Nielsen, J (1992) 'Islam, Muslims, and British Local and Central Government', Paper presented at conference on Muslims in Europe, Turin, 4–5 May 1992

Lord Nolan, Rt Hon (1997) 'The Judiciary', in Rt Hon Lord Nolan and Sir Stephen Sedley *The Making and the Remaking of the British Constitution*, London: Blackstone, pp 67–78

Oyètádé, BA (1993) 'The Yorùbá community in London', in Vol 6, No 1 *African Languages and Cultures*, pp 69–92

Parashar, A (1982) 'Polygamous marriage in conflict of laws', in Vol II, No 3 *Islamic and Comparative Law Quarterly*, pp 187–208

Parekh, B (1989) *Gandhi's Political Philosophy. A Critical Examination*, Basingstoke: Macmillan

Parekh, B (1998) 'Integrating minorities', in Blackstone, T, Parekh, B and Saunders, P (eds) *Race Relations in Britain: A Developing Agenda*, London and New York: Routeledge, pp 1–21

Parekh, B (2000a) *Rethinking Multiculturalism: Cultural Diversity and Political Theory*, Basingstoke: Palgrave

Parekh, B (2000b) *The Future of Multi-ethnic Britain: Report of the Commission on the Future of Multi-Ethnic Britain*, London: Profile

Paul, K (1997) *Whitewashing Britain. Race and Citizenship in the Post-war Era*, Ithaca and London: Cornell UP

Peach, C (ed) (1996) *Ethnicity in the 1991 Census. Volume 2: The Ethnic Minority Populations of Great Britain*, London: HMSO

Pearl, D (1972) 'Muslim marriages in English law', in Vol 30, No 1 (April 1972) *Cambridge Law Journal*, pp 120–43

Pearl, D (1986) *Family Law and the Immigrant Communities*, Bristol: Jordan and Sons

Pearl, D and Menski, W (1998) *Muslim Family Law*, 3rd edn, London: Sweet & Maxwell

Phillips, A (2003) 'When culture means gender: issues of cultural defence in the English courts', in (July 2003) Vol 66, No 4 *Modern Law Review*, pp 511–31

Phillips, A and Morris, HF (1971) *Marriage Laws in Africa*, London: Oxford University Press, for International African Institute

Phillips, M and Phillips, T (1998) *Windrush: The Irresistible Rise of Multi-racial Britain*, London: Harper Collins

Phillips, T (2004) 'Britishness and the 'M' word', in [Spring 2004] *Connections*, pp 12–13

Pilkington, E (1996) 'The West Indian Community and the Notting Hill Riots of 1958', in Panayi, P (ed) *Racial Violence in Britain in the Nineteenth and Twentieth Centuries*, London and New York: Leicester University Press, pp 171–84

Pollard, D, Papworth, N and Hughes, D (1997) *Constitutional and Administrative Law: Text with Materials*, London: Butterworths

Poulter, S (1986) *English Law and Ethnic Minority Customs*, London: Butterworths

Poulter, S (1987) 'Ethnic minority customs, English law and human rights', in Vol 36 *International and Comparative Law Quarterly*, pp 589–615

Poulter, S (1989) 'The significance of ethnic minority customs and traditions in English criminal law', in (October 1989) Vol 16, No 1 *New Community*, pp 121–28

Poulter, S (1990a) *Asian Traditions and English Law*, Stoke-on-Trent: Runnymede Trust and Trentham Books

Poulter, S (1990b) 'The claim to a separate Islamic system of personal law for British Muslims', in Mallat, C and Connors, J (eds) *Islamic Family Law*, London: Graham and Trotman, pp 147–66

Poulter, S (1995) 'Multiculturalism and human rights for Muslim families in English law', in King, M (ed) *God's Law Versus State Law: The Construction of an Islamic Identity in Western Europe*, London: Grey Seal, pp 81–87

Poulter, S (1998) *Ethnicity, Law and Human Rights*, Oxford: Clarendon

Probert, R (2003) *Cretney's Family Law*, London: Sweet & Maxwell

Radzinowicz, L (1966) *Ideology and Crime: A Study of Crime and its Social and Historical Context*, London: Heinemann Educational Books

Ramdin, R (1999) *Reimaging Britain: 500 Years of Black and Asian History*, London: Pluto

Reid, K (1998) *A Practitioner's Guide to the European Convention of Human Rights*, London: Sweet & Maxwell

Robinson, V (1986) *Transients, Settlers and Refugees: Asians in Britain*, Oxford: Clarendon Press

Rose, EJB *et al* (1969) *Colour and Citizenship: A Report on British Race Relations*, Oxford: Oxford University Press

Rosen, L (2000) *The Justice of Islam*, Oxford: Oxford University Press

Sachdeva, S (1993) *The Primary Purpose Rule in British Immigration Law*, Stoke-on-Trent: Trentham

Saggar, S (1996) 'The politics of racial pluralism in Britain and problems of evaluation', in Barot, R (ed) *The Racism Problematic: Contemporary Sociological Debates on Race and Ethnicity*, Lewiston: The Edwin Mellen Press, pp 166–92

Salvadori, C (1989) *Through Open Doors: A View of Asian Cultures in Kenya*, 2nd edn revd, Nairobi: Kenway Publications

Santos, B de S (2002) *Toward a New Legal Common Sense*, London: Butterworths

Sappal, P (2002) 'In demand: transcultural managers', in *Expatica Jobs* at www.expatica.com

Serajuddin, AM (2001) *Shari'a Law and Society: Tradition and Change in South Asia*, Oxford: Oxford University Press

Sewell, T (1996) *Black Masculinities and Schooling*, Stoke-on-Trent: Trentham Books

Shah, I (1999) *Darkest England*, London: The Octagon Press

Shah, P (1994) 'Legal pluralism – British law and possibilities with Muslim ethnic minorities', in Nos 66/67 *Retfærd*, pp 18–33

Shah, P (1995) 'The effects of British nationality and immigration law on the people of Hong Kong', in Menski WF (ed) *Coping with 1997: The Reaction of the People of Hong Kong to the Transfer of Power*, Stoke-on-Trent: Trentham, pp 57–119

Shah, P (2000a) 'Ethnic minorities and the European Convention on Human Rights: a view from the UK', in Edge, I (ed) *Comparative Law in Broader Perspective*, Ardsley, New York: Transnational Publishers, pp 387–410

Shah, P (2000b) *Refugees, Race and the Legal Concept of Asylum in Britain*, London: Cavendish

Shah, P (2001) 'British nationals under Community law: the *Kaur* case', in Vol 3, No 2 *European Journal of Migration and Law*, pp 271–78

Shah, P (2002a) 'An unhelpful approach to the validity of South Asian marriage', in Vol 16, No 1 *Immigration, Asylum and Nationality Law*, pp 32–34

Shah, P (2002b) 'Children of polygamous marriage: an inappropriate response', in Vol 16, No 2 *Immigration, Asylum and Nationality Law*, pp 110–13

Shah, P (2003a) 'Attitudes to polygamy in English law', in (April 2003) Vol 52 *International and Comparative Law Quarterly*, pp 369–400

Shah, P (2003b) 'Preliminary reflections on teaching about ethnic minorities in law', in Vol 37, No 1 *The Law Teacher*, pp 18–35

Shah, RKD (1992) 'Britain and Kenya: some immigration and nationality issues', in Vol 6, No 2 *Immigration and Nationality Law and Practice*, pp 35–39

Shah, RKD (1999) 'A thirty year wrong – remnants of Empire', in Vol 13, No 1 *Immigration and Nationality Law and Practice*, pp 9–13

Shah, RKD (2003a) 'Being British: rites of passage', in Vol 17, No 4 *Immigration, Asylum and Nationality Law*, pp 250–54

Shah, RKD (2003b) 'A wrong righted: full status for Britain's other citizens', in Vol 17, No 1 *Immigration, Asylum and Nationality Law*, pp 19–24

Shah-Kazemi, SN (2001) *Untying the Knot. Muslim Women, Divorce and the Shariah*, London: Nuffield Foundation

Sharma, A (2003) *Hinduism and Human Rights: A Conceptual Approach*, Oxford: Oxford University Press

Shaw, A (1988) *A Pakistani Community in Britain*, Oxford: Basil Blackwell

Shaw, A (2000) *Kinship and Continuity: Pakistani Families in Britain*, Amsterdam: Harwood

Simmons, A (1994) 'French nationality law', in Vol 8, No 1 *Immigration and Nationality Law and Practice*, pp 13–17

Smith, JC (1996) *Criminal Law*, London: Butterworths

Sondhi, R (1987) *Divided Families: British Immigration Control in the Indian Subcontinent*, London: The Runnymede Trust

Spalek, B (2002) 'Religious diversity, British Muslims, crime and victimisation', in Spalek, B (ed) (2002) *Islam, Crime and Criminal Justice*, Cullompton, Devon: Willan Publishing, p 118

Spijkerboer, T (2000) *Gender and Refugee Status*, Aldershot: Ashgate/Dartmouth

Staal, F (1996) *Ritual and Mantras: Rules Without Meaning*, Delhi: Motilal Banarsidass

Steel, D (1969) *No Entry: the Background and Implications of the Commonwealth Immigrants Act 1968*, London: C Hurst & Co

Stein, B (1980) *Peasant, State and Society on Medieval South India*, Delhi: Oxford University Press

Stevens, D (2004) *UK Asylum Policy: Historical and Contemporary Perspectives*, London: Sweet & Maxwell

Tamanaha, B (2001) *A General Jurisprudence of Law and Society*, Oxford: Oxford University Press

Thakur, U (1978) *An Introduction to Homicide in India*, New Delhi: Abhinav Publications

Tibballs, G (1998) *Legal Blunders*, London: Robinson

Tomaney, J (2000) 'The Governance of London', in Hazell, R (ed) *The State and the Nations: The First Year of Devolution in the United Kingdom*, Thorverton: Imprint Academic, pp 117–48

Turpin, C (1995) *British Government and the Constitution: Text, Cases and Materials*, London: Weidenfeld and Nicolson

Uberoi, P (1993) *Family, Kinship and Marriage in India*, Oxford: Oxford University Press

United Nations Development Programme (2004) *Human Development Report 2004: Cultural Liberty in Today's Diverse World*, New York: UNDP

van Caenegem, RC (1987) *Judges, Legislators and Professors: Chapters in European Legal History*, Cambridge: Cambridge University Press

van Zyl Smit, D (2002) *Taking Life Imprisonment Seriously in National and International Law*, The Hague: Kluwer Law International

Vincenzi, C (1998) *Crown Powers, Subjects and Citizens*, London: Pinter

Vincenzi, C and Marrington, D (1992) *Immigration Law: The Rules Explained*, London: Sweet & Maxwell

Visram, R (2002) *Asians in Britain: 400 Years of History*, London: Pluto

Wainwright, M (2001) 'Some Bradford Muslims "act like colonists"', in *The Guardian*, 12 September 2001

Welhengama, G (2000) *Minorities' Claims: From Autonomy to Secession, International Law and State Practice*, Aldershot: Ashgate

Werbner, P (1979) 'Avoiding the ghetto: Pakistani migrants and settlement shifts in Manchester', in Vol 7, No 3 *New Community*, pp 376–89

Werbner, P (2002) *Imagined Diasporas Among Manchester Muslims*, Oxford: James Currey

Wilson, W (2003) *Criminal Law: Doctrine and Theory*, 2nd edn, London and New York: Longman

Wray, H and Quayum, M (1999) 'Entry clearance application for spouses where sponsor is on benefits', in Vol 13, No 4 *Immigration and Nationality Law and Practice*, pp 133–35

Wu, K-M (1998) *On the Logic of Togetherness: A Cultural Hermeneutic*, Leiden: Brill

Yardley, DCM (1978) *Introduction to British Constitutional Law*, 5th edn, London: Butterworths

Yardley, DCM (1990) *Introduction to British Constitutional Law*, 7th edn, London: Butterworths

Yeboa, KY (1993–95) 'Bigamy and Islamic marriages in the law of Ghana: the legislator's dilemma or studied silence', in Vol XIX *Review of Ghana Law*, pp 69–83

Yeo, S (1998) *Unrestrained Killings and the Law. A Comparative Analysis of the Law of Provocation and Excessive Self-defence in India, England and Australia*, Delhi: Oxford University Press

Yilmaz, I (1999) *Dynamic Legal Pluralism and the Reconstruction of Unofficial Muslim Laws in England, Turkey, and Pakistan*, PhD Thesis, London: School of Oriental and African Studies

Yilmaz, I (2000) 'Muslim law in Britain: reflections in the socio-legal sphere and differential legal treatment', in Vol 21, No 2 *Journal of Muslim Minority Affairs*, pp 353–60

Yilmaz, I (2001) 'Law as chameleon: the question of incorporation of Muslim personal law into the English law', in Vol 21, No 2 *Journal of Muslim Minority Affairs*, pp 297–308

Yilmaz, I (2002a) 'The challenge of post-modern legality and Muslim legal pluralism in England', in (April 2002) Vol 28, No 2 *Journal of Ethnic and Migration Studies*, pp 343–54

Yilmaz, I (2002b) 'Secular law and the emergence of unofficial Turkish Islamic law', in Vol 56, No 1 *Middle East Journal*, pp 113–31

Yilmaz, I (2004) 'Marriage solemnisation among Turks in Britain: The emergence of a hybrid Anglo-Muslim Turkish law', in Vol 24, No 1 *Journal of Muslim Minority Affairs*, pp 57–68

Yilmaz, I (2005) '*Inter-madhhab surfing, neo-ijitihad*, and faith-based movement leaders', in Vogel, F Bearman, P and Peters, R (eds) *The Islamic School of Law: Evolution, Devolution and Progress*, Cambridge, Mass: Harvard University Press, (forthcoming)

Young, C (1998) 'Political representations of geography and place in the introduction of the UK Asylum and Immigration Act (1996)', in Nicholson, F and Twomey, P (eds) *Current Issues of UK Asylum Law and Policy*, Aldershot: Ashgate, pp 34–51

Zander, M (1989) *The Law-making Process*, 3rd edn, London: Weidenfeld and Nicolson

Index

Angrezi shariat 118-19

Bangladeshi legal
   pluralism **123-40**
   Bangladeshi immigration to
     Britain 123
   case studies in legal ethno-
     cracy 131-37
     distortion of Bangladeshi legal
       culture 131
     genuineness of 'marriage
       deed' 133
     legitimacy of children 134-37
     sanctity of marriage or over-
       reliance on kagzi
       evidence 132-34
     widow's pension 132-34
   immigration restrictions 128-31
     establishing right of abode
       status 130
     family reunion, and 129
     'patriality' provisions of
       Immigration Act
       1971, ...129-30
     polygamous marriages,
       and 130-31
     shift from 'international
       commuter' 128
     tightening of 128
   interplay of legal systems 124-27
     Bangladeshi legal system 125
     bideshi habits 126
     centrality of state law 124
     creation of 'secondary' rule..127

     ethnocentrism within legal
       system 124
     legal patterns followed at
       personal level 125-26
     personal laws 125
     process of developing living
       law 126
     status of emergent Muslim
       law 127
   reconstruction of diasporic
     group 123
   towards a Londoni-Bangala
     law 137-40
     change of child's name ...137-38
     community context 139
     'quamic' 139-40
Begum, Shabina
   right to wear jilbab 173
Bigamy *see* Polygamy
Britain
   balance of law founding elements
     in, ...11-13
   see also Identity postulate
British constitutional order
   diasporic challenge to
   see Diasporic challenge
British nationality **149-71**
   British Nationality Act 1981, ...160-
                    65
     de facto stateless British
       nationals 164
     Hong Kong transfer of power,
       and 163
     nationality for Community

purposes 163
people who had lost right of
    abode 161
split between nationality and
    immigration status 160
which nationals qualify for free
    movement rights 162-63
Community law freedoms 149
European context, in 149-71
    first UK Declaration on
    Nationality 153-60
Immigration Act 1971, and ..153-60
    Commonwealth citizens 155
    complexity of British
        immigration law 156
    definition of British
        nationals 157
    EEC negotiations, and 155
    Falkland Islanders 158
    free movement of workers,
        and 158-59
    link between racism and
        immigration control 154
    migration implications of EEC
        membership 156
    right of abode, definition 154
    tension between territorality
        principle and
        ethnicity 157-58
immigration and nationality law
    prior to EU membership...151-53
    Citizens of the UK and
        Colonies (CUKCs) 151
    legal entry from East
        Africa 153
    passports issued in British High
        Commission 152
    return of white
        migrants 151-52
Manjit Kaur case 165-71
    narrow legal effect of 169
second UK Declaration on
    Nationality 160-65

sub-citizenships of UK
    nationality 150
Britishness
    defining 44-48

Centre-locale relation
    legal postulates of 60-66
Children
    legitimacy of 134-37
Constitutional law
    limits of dominant perspectives
        on 54-57
Criminal justice
    South Asians and homicide law
        see Homicide law
Cultural diversity
    immigration law responsibility
        for managing 13-14

Desh bidesh 126
Diasporic challenge 43-66
    avoiding pluralism 48-50
    assimilation 48
    controlling family-based
        migration 49-50
    exclusionary mechanisms 50
    passing of 1971 Immigration
        Act 49
    'rotating' migrants 48
    British constitutional order,
        to 43-66
    defining Britishness 44-48
    character of migration
        patterns 45
    ethnically driven controls 46
    European angle 46-47
    imperial norm of
        citizenship 45
    judicial decisions 46
    Kenyan Asians exodus 45
    post-war labour shortages 44
    redefining national identity ...48
    rights of citizenship 47

disruption to pre-existing
  constitutional system 43
legal postulates of centre-locale
  relation 60-66
  conflict between state and
    self-regulatory orders 66
  custom as source of law 62
  effects of suppression 65-66
  litigation, and 65
  modernity-focused research ..61
  recreation of Asian and African
    legal orders 64
  ruler's discretion 63
  shari'a law 63
  'soft' state 62
  two models of legal
    regulation 64-65
  understanding of non-Western
    cosmologies 61
limits of dominant perspectives on
  constitutional law 54-57
  changing social scenario 55
  immigration judicial review ..56
  implication of changed ethnic
    character 57
  influence of immigration of
    legal cultures 55
  putative power of Crown to
    exclude aliens 55
  representative nature of voting
    systems 56
  uncertainty about ethnic
    diversity at official level ...54
overcoming hegemonic
  ideology 57-60
  'ethnic niche' 59
  legal postulates of centre-locale
    relation 60-66
  political theory perspective ...57
  value pluralism 58
  world view 59
representing ethnic diversity 50-54
  1991 Census, and 50

ethnographic information 53
failure of immigration control
  system 50
freedom of movement 52
geographical concentration ...53
hybrid identifications 52
non-European ethnic minority
  population 53
'religions' in Asia 52
white immigrant minorities ..51
'white' minorities 51
self-concept of British polity 43

English law
  framework 70-72
  polygamy under *see* Polygamy
Ethnic minority legal studies 27-42
  curricular concerns 40-42
    articles from minority press ..41
    immigration law 40
    separate optional offerings 41
    teaching materials 40
  ethnic diversity in UK 29-31
    capturing character of ethnic
      minority presence 30
    deprivationist frame 30
    inner dynamics and value
      systems 31
    methodological implications .31
    minorities of key interest 29
    Muslim spokespersons, and ..31
  problematising prevailing
    paradigms 32-37
    assumptions and limitations of
      prevailing jurisprudence ..32
    conflicts of law approach 34
    definition of 'radical groups' ..33
    delimiting scope of ethnic
      minority laws 35
    demands for conformity 36
    diverse coverage in 1980s 34
    'ethnic minority customs' 35
    'ethno-cratic' 36

'foreign' legal rules in English
   courts 34
group issues 33
Islamic law in Britain 36
Macpherson inquiry
   report 32-33
reintroduction of teaching of
   laws of religions 35
tradition of legal responses ...32
student and academic
   perceptions 27-29
inter-culturalité 27
topics taught 29
white students, attitudes
   of 28
teaching and doing legal
   pluralism 37-40
agency-oriented approach 38
'black-letter' renderings 37
ethnic minority awareness
   training 39
existing teaching tools 39
expert background
   information 39
feminist legal studies 38
overemphasising top-down
   structures 38
positive framework of
   inquiry 37
Ethnic minority studies 1-26
British Census 2001, ...1
cultural diversity 1
legal pluralism, ...2-7
   see also Legal pluralism
Ethno-cracy
case studies in 131-37
Expiation
concept of 82

Falkland Islanders 158

Gujarati
socio-cultural norms 143-44

Hegemonic ideology
overcoming 57-60
Homicide law 67-87
criminal law
   expression of 'public' values, as
  68-69
English law framework 70-72
consequences of murder
   finding 70-71
discrimination against ethnic
   minorities 71
idealised idea of criminality .71
juries, role of 71-72
life sentences 70
state-centred presuppositions
   of 72
foundations of Euro-American
   societies 67
high levels of Afro-Caribbean
   imprisonment 69
liberal attitudes to crime 67
consequences of 68
modernist antipathy to religion ...70
South Asians and English
   homicide law 79-87
additional barriers faced by
   ethnic minorities 87
concept of expiation 82
criminalisation of minorities .83
culture-specific issues leading
   to homicide 80
lack of culturally informed
   approach 86
material regarding 79-80
'public interest', and 86
Ram, Satpal, case of 81-82
'scientific' evidence, lack of ...86
Shah, Zoora, case of 83-85
South Asian laws establishment
   in England 80
traditional South Asian laws,
   under 72-79
acts of revenge 75

complexity of 72-73
diverse origins of diaspora
  in Britain 72-73
Hindu determinant of
  guilt 75
Hindu and Muslim 'families
  of law' 73
Hindu shaastric literature 74
honour killings 77
Indian notions of justice 79
Islamic punishment for
  killing 76-77
karma 74-75
killing of children 75-76
killing under Muslim law 76
problems with defences to
  murder 78
tension between tradition and
  modernity 78

Hong Kong
transfer of power in
  nationality status, and 163
Honour killings 77
Human rights
polygamous marriages,
  and 116-17

Identity postulate
British legal order, seeking 10-17
balance of law founding
  elements in Britain 11-13
centralising common law 11
codification 11
common law as means of
  ensuring social
  responsiveness 12
coping with presence of new
  ethnic minorities 14
cultural crisis 10
immigration law 13-14
international treaties, and 16
jurisprudence of difference ...13
legislation, and 13

managing legal pluralism in
  conflict 13-17
Napoleonic law, and 11-12
official recognition of religious
  diversity 17
promotion of equal
  opportunity 15
Race Relations Act 15
response to Afro-Asian
  presence 16
strong state ideology 14
unity of culture 12
Immigration cases 141-47
expert opinions on South Asian
  laws in 141-47
  academic value 146-47
  interaction with legal
    advisors 141-43
  'legal' or 'non-legal'
    information 143-44
  overcoming dominant legal
    approaches 144-46
Immigration law 10
responsible for managing cultural
  diversity 13-14
India
notions of justice in 79
Indigenous law
identity postulate of 6
Infanticide
South Asian homicide law,
  and 75-76
Islamic law
influences 4

Japan
foreign legal elements in 6
Judges
discrimination by 71
Juries
role of 71-72

Kagzi evidence 132-34

Karma **74-75**

Law founding elements
three of 5
Legal advisors
interaction with 141-43
Legal education **174**
Legal pluralism **2-7**
Bangladeshi
see Bangladeshi legal pluralism
conflict and subjectivity, in 7-10
immigration law 10
law in objectivity 8-9
law in subjectivity 8
legal hybridity 9
neglected study of 7-8
situation of ethnic minorities
under English law 8
'wisely' managing conflicts in
legal pluralism 9
legal postulates 3
model jurisprudence 2
teaching 37-40
threefold structure of law 3
tool for ethnic minority studies, as
see Ethnic minority studies
Legal postulates **3**
centre-locale relation, of 60-66
Legal transplantation
two directions of 7

Macpherson inquiry report **32-33**
Manjit Kaur case **165-71**
Model jurisprudence **2**

Para-mentalites **7**
Polygamy **89-121**
attitudes to in English
law 89-121
ban on second wives 110-18
attempts to circumvent 114
continuance of 'alien'
customs 113

control of settlement of South
Asians 110
granting of entry to
children 116
human rights, and 116-17
Immigration Act 1988 and
accompanying
restrictions 111-13
intervention of statutory
control 110-18
judicial review challenge to
Immigration Rules 113-14
one-wife policy in
courts 113-18
position of children of
polygamous marriages ...116
right of abode for polygamous
wives 111
talaq divorces, and 113
women's equality, and 112
comparative law context 90-94
Africans in Britain, lack of
case law 93
emphasis on uniformity 91
maintenance of personal law
systems 90
Muslim law 93
polygamy as social practice ..92
polygamy legislation 92
recognition of polygamy by
official legal sphere 91
control through choice of
law rules 94-110
application of alternative
tests 110
Bangladeshi migrant men ...102
British recognition of existence
of other states 95-96
challenge to 'traditional'
test 108
changing migration pattern
1970s 102
codification 98

consequences of social
scenario 99
consideration of overseas
law 109
decriminalisation of
homosexual activity 95
domicile as key determinant...98
emergence of immigration
related cases 105-10
English private international
law 94-101
entry into UK of second
wives 104
failure to distinguish between
personal law and
jurisdictional law..............101
family reunion and
immigration control ...101-05
further ceremony in UK
requirement 104
injustice behind decisions
refusing entry 107
'international commuters' ...102
legislative provision in
1970s 94
neglected wife's right of
recourse 96
potential polygamy, case
law 95
recognition of marriages
abroad 100
refusal to *see* personal
law 94-101
reinterpretation of Kenyan and
Indian law 96-97
retention or loss of
domicile 107
routine enquiries about validity
of marriages 103
status of children 104-05
statutory reforms 97
termination of polygamous
unions 97-98

use of Rules to admit
polygamous wives 106
validity of marriages on basis
of polygamy 103
*Zahra and Another v Visa Officer
Islamabad* 105-06
English developments in
law of 89-90
Eurocentric perceptions of
non-Western law 89
family reunion immigration
law 90
illustrative of problem of ethnic
minority laws, as 118-21
'angrezi shariat' 118-19
unsatisfactory official
position on 120

Qisaas offence
killing as 76
Quamic **139-40**

Race Relations Act
reception given to 15
Ram, Satpal
case of 81-82

Shaastric literature **74**
Shah, Zoora
case of 83-85
Shari'a law **63**
polygamy, and 119
South Asians
homicide law, and
see Homicide law
law in immigration cases
see Immigration cases
State law
approach to place of 5

Talaq divorces **113**
Teaching
legal pluralism 37-40

Trans-state law 4

Transplanted law 4

United Kingdom
  ethnic diversity in 29-31

Widow's pension
  entitlement to 132-34

*Zahra and Another v Visa Officer
Islamabad* **105-06**